Working the Spaces of

Working the Spaces of Neoliberalism

Activism, Professionalisation and Incorporation

Edited by

Nina Laurie and Liz Bondi

First published 2005 by Blackwell Publishing Ltd

Library of Congress Cataloging-in-Publication Data has been applied for

ISBN 1-4051-3800-9

A catalogue record for this title is available from the British Library.

Set in Pondicherry, India
by Integra Software Services Pvt Ltd, India
Printed and bound in Great Britain
by TJ International Ltd, Padstow, Cornwall

The publisher's policy is to use permanent paper from mills that operate a sustainable forestry policy, and which has been manufactured from pulp processed using acid-free and elementary chlorine-free practices. Furthermore, the publisher ensures that the text paper and cover board used have met acceptable environmental accreditation standards.

For further information on
Blackwell Publishing, visit our website:
www.blackwellpublishing.com

Contents

Introduction

Liz Bondi and Nina Laurie

The project brought to fruition in this collection began with the discovery that the two of us shared an interest in the extension of processes of professionalisation into very different arenas (voluntary sector counselling and indigenous knowledges). We also shared a sense of uncertainty, ambivalence and perplexity about the politics of the processes we were observing and analysing. As we explored these commonalities, we talked about our own and others' complex positioning in relation to neoliberalism and neoliberalisation. We began to think about our respective projects as two of many examples of how the negotiation of the spaces of "actually existing neoliberalism" (Brenner and Theodore 2002:349) deploy, or are bound up with, processes of professionalisation. In other words, we felt that we were trying to get to grips with questions of how people "work" the spaces of neoliberalism and how such "work" engages—intentionally or unintentionally—with processes through which professions are constituted. Our conversations led (via the organisation of a conference session) to the production of this collection, in which we include examples drawn from our own and seven other research projects. In its totality, this collection argues that processes of professionalisation form an integral part of the production of the globalised spaces of neoliberal governance.

Throughout the unfolding of this project, we remained committed to bringing together research from diverse contexts, including perhaps especially from the global South and the global North. As well as juxtaposing studies that are too often produced, published and read in isolation from each other, the various contributions bring into focus tensions and connections between activism and processes of professionalisation in relation to neoliberalism. Individually and collectively they help to illuminate links between the framing context of neoliberal restructuring and the ways in which professionalisation involves processes of representation, negotiation and embodiment as activism feeds into "scaled up" policy making. In so doing, these studies elaborate how the spaces of neoliberalism are "worked" in two related senses, namely how neoliberalisation incorporates, co-opts, constrains and depletes activism, and how professional(ised) subjects inhabit and sometimes subvert the opportunities neoliberalisation opens up. In this introduction we set in context the substantive contributions by outlining key aspects of the links between neoliberalism, activism and professionalisation.

Neoliberalism has travelled with remarkable ease. Characterised initially by economic liberalisation and an emphasis on "rolling back the state" (especially the welfare state), it rose to global prominence in the 1980s as the cornerstone of the overtly right-wing programmes of Thatcherism and Reaganism. Nevertheless, its antecedents can be found in social democratic regimes (perhaps most notably New Zealand) as well as the economics of General Pinochet's dictatorship in Chile, inspired by the Chicago Boys. Neoliberalism swiftly extended its reach globally via the activities of leading international organisations including the International Monetary Fund, the World Trade Organisation and the World Bank, where the influence of the USA and the UK, among others, was strong. These multilateral organisations promoted "packages of reform", which sought to disseminate what they saw as neoliberal "best practice" in economic policy making. In so doing, they transferred policies from one context to others, wresting the specific socio-political contexts and relationships through which they had been forged, and imposing them elsewhere with minimal regard for distinctive features of policy-making and policy-receiving environments. As a result, public sector and privatisation packages developed in one place could be copied elsewhere with little reference to the social and political climate in which they had been developed and would now be implemented. To take a specific example, the introduction of Chilean-style pension reform in the UK under a "New Labour" government in the late 1990s bears testimony to the longevity and de-contextualised global reach of neoliberal thinking, which clearly goes far beyond the now notorious alliance between the Iron Lady (Margaret Thatcher, British prime minister from 1979 to 1989) and her discredited South American dictator friend General Pinochet. That an abstract economic theory might become so patently commonsensical to be adopted by ideologically divergent political parties so swiftly and easily has disturbed numerous commentators (for example, Bourdieu and Wacquant 2001). It has also been a motivating force in the rise of a global anti-capitalist protest movement that seeks to question the grip of neoliberal thinking on the major lending agencies and expose the fiction of neoliberal best case scenarios.

In an influential theorisation of the spatial dynamics of neoliber-alisation, Jamie Peck and Adam Tickell (2002) draw attention to historical shifts from "proto-" to "roll-back" neoliberalism (during which, abstract free-market economic theory was operationalised through strategies such as deregulation and privatisation), and from "roll-back" to "roll-out" neoliberalism (signalled by the proliferation of regulatory systems through which quasi-market mechanisms have been extended into an ever-widening range of activities). They show how places themselves are increasingly drawn into market-style competition for public funds, and how these market mechanisms produce spatial differentiation.

In this context, one of the ways in which critical social scientists have sought to avoid merely reaffirming the global hegemony of neoliberalism is by considering its variability. Neil Brenner and Nik Theodore, for example, note that "[t]he global imposition of neolib-eralism has ... been highly uneven, both socially and geographically" (2002:350). A key task for critical geographers, therefore, has been to examine the production of a plurality of neoliberal spaces. In this vein, research has explored the differentiated nature of neoliberalism in a wide variety of contexts. Examples include studies of how the spaces vacated by "roll-back" neoliberalism are colonised in diverse ways that enable different forms of "roll-out" neoliberalism to proceed.

In Bolivia, for example, comprehensive neoliberal reforms directed at decentralisation and privatisation of key industries occurred in the early 1990s (Kohl 2002), but dreams of modernisation based on public ownership of important resources like water continued to shape struggles over regional development (Laurie and Marvin 1999). Subsequently, Bolivian activists have been persistent in attempts to overturn state and donor-backed water privatisation policies (Laurie 2005; Laurie and Crespo 2005), with their activities providing clear examples of the contested and unevenness of neoliberalism. The example of Bolivia further illustrates what Jamie Peck (2004:395) refers to as the "contingent outcomes" of neoliberalism associated especially with "less government and more governance". Thus, a new Bolivian constitution, giving groundbreaking recognition to indigen-ous rights, was ushered in as part of these neoliberal reforms (see also contribution by Laurie, Radcliffe and Andolina). While its ethos implied incorporating the poorest groups into the economy as the active self-governing citizens of neoliberalism, it nevertheless opened up space for contestation within the policy-making processes (compare with contributions by Bondi, and Larner and Craig). Chiming both with vociferous indigenous demands for appropriate forms of development and international donor interests in moving away from harsh economic restructuring towards "adjustment with a human face", these circumstances came together to help generate a specific type of multicultural neoliberalism (Andolina, Laurie and Radcliffe 2005). In turn, Bolivian neoliberal multiculturalism has become established as "best practice" in donor circles, completing the circuit of what Jamie Peck and Adam Tickell (2002) call "roll-out" neoliberalism.

In the very different context of British and North American cities, critical geographers, including Jennifer Wolch (1990), Katharyne Mitchell (2001), Nick Fyfe and Christine Milligan (2003) and Michael Brown (2004), have traced how the spaces vacated by the "rolling back" of welfare state provision become populated by a range of non-profit activities, which are drawn into a variety of positions within, and in relation to, regulatory frameworks characterising roll-out neoliberalism. Posing the question of how "the process of neo-liberal expansion *actually work*[s]", Katharyne Mitchell (2001:166, original emphasis), for example, has explored how a locally distinctive form of transnational multicultural neoliberalism took shape in British Columbia in the 1990s. During the 1980s a federal immigra-tion policy that encouraged "business" migrants had proved to be especially attractive to affluent migrants from Hong Kong. At the same time, economic neoliberalism was on the rise across Canada, exemplified by international free trade agreements, financial deregulation, and withdrawal of federal and provincial government from welfare provision. Affluent, entrepreneurial immigrants arriv-ing in Vancouver in this context swiftly and easily invested in the fabric of the urban environment. In the conflicts with other residents that ensued, these landed immigrants soon discovered that socio-cultural acceptance was more problematic than the acquisition of legal citizenship rights. Philanthropic and volunteering activities turned out to be one of the means through which they countered such resistance. The charitable activities in which they participated included social service provision for other immigrants who lacked their own readily transferable resources. During the 1990s these charitable organisations competed successfully for government con-tracts for social welfare, which aimed to fill in at least some of the gaps produced by the decline of public sector provision (exemplifying the combined processes of roll-out and roll-back neoliberalism). With the backing of major donors, several were successfully drawn into close relationships with state agencies while other mutual aid organisations lacking such backing were increasingly squeezed out (compare contribution by Nightingale). Becoming part of what Jennifer Wolch (1990) has called "the shadow state", successful charities supported by affluent Hong Kong immigrants facilitated the extension of governance in the context of less government, and simultaneously lubricated socio-cultural frictions between different groups of citizens (see contributions by Dolhinow and Fyfe). As well as illustrating the contingent outcomes of neoliberalism, this example highlights the complex interweaving of its economic, political and cultural dimensions.

In response to the geographically variable but nevertheless seemingly inexorable extension of neoliberalism, Jamie Peck and Adam Tickell have called for "a far-reaching *deliberalization* of spatial relations" (2002:401, original emphasis). Quite how spaces might be "deliberalized", and how resistance to neoliberalism might be fostered, remain important and troublingly difficult questions. In numerous contexts, the very real achievements of popular social movements in influencing policy agendas generate pressing dilemmas about the dangers and the benefits of incorporation within "mainstream" structures. As Michael Brown (1997) has illustrated in the case of AIDS activism, when political agitation results in funding, activists may be recruited to deliver services. Their occupational positions are linked to wider structures within which the dynamics of professionalisation and bureaucratisation often loom large. Neoliberal systems of governance and the accompanying forms of restructuring increasingly condition these developments (also see Brown 2004). In a different context, Janet Townsend, Gina Porter and Emma Mawdsley (2002) point to the ways in which the rise of "new managerialism" in the development industry reflect the increasing tendency of donors to emphasise issues of governance, which often effectively override as well as precede questions of the capacity to relieve poverty, and simultaneously undermine grassroots organising (compare contribution by Fyfe). Activist–funder relationships are circumscribed and limited by audit cultures, while the increasingly professional network relationships involved in the burgeoning transnational community of non-governmental organisations (NGOs) make it especially difficult for the voices of southern NGOs to be heard (Mawdsley, Porter and Townsend 2005; Townsend, Porter and Mawdsley 2002).

A suggestion elaborated in this collection is that incorporation into the discursive framework of neoliberalism is not so much a danger about which activists must be vigilant, nor an inevitability about which nothing can be done, but might instead be more usefully understood as a process that calls upon activists and intellectuals to rethink the parameters of political agency. The swift rise of neoliberalism owes much to the "fit" between the terms of its economic theory and liberal democracy. Neoliberalism defines subjects as self-governing individuals who exercise economic and political choices as citizen-consumers (see contributions by Bondi, Richardson and Simpson). However limited many of the choices we make might seem to be, the appeal of self-governance is one that is extremely difficult to resist. However much we might contest the adequacy of this model of subjectivity, every contestation effectively mobilises the contesting subject's claim to be able to think for her- or himself, and therefore the salience of self-government (Rose 1985, 1990). Notwithstanding the scope to theorise self-governance *within* relational approaches to the subject (for example, Mackenzie and Stoljar 2000), neoliberalism (mis)recognises such features of subjectivity as consistent with its own framework. Conversely, the rhetoric of neoliberalism offers political actors undeniable, if problematic, opportunities. Not surprisingly, activists (and academics) take up these opportunities even if they also contest and seek to reframe neoliberal definitions of subjectivity. Drawing especially on feminist geography methodologies (for example, Gibson-Graham 1994), we argue that approaching neoliberalism as a constructed social terrain or field turns notions of inevitability into potential resources in the long-term political project of "deliberalizing" space. This is, of course, a contentious suggestion, and it is not necessarily one with which all contributors to this collection would agree. Nevertheless, the contributions are underpinned by a determination to examine how "deliberalisation" might be enabled by analysing and engaging with its strengths, rather than by focusing on margins and interstices potentially available for alternatives. Thus, rather than attempting to identify neoliberalism's "flanks of vulnerability" (Peck and Tickell 2002:77), this collection is more concerned with possibilities for the transmutation of its core. Central to this core—and perhaps to its transmutation—are processes of professionalisation.

Professionalisation positions individuals in dynamic relationships with collectives, including collectives with which they identify themselves and those from which they seek to distance (or dis-identify) themselves, and in different ways, the contributors examine these relationships and positions. In so doing, they aim to explore the dilemmas faced by a variety of actors for whom accessing spaces or positions outside the purview of neoliberalism is a very difficult, unattractive, and perhaps impossible task. But, rather than focusing on its apparent inevitability, the contributors highlight the agency of a diverse array of politically engaged and reflexive actors, who are to varying degrees alert to the power and the pitfalls of professionalisation in their various contexts. If neoliberalism "recognises" political resistance as the performance of neoliberal subjectivity, there is no way of resisting that which remains wholly outside neoliberalism. In other words, there is no uncontaminated form of, or space for, political resistance. We would argue that the activists discussed in this collection are well aware of these dilemmas and resist representations of their actions and their selves as if they are merely naïve victims of neoliberalism and/or ingénues in their political encounters. There are also four commentaries, which, in different ways, reflect further on some of the contradictions and negotiations of neoliberalism that are analysed within the nine contributions.

In this way, we aim to add to and shape the growing body of work that seeks to explore economic sociologies (Peck 2005). By drawing together studies from North and South, we also seek to profile how "epistemologies of the South" (Santos de Sousa 2004:236, quoted in Gibson-Graham 2005) reach far into northern territories, constituting new spaces along the way (see contribution by Kothari). As Gibson-Graham (2005) argues, this requires "venturing into a creative field in which the possibilities of reconfiguration and experimentation are linked to contingency and unpredictability". The field we seek to create is one in which we strive to represent social movement actors respectfully, acknowledging their awareness of where they come from and where they might be going. It is also one in which geographies of the North and South are not only bound together, but have important stories to tell each other that challenge how we do geography.

References

Andolina R, Laurie N and Radcliffe S (2005) *Multi-ethnic Transnationalism: Indigenous Development in the Andes*. Durham: Duke University (forthcoming)

Bourdieu P and Wacquant L (2001) NeoLiberalSpeak: Notes on a new planetary vulgate. *Radical Philosophy* 105:2–5

Brenner N and Theodore N (2002) Cities and geographies of "actually existing neoliberalism". *Antipode* 34:349–379

Brown M P (1997) *RePlacing Citizenship. AIDS Activism and Radical Democracy*. New York: Guilford

Brown M (2004) Between neoliberalism and cultural conservatism: Spatial divisions and multiplications of hospice labor in the United States. *Gender, Place and Culture* 11:67–82

Fyfe N R and Milligan C (2003) Out of the shadows: Exploring contemporary geographies of voluntarism. *Progress in Human Geography* 27:397–413

Gibson-Graham J-K (1994) "Stuffed if I know!" Reflections on post-modern feminist social research. *Gender, Place and Culture* 1:205–224

Gibson-Graham J-K (2005) Surplus possibilities: Postdevelopment and community economies. *Singapore Journal of Tropical Geography* 26:4–26

Kohl B (2002) Stabilizing neoliberalism in Bolivia: Popular participation and privatization. *Political Geography* 21:449–472

Laurie N (2005) Establishing development orthodoxy: Negotiating masculinities in the water sector. *Development and Change* (forthcoming)

Laurie N and Crespo C (2005) Deconstructing the best case scenario: Lessons from La Paz-El Alto, Bolivia. *Geoforum* (forthcoming)

Laurie N and Marvin S (1999) Globalisation, neo-liberalism and negotiated development in the Andes: Bolivian water and the Misicuni dream. *Environment and Planning A* 31:1401–1415

Mackenzie C and Stoljar N (2000) Introduction: Autonomy refigured. In C Mackenzie and N Stoljar (eds) *Relational Autonomy* (pp 3–31). Oxford: Oxford University Press

Mawdsley E, Porter G and Townsend J G (2005) Whose ideas count? How can Southern NGOs challenge global development fashions. *Development in Practice* 15:77–82

Mitchell K (2001) Transnationalism, neo-liberalism, and the rise of the shadow state. *Economy and Society* 30:165–189

Peck J (2004) Geography and public policy: Constructions of neoliberalism. *Progress in Human Geography* 28:392–405

Peck J (2005) Economic sociologies in space. *Economic Geography* (forthcoming)

Peck J and Tickell A (2002) Neoliberalizing space. *Antipode* 34:380–404

Rose N (1985) *The Psychological Complex*. London: Routledge and Kegan Paul

Rose N (1990) *Governing the Soul*. London: Routledge

Santos de Sousa B (2004) The WSF: Toward a counter-hegemonic globalization. In J Sen, A Anand, A Escobar and P Waterman (eds) *World Social Forum: Challenging Empires* (pp 235–245). New Delhi: The Viveka Foundation, http://www.choike.org/nuevo_eng/informes/1557.html

Townsend J G, Porter G and Mawdsley E (2002) The role of the transnational community of non-government organisations: Governance or poverty reduction? *Journal of International Development* 14:829–839

Wolch J (1990) *The Shadow State: Government and Voluntary Sector in Transition*. New York: The Foundation Centre

After Neoliberalism? Community Activism and Local Partnerships in Aotearoa New Zealand

Wendy Larner and David Craig

Introduction: Partnership, Neoliberalism and Community Activism

According to a welter of rhetoric, policy documents and new initiatives, in Aotearoa New Zealand neoliberalism has been replaced by a new form of joined up, inclusive governance characterised by relationships of collaboration, trust and, above all, partnership. The new emphasis on partnership extends across economic, social and environmental governance ambits, and out into the very future well-being of the nation. A recent high-level policy document states:

> Partnership is at the heart of the sustainable development approach. We want to engage with others who have a stake in the issues, and work together to develop and implement the programme of action. We want to build an innovative and productive New Zealand. The sustainable development approach will help us find solutions that provide the best outcomes for the environment, the economy and our increasingly diverse society. New Zealand's success in the modern world depends on this—so too does the wellbeing of future generations ... The government expects that others will recognise the partnership approach as our normal way of doing business. (Department of Prime Minister and Cabinet 2003)

The academic debate about the significance of the new partnership ethos, and its wider Third Way accoutrements, is much less conclusive. Indeed, there is acknowledged "methodological anarchy and definitional chaos" (Ling 2000:82) in this literature. Some see the rise of partnerships as an example of a "flanking compensatory mechanism for the inadequacies of the market mechanism" (Jessop 2002:455), whereas others venture that partnerships may represent a new form of social governance based on trust and collaboration (Clarke and Glendinning 2002; Newman 2001; Rhodes 2000).

Partnerships might signal a wider hybridisation process between markets and societies, wherein market competition and contractual obligations are "re-embedded" in an "inclusive" post-neoliberal consensus (Polanyi 1957; Porter and Craig 2004). Seen in this context, partnership could be part of the "roll out" of neoliberalism itself (Peck and Tickell 2002), the contested processes of experimentation through which various state agencies are trying to distance themselves from the more-market approaches of "roll back neoliberalism" and recreate conditions for social integration and the regulation of capitalism (Keil 2002:586). Or does partnership mark a return to a very old liberalism, the "positive" or "social liberalism" of enhancing capability, social investment and human capital stretching from J S Mill forward to Amartya Sen (1999) (itself powerfully implicated in the political legitimation and accommodation of liberal market economics)?

National and regional differences further complicate the academic analysis of partnerships, just as they complicate and change our accounts of neoliberalism. Edwards et al, for example, stress that: "Partnership is neither a neutral term, nor one with a fixed definition; rather the meaning of 'partnership' is discursively constructed and contested through political rhetoric, policy documentation, programme regulations, and grassroots practice" (2001:295). Indeed, even in the United Kingdom, where partnerships have received considerable academic attention over the last decade, the discursive mobilisation of partnership is variously attributed to Thatcherism (Clarke and Newman 1997; Hastings 1996), the European Union (Edwards et al 2001:294), and Third Wayism (Newman 2001). Country-specific studies of the place of partnerships in restructured institutions, organisations and social relations also reveal significant differences. The Irish case, for example, is characterised by a neo-corporatist version of partnership that is the legacy of a national level tripartite agreement between sectoral interests (Walsh, Craig and McCafferty 1998), whereas in Canada the rise of partnership is usually attributed to the effects of neoliberal restructuring, the rise of contractualism, and the distancing of governments from direct service delivery (Brock 2002). More generally, there is also a long history of co-operation between public and voluntary agencies in the context of the "mixed social economy" of welfarism (Valverde 1995).

Seen collectively, these debates about the relationships between neoliberalism and partnership have the virtue of moving our understandings of neoliberalism well beyond that of a monolithic political project and the preference for a minimalist state. Further examination of this literature also suggests that strange organisational formations are emerging under the umbrella of partnership, and contradictory demands and tendencies are embedded within them. Indeed, as some commentators have observed, the contradictory, historically contingent, features of partnerships may well be their most interesting feature—practically, politically and analytically (Clarke and Glendinning 2002:45). If so, understanding the specificities of partnership might help inform more adequate conceptualisations of neoliberalism, conceptions which are attentive to the contingency, political complexity and the different versions of neoliberalism found in different places (Larner 2000).

We ground our interest in these theoretical debates about the relationships between neoliberalism and partnership through an empirical focus on those people centrally involved in the creation and consolidation of local partnerships in Aotearoa New Zealand. To date, there has been analytic silence around the social characteristics, backgrounds and skills of the exponents and practitioners of partnership: those *working* the spaces of (and beyond?) neoliberalism. Rather, the "who" of partnerships has tended to focus on the different types of agencies and sectors involved, even though practitioner-oriented "how to" guides stress that "partnerships start with individuals, not organisations" (Wilson and Charlton 1997:25). Where particular social actors have received attention, it has tended to be in the context of demands for new skills. In the social policy literature, for example, it is argued that whereas earlier forms of social governance required managers with bureaucratic skills, partnership working requires management skills based on ability to network and promote change (Salamon 2002). In our research we have coined (or rather co-opted) "strategic brokers" (Reich 2001) as a new term for these people. But a new nomenclature still begs the question: just who are these so-called "partnership champions" (Audit Commission 1998)? What implications do their activities have for the forms local partnerships take in Aotearoa New Zealand? And what can we learn about neoliberalism from all this?

Our observation is that in Aotearoa New Zealand advocates of local partnerships are very often community activists who have been forced into, opted for, or been recruited into new "professionalised" roles in their efforts to advance social justice in a context marked by the legacy of nearly two decades of neoliberal experimentation, most notably (and locally) manifest in increased socio-spatial polarisation. Many see their current work as expressly about rebuilding the social links neoliberalism severed. As such, these new strategic brokers might be considered as prime exemplars of Polanyi's (1957) "enlightened reactionaries" seeking to re-embed market society relations, or alternatively as pragmatic improvisers who unwittingly contribute to the hybrid, contested "rolling out" of neoliberalism. Their activities focus on "etho-political" (Rose 1999) forms of social governance, manifest in the re-territorializing, re-moralising emphases on community, locality, civil society and family characteristic of "inclusive" liberalism (Craig 2003; Larner 2005; Porter and Craig 2004). Jessop (2002:461) associates this "neo-communitarian approach" with the "Schumpertarian Workfare Post-national Regime" (SWPR), which emphasises the contribution of the so-called "third sector" to economic development and social cohesion. He argues these efforts to empower community and citizen groups, which are focused on less competitive economic spaces such as inner cities, are "linked to efforts to manage issues of social exclusion and social cohesion at the urban level even in the most strongly neoliberal cases".

In the discussion that follows we both historicise and politicise the rise of local partnerships and strategic brokers in Aotearoa New Zealand. In turn, this discussion complicates and nuances analyses of neoliberalism. We show that while efforts to develop partnerships were initially ad hoc and focused on bottom-up "grassroots" or "flax roots" initiatives, they have now begun to feed into new forms of local strategic policy making and co-ordinated service delivery. In turn, this has created a new role for community activists. One of the most visible signs of this new role is the formal identification by government agencies of "partnership managers" and "social entrepreneurs" as new types of networked policy and community actors. Both specifics and generalities of grassroots and wider politics enter the frame: we are particularly concerned that existing accounts may have overlooked the sheer hard work and long-standing efforts of social movements, community organisations and other grassroots organisations to make their voices heard in governmental processes (Brodie 1996a, 1996b; Larner 2000). In turn, these processes and features have implications for the specific forms local partnerships take in Aotearoa New Zealand. In the wake of profound neoliberal fragmentation, the complexity of the re-joining task is such that these agents find themselves palpably stretched, often carrying personally the enormous costs of reintegration. In this regard, the new strategic brokers appear not just to be governmentalised in their professional functions, but in their personal and political commitments too. If this is true, then the new form of governance being rolled out is not just embedded, it is also feminised and domesticated.

To substantiate these claims, we draw on the findings of a large project on local partnerships in Aotearoa New Zealand (see http://www.lpg.org.nz). We focus on developments at the national level and in Waitakere City, which is a key site both for the research project and for the development of local partnerships more generally. At the national level, we have examined 27 "headline" partnership programmes that bring together government agencies, local institutions and community organisations in new collaborative relationships. We have collated relevant background documentation, conducted key informant interviews, and held two workshops in which our interim findings were shared with strategic brokers from central and local government. In Waitakere City, these more targeted exercises have been supplemented by extended participant observation and four "shared learning groups" that brought together academics, local politicians, policymakers and community-based practitioners. The findings from these exercises inform an analysis presented as follows. First, we overview and analyse the rise of local partnerships in Aotearoa New Zealand, identifying the role that community activists have played in shaping their distinctive characteristics. The following section shows that local partnerships are now being transformed from relatively ad hoc initiatives to formal governmental strategies. We identifiy and discuss the role of strategic brokers in this context, exploring the range of issues, including aspects of gendered professionalisation, that are arising as new positions are created for community activists in mainstream institutions. We conclude by returning to contemporary theorisations of neoliberalism and discussing the implications of our account.

Partnerships in Aotearoa New Zealand: History, Locality and Political Struggle

Aotearoa New Zealand is an ideal empirical research case from which to engage debates about the nature of neoliberalism, partnership and community activism. As a commentator observed in the late 1990s:

> The neoliberal experiment in New Zealand is the most ambitious attempt at constructing the free market as a social institution to be implemented anywhere this century. It is a clearer case of the costs and limits of reinventing the free market than the Thatcherite experiment in Britain (Gray 1998:39).

Jessop (2002:457) also describes New Zealand during this period as the "least impure form of neoliberalism". However, whereas during the 1980s and 1990s the policy emphasis was on marketisation, the "level playing field" and a minimal state, new issues have emerged as a consequence of sustained efforts to address issues of economic and social development in a context characterised by globalising economic processes, social polarisation and racialised poverty. Indeed, it can be argued that New Zealand's neoliberal project has now been through three distinct "phases": during the 1980s the state withdrew from many areas of economic production, while at the same time attempting to preserve—and even extend—the welfarist and social justice aspirations associated with social democracy; the more punitive phase of the early 1990s which saw an extension of the marketisation programme accompanied by the introduction of neo-conservative and/

or authoritarian policies and programmes in the area of social policy; a third phase in the late 1990s characterised by a "partnering" ethos and in which discourses of "social inclusion" and "social investment" sit awkwardly alongside more obviously neoliberal elements such as economic globalisation, market activation and contractualism (Larner 2003).

Partnerships have only recently explicitly entered into policy discourse in Aotearoa New Zealand and are most commonly understood to be an integral aspect of the third phase of neoliberalism: a response to the fragmentation of services associated with the earlier phases of neoliberal reforms. They are explained as effect of the efforts of the fifth Labour government to develop a local variant of "Third Wayism" (James 2002; Kelsey 2002). Certainly, there has been a great deal of inter-state policy learning with, for example, compacts between the government and the voluntary sector in Canada, the United Kingdom and New Zealand involving considerable consultation and mutual exchange amongst policy networks (Craig 2003; Phillips 2001). There is also a proliferation of pilot partnership programmes in which efforts are being made to link up central government, local institutions (including schools, hospitals and local government) and/or community and voluntary sector groups and Iwi/Maori groups. Our research has identified a wide range of these projects including community health plans; interagency well being strategies; Iwi and urban-Maori service delivery; full service schools; health and education action zones; safer community programmes; area-based employment and training projects and "one stop shops" for government services. In the most general terms, the aspiration is that these multi-level collaborative arrangements will meet local needs, solve seemingly intractable social problems, build community capacity and support local development efforts (Loomis 2002). We are calling these initiatives local partnerships in an effort to distinguish them from other forms of interagency and collaborative working.

Our claim is that these local partnerships have their antecedents in earlier periods. Specifically, many of the initiatives now called local partnerships have their origins in the long-standing efforts of local activists and community development advocates to resist policies and processes associated with the earlier versions of neoliberalism. We begin by observing that partnership as a principle of working in social services has a long provenance in New Zealand. For example, a prominent entry into policy discourse came in the 1970s when lottery funding allowed a plethora of so-called "non-statutory" (or voluntary) sector agencies with health, disability and welfare foci to take their place alongside more established community agencies such as the Intellectually Handicapped Children's Association (founded in 1949) and the Marriage Guidance Service (founded in 1948, linked to Department of Justice funding since 1960). During the 1980s, following the election of the fourth Labour government, there were partnership initiatives in housing (Housing Corporation of New Zealand 1990), employment training and work skills development, community welfare, day and foster care (Social Advisory Council 1986). Community development networks were actively promoted, sometimes from within offices of the Department of Social Welfare, and also in umbrella forums (McClure 1998:148). Perhaps most crucially, however, during this period the emergence of "partnership" as a core rubric in debates around the Treaty of Waitangi gave a particular urgency to the development of new relationships between government and community (see, for example, Ministry of Maori Affairs 1988; State Services Commission 1989).

Yet, despite these early examples of partnership working, by the late 1980s the dominant ethos was that of competitive contractualism, reflecting the sustained move towards managerialism in the public sector. This move was cemented by the introduction of the Public Finance Act (1990) and a new focus on output-based accountability regimes. It has been widely discussed how the shift to contract culture saw an expansion in the accounting and reporting infrastructure of community and voluntary organisations, with an associated need for staff to perform these functions (Conradson 2002). Not only did this see an expansion in the size and scale of many organisations, it also saw increasing professionalisation as volunteer's roles were formalised with an associated increase in training and skill development. However, in contrast to other countries, in New Zealand these individuals were often self-motivated and self-funded (Wilson et al 2001). Increasing numbers of people within subcontracting agencies and organisations, including many with years of practical and political engagement, began (or were forced) to gain formal qualifications, as the new skills were required of them. A good example is provided by the workshops the Women's Refuge ran on contractualism, based on a handbook produced for them by a legal academic (Seuffert and McGovern 2000). One consequence was that community organisations increasingly became a key site for de-centralised professional and technical capacity. In many cases this gaining of professional and technical expertise was complemented by hearty political engagement, powerfully motivated by anger over the impact of neoliberalism. As one interviewee emphasised:

> You know, we grew our leaders through experience. Years and years of taking the hits, surviving the hits, and forming our views.

For many community activists the impact of competitive contractualism on existing collaborative modes of working was devastating. Explicit competition undercut trust, and contractual obligations narrowed operational focus to individual clients and specific objectives.

Community workers found themselves compelled to devote disproportionate time representing their work through reporting frameworks they found objectionable and alien. Client focus, teamed with a new emphasis on confidentiality, served to undermine day-to-day interagency practice. New providers entering the market profoundly and continually fractionated existing fields of working. Relationships with central government funding agencies were characterised by bruising and repetitive negotiations, and the emphasis on narrowly specified outputs submerged issues widely understood as needing more broad-based and longer-term interventions.

This new ethos also radically reconfigured public sector accountabilities, expressing them in objectified output terms that encouraged public servants to define and delimit their "core business". New departmental demarcations and sharply focused job descriptions, developed in a context that expressly valorised competition and greatly impinged on the ability of public servants to work across departmental boundaries. Moreover, the new distinction between policymaking and service provision that arose out of the discourse of "provider capture" led to the "disembedding" of the content-based knowledge previously integral to the public sector. In management positions, actors such as medical directors and school inspectors were increasingly displaced and subordinated by those with more generic forms of knowledge (managers, accountants and auditors). One consequence was that many of those in the public sector with a political commitment to more collective modes of working found official agencies increasingly alien environments and exited—frustrated, even bitterly disappointed.

Despite, or perhaps because of, the hostile environment many contemporary partnerships have their basis in this period. For those in the social services, in part because of their "client" focus and basis in shared professional aims and practice, the high cost and destructiveness of competition was obvious. Among these actors, there was both an expressed preference to work in more collaborative ways, and a sense of relationships that might frame this action. Further, because competitive contractualism didn't explicitly fund coordination, it created a vacuum into which agencies such as Barnadoes and Presbyterian Support Services could move in order to contest neoliberalism on the basis of a shared orientation to local issues. Indeed, it could be argued that their strong values and sense of common imperatives were actually sharpened by lack of funding, and by the seeming intransigence of central authorities in the face of local needs. Local collaboration, often on "the smell of an oily rag", became a rallying issue for both organisations and professionals, an issue that sharpened their position and practice against prevailing winds seen as socially divisive.

During the 1990s a range of central government initiatives created new forums in which locally based skills in advocacy and contest could be further developed, including the establishment of locality-based social programmes such as Regional Employment and Access Councils (REACs), Social Welfare District Executive Committees (DECs), and the Community Organisation Grants Scheme (COGS). Later, short-lived area health boards offered local opportunities for community interventions around health. Local government reform also created territorial authorities with comparatively large resource bases and significant planning responsibilities. Reluctance on the part of central government agencies to devolve mandates or share revenue with these local authorities created a domain of contestation and some local councils began to adopt advocacy and coordinating roles around issues such as social well-being. Together, these initiatives further raised the prospect of an increasingly professionalised cadre of local actors who had advocacy roles linked to central government, relationships with other professionals and practitioners, and ties with community and voluntary networks. The story below is not unusual:

> I had been involved in setting up a co-operative that was done in a very community development way. And then there was the establishment of a community initiative to address unemployment and self-employment issues. This small unit was the precursor to the current Community Employment Group so when that was set up and space was made for a 0.5 fieldworker, I became that. I was also on the REAC committee. Then the unit was amalgamated with other small units of a similar ilk. And the new boss, after a couple of conversations, said to me I want you to come and work in Wellington for six months. So I went to Wellington and was suddenly involved in developing and implementing funding programmes, writing briefing notes to the Minister of Finance, helping with the reorganisation and amalgamation process.

There was also a local dimension to these career trajectories, especially in greenfield suburban and urban fringe developments of the 1960s and 1970s, where social services were not yet well established, and activists were able to move up through voluntary organisations into senior roles. As one activist manager recalls:

> … we strongly believed in the need to have our own identity, to be in control of our own destiny. People together making decisions for themselves—not being "done to". We just did it. We had a strong belief in it and in our ability to do it. It was for the benefit of our children and we grew strong as a community from it. Playcentre gave me, and many other women in the community, the opportunity for

personal growth through the training programme. That was a major turning point for me and set me off on an unintended career path.

It is important not to underestimate the identity politics to all of this. Feminists and Maori (sometimes embodied in the same person) played central roles in these processes, as did locality-based solidarities. Thus, while these "social movements" had begun from grassroots struggles defined in opposition to mainstream institutions, during this period activists were more increasingly likely to engage from within these institutions. Nor is it coincidence that this was the period of mass participation in tertiary education. The increasing numbers of people entering into formal study, particularly in education, health and the social sciences, further fostered both the development of new professional capacities in social sector organisations (as the demand for contract managers and financial expertise continued to grow) and further professionalisation of community actors and activists. The story below is typical:

> I moved from being a Mum, doing my training, and I went and worked at the HELP Foundation doing crisis work with raped, abused women. Then I became involved in a group that wanted to set up services in Waitakere ... What was a very organic community based service then grew from people getting together with the statutory agencies ... identifying the needs, going to the City Council.

Finally, these institutional developments had a symbiotic relationship with the rise of a new cohort of activists. In the context of growing inequality, and with the funding and professionalisation imperatives described above, some community groups began to refocus their efforts. Often these struggles involved efforts to embed policies and programmes in particular places and communities by emphasising the importance of local knowledges and local accountabilities. While the so-called "Maori renaissance" was a strong and leading case for this politicisation, with wider ripple effects, long--standing community development discourses were also central to these efforts. Although these were framed as the political claims of the flaxroots/grassroots, often key community representatives and NGOs found themselves cast in the position of "surrogates" for community voices. New types of community entrepreneurs thus began to play an important role in articulating the claims of a transformed grassroots that more fully understood the political significance of strategic networks and the reform of governmental programmes as a key aim.

Overall, therefore, the changes associated with earlier forms of neoliberalism involved an enormous shifting upwards of gears for non-government service providers, community agencies and political activists. This provides a crucial context for understanding the rise of local partnerships in Aotearoa New Zealand. Many of these organisations and activists struggled for over two decades to maintain themselves in the context of competitive contractualism. In this process, they survived the thin promises and often frank duplicities of the neoliberal engagement with "civil society". They also learned new ways of contesting policy agendas and how to position themselves in relation to local competitors, particular populations and local needs. Thus a crucial, yet unexpected, consequence of the earlier periods of neoliberalism was the emergence of community activists both as highly skilled and articulate organisational leaders and lobbyists. But should we think about these people in the "positive liberal" terms of newly capable, active liberal subjects working in new domains of empowerment, and doing the same by enabling their clients? To answer this question, we need to consider the wider context in which they now operate.

Governmentalising Partnership: The Rise of Mandatory Partnership Working

It was the election of the fifth Labour government that saw sustained efforts to formalise partnerships, manifest in the recent *Statement of Government Intentions for an Improved Community–Government Relationship* (New Zealand Government 2001), which expresses the desire to develop new relationships between national government, local institutions and communities. From the highest levels, partnership working is urged in normative terms. Policy makers argue that strengthening local communities through the mechanism of local partnerships will help New Zealanders to respond more positively to economic and social change. There is a broad consensus amongst politicians and practitioners alike that rebuilding institutional infrastructure through the fostering of collaborative relationships will allow for the sharing of "best practice" knowledge and practices, and more nuanced understandings of the local needs those practices must meet. In both economic and social arenas there is a marked effort to institutionally re-embed a wide range of activities that during the previous period were seen through "more market" lenses. In turn, this is giving rise to new hybrid forms of governance that fuse policy-makers and communities, and erode the purchaser–provider split that was previously so important in the New Zealand context. Nor is this simply rhetoric. Considerable resources are now being devoted to linking together various initiatives, encouraging mutual learning and identifying "best practice" partnerships.

It is in this context that local partnerships have come to the centre stage politically and practically. One consequence is a shift from partnerships as localised initiatives that emerge out of the activities of a group of like-minded individuals and/or organisations, to partnership working as a "mandatory tool" in the social sector. In other words, local partnerships are now being codified and made governmental (Larner and Butler 2005). Despite scepticism in the international literature on partnerships, and indeed amongst some of the players themselves, it is widely assumed that partnerships are mutually beneficial and that efforts to "join together" different organisations will create more than the sum of the parts. The ambition is that these partnerships will draw together the otherwise separate institutional worlds of central, local government and community organisations, and allow these to be more closely aligned with the needs of specific locales. Not surprisingly, given the context outlined above, this was by no means a one-sided, top-down development:

> What happened out here—and it wasn't a new start, what they did was build on what was already there—organisations got together. Those delivering either similar sorts of services, or services that could be running parallel or linking up in some way, and said Let's plan *together*. So, for instance, in Mental Health Services, all the Mental Health organisations got together, *with consumers*, and that's when "shared vision" was created … What they did was set up a way, that when they wanted to put proposals forward for funding, they actually got the mandate of the wider group. So in other words, they were working collaboratively in a competitive environment. The same thing happened with services for abuse and trauma, sexual abuse and so on. They've set up the best practice stuff. They've set up, too, a whole lot of networks. They've set up organisations and umbrella groups and networks.

This governmentalisation of local partnerships is embedded within distinctive policy rationales. In particular, the shift in policy documents from the discourse of community development to that of social capital is notable. Indeed, it is the strong influence of social capital discourse that underpins current efforts to map local services, measure community resources and create inventories of social service organisations and activities. In turn, this is reshaping understandings of community. Rather than "community" being a self-sufficient sphere separate from "state" and "market", consider the following claim; "Communities are the point where the public sector, private sector and voluntary sector meet and interact" (Loomis 2002:6). Moreover, "strengthening" communities is defined as a capability/investment process. Not only is the "social capital" of different "communities" calculable (see Robinson 1997), so too can it accumulate and grow through the mechanism of local partnerships. Moreover, the joining up of the etho-political domains of community under rationales of collaboration, consensus and partnership is at once de-politicising and embedding of previous disaggregations (Harriss 2001; Porter and Craig 2004). But from an "on the ground" perspective, community is also a natural, doable field of operations: a field that locally based brokers can mobilise:

> We recognised it was really important to work with the really active groups that we had out here anyway, keeping *close* contact with environmental groups, ratepayer groups, particularly the key ones in those early days ... They were far more active in working with the other groups. Then there were key people in the community that also needed to be kept on board with it. So what we did, we made sure that we were actually involving them right from the very early stages with talking about what we might be doing. They could see that it wasn't our idea, that what we were doing was actually pulling together into a framework the stuff that they'd been pushing for, for so long.

The actual techniques through which local partnerships are being codified are varied. For example, government departments are supporting the construction of databases, searchable web pages, funding guides, checklists, and best practice manuals. As part of this process, partnerships are being increasingly delineated from other less formal forms of inter-agency working (such as alliances, collaborations, coordination, cooperation, networks, joint working, multi-party working groups).[1] There is a growing consensus that partnerships are characterised by formal agreements. At the same time, the new approach is understood to require ways of working that are more citizen focused, relationship based and collaborative. The most common solution to the apparently contradictory demands for both formal agreements and more consensual ways of working are Memorandums of Understanding, which establish the respective roles and responsibilities of the partners. In these highly aspirational agreements there is a strong emphasis on values as the basis for relationships between different levels of government and the community sector (keywords include honesty, trust, diversity, integrity, compassion and caring). Thus "relational contracting" is emerging as a key mechanism for government agencies, replacing the more hierarchical contracts that predominated in earlier periods.

Finally, as partnerships are being formalised and distinguished from contracts, consultation and collaboration, government departments are now starting to employ individuals whose task is to build partnerships and other collaborative relationships between government departments, non-governmental organisations, Maori, local government and communities. These actors are focused on both growing local capacity and central government's new concerns to efficiently and effectively "join up" local services towards wider policy ends (Review of the Centre 2002). As we saw above, these changes have been driven in part by the rising capacity of professional activists and others at local and central levels. However, with the governmentalisation of partnerships, it is now the official discourses of partnership that nurture the expansion of partnership working. What implications does this have for the roles of the community activists? The next section focuses more specifically on the rise of "strategic brokers" and the new roles they have begun to play.

Strategic Brokers: Activism, Inclusion and Networks

Our argument is that, with the rise of mandatory partnership working, community activists have begun to take on new roles, wherein not just their professional skills and their relationships with civil society organisations are recognised, but also their "soft skills" and commitments: networking, relationship management, and local/sectoral activism. Most immediately, the governmentalisation of local partnerships is reinforcing the role of those strategic brokers who in multiple institutional and community sites emerged as advocates for both their organisations and more relational forms of practice during the earlier neoliberal periods. There have long been local network coordinator roles in community development and social services. These new roles bring not just all those responsibilities, but also an ability to articulate them into the multiple levels of governance now emerging as vital partnerships contexts. There is also a growing demand for what the social policy literature calls "partnership champions" (Audit Commission 1998) or "reticulists" (Challis et al 1988); those committed and charismatic individuals who can drive changes through organisations in a context where the role of key individuals, and the relationships between them, is understood as central to the successful creation of local partnerships.

It is widely recognised by both academics and practitioners that the most successful partnership working has strong leadership. Moreover "partnership champions" require a different skill set to that emphasised by competitive contractualism. Hudson et al. (1999: 251), for example, claim that their characteristics are likely to include not only technical or competency-based factors, but also social and interpersonal skills. Similarly, Rhodes (2000:355–356) notes that the attribute of "diplomacy" or "management by negotiation" lies at the heart of successful managerial strategies in the current period (he contrasts this with the "hands off" management or the arms-length relationships associated with the "macho manager"). More generally, it is understood that effective partnership working requires the ability to build trust, reciprocity, understanding and credibility. In particular, the value of individuals who can work across boundaries is increasingly recognised, as are "enablement" skills required to engage multiple partners. It is these skills we recognise through our use of the term strategic broker:

> Relationships are about personal management. The strategic broker is operating at both an organisational and individual level.

In the New Zealand context, at least two distinct roles have emerged for the new strategic brokers: "partnership managers" who are most likely to be located within government agencies, and "social entrepreneurs" who are more likely to be locally based in either territorial authorities or community organisations. In each case, however, these roles are now being formally identified in restructured institutional structures, policy documents and programme design. Moreover, in addition to the technical knowledges vital to both professional practice and wider policy strategy, these new institutional actors are required to have the new "soft skills" identified above. As one put it:

> The difference between coordination and strategic brokering is that a coordinator just brings people together, yet a strategic broker brings them together and sees what needs to happen to take things further, and gets on and does it. They have the vision, the networks and the practical implementation skills to take things a whole step further.

"Partnership managers", for example, must have not only sectoral and technical expertise, but also knowledge of government and community networks. Moreover, it is assumed they come with this knowledge rather than these being skills learned on the job. We note with interest that existing knowledge of particular networks is now being regularly written into job descriptions. The Partnerships Manager for Housing New Zealand, for example, is required to have not only "knowledge of third sector housing", but also "excellent networking abilities" and fluency in Maori and/or Pacific languages is also identified as an advantage. Similarly, the Ministry of Education recently created a position for a Senior Partnerships Advisor focused on Iwi and Maori education partnerships. This position, which deals with issues of strategic planning, risk assessment and financial management, requires not only sectoral expertise, but also "an understanding of partnership and effective relationship management" and "the ability to operate effectively in a predominantly Maori environment". As one relationship broker recently noted in a workshop, for the first time her skills in maintaining quality relationships are being formally recognised in her national strategic partnerships role. As another put it:

> There is a lack of boundaries, the expectations are ridiculous. There is a need for all sorts of things in the job, from multiculturalism to self-inspection/reflection.

In contrast to the partnership managers, those named as "social entrepreneurs" are more likely to be firmly rooted in the local or community context, often affiliated to voluntary or community organisations. Unlike partnership managers who are networked to other government agencies as well as their "partners", the priority for social entrepreneurs is that they have local knowledge. "Social entrepreneurs", says Loomis (2002) are "community advisors who empower, mentor and facilitate". The Minister for Social Services explains: "By taking the same approach to risk, opportunity and innovation as a business entrepreneur, social entrepreneurs grow social capital in the same way those in the business world build their balance sheets". He goes on to explain: "A key feature of social entrepreneurship is the use of partnerships" (Maharey 2001). As with the partnership managers, the once informal networking of these local actors is being increasingly formalised. For example, at the end of 2001 the first New Zealand Conference on Social Entrepreneurship was held (in the capital city of Wellington!). There is also a growing tendency for social entrepreneurs to be institutionally located because this gives them access to funding and resourcing. To give an example, the government recently committed three years of salary to pay for a social entrepreneur in Highbury, a poor suburb in a provincial town that had been experiencing gang-related issues.

In both cases, however, these "strategic brokers" spend a great deal of time building and maintaining relationships because no policy or strategy is now complete or legitimate without evidence of consulta-tion and/or collaboration. In the broader strategic context it is also important to avoid overlaps, sort out niches, and create wider plat-forms to legitimate the work of their organisations. This is precisely the domain of their expertise: explicitly geared to *process* issues, they can facilitate, mediate and negotiate, nurture networks, and deploy cultural knowledge and local knowledge in ways that enable tradition-ally "silent" voices to be heard along with the articulate, persistent and powerful (Community and Voluntary Sector Working Party 2001:70). These skills are both embodied and deeply personalised, and rely on well-developed abilities to network; although, more recently, elec-tronic means of consultation and strategy have been used, including the web pages and databases mentioned previously.

But these are not the only knowledges that strategic brokers require. The new forms of professional knowledge and practice require not only knowledge *of* communities but also knowledge *about* communities. Technical knowledges around emerging social issues are developing rapidly, including developments in population information (surveys, social mapping, area-referenced social deprivation indices) and public health information based on social epidemiology. While initially harnessed to neoliberal attempts to better target government resources, these tools are now being used to support the arguments for the redistribution of social services amongst local populations. While by no means uncontested by other modes of local political power (most notably, clinical medicine; see Tenbensel 2001), such information is being used by the strategic brokers to provide hard evidence of the misdistribution of services and resources, and the cross cutting aspects of social deprivation, health, well-being, safety, employment and education. All of these issues emerge as conspicuous within particular local places, strengthening the ambit of the brokers who are developing local partnerships to address social issues.

Thus, in the composite forms of governance emerging under the umbrella of "local partnerships", new roles are being created for those who once understood themselves as oppositional voices. In turn, this marks a new phase in the professionalisation of community activists as once informal activities are increasingly formalised. This phase is being further facilitated by an increasing tendency for movement of personnel between government departments, local government and community groups, both through permanent movements and through mechanisms such as secondments. Inevitably, because of the mix of skills needed, those who fill these positions will not only be required to exercise new forms of leadership and management skills, they are also expected to introduce new cultures of working and learning into their institutions. Their positions involve commitment and enthusiasm, as well as ongoing attempts to link personal and organisational values. Of course, the demand for constant networking also often leads to over commitment and the intensification of labour. Finally, perhaps unsurprisingly, the vast majority of these actors are women:

> Quite simply, women, often because they raise families, are the relationship builders and therefore it's not surprising that they are more process-oriented because they are used to looking after people, trying to look after their interests, hearing their voices, trying to work out ways of dealing with things.

All this could be cast in empowering, socially progressive terms. However, its gendered inflection also raises suspicions about the broader implications of strategic brokerage. As Roelvink and Craig (2005) argue, women are not only charged with the usual double shift of professional earnings and homemaking/housework, there is now a new version of a third shift in which their domesticated duties and practices spill over into the "emotional labour" (Hochschild 1983) required by these new forms of governance. Given the enormous transaction costs involved in re-embedding economic and social activities after "more market" oriented forms of neoliberalism, this mobilisation of un- and underpaid labour, and the expansion of governmentalising ambits into feminised and domesticated realms, becomes perhaps a bit less surprising. Moreover, what is happening in this new form of governance is that local coordination (and strategic brokers) is compensating for the inability of government agencies to overcome a highly silo-ised, vertically accountable regime in an effort to achieve social change. While the shifting of responsibilities and shared accountabilities to the local level legitimates "after neoliberalism", and may be seen to address the worst failings of earlier forms of neoliberalism, this it is not the same as government agencies and communities being jointly accountable for social outcomes.

Conclusion: After Neoliberalism?

We have emphasized how local partnerships in New Zealand depend on strategic brokers. These are often community activists whose role and function is now attaining more specific recognition within organisations and in job descriptions. However, the political context of their work remains fraught, with their activities directly linked to the politicisation of local issues, while at the same time they are increasingly required to make their political claims technical, or turn their contests into collaboration. Moreover, while their expertise in process often enables shrewd political positioning, the wider contexts of political contest, organisational pluralism, identity politics, as well as rapidly developing technologies of information, consultation and surveillance continue to stretch strategic brokers in their day-to-day practice. We have also emphasised that the emerging partnership ethos is profoundly gendered, with women disproportionately represented in these brokering roles. But what does this tell us about the broader, "post-neoliberal" political environment within which these partnerships and the strategic brokers are operating?

This process we have described could be interpreted as exemplifying increased state penetration into the community and voluntary sector by a state seeking partners with whom it can act out community consensus without reducing core market orientations. Here, the "shadow state" (Wolch 1990) is being given wider ambit, but with its increased political capability firmly channelled into minimising the fallout from earlier phases of neoliberalism, which has barely had its core tendencies otherwise reined in. In this way, the neoliberal state gets to have its contractual cake, and eat it too, courtesy of the expanded domestic domains of feminised strategic brokers. Because there are no preconceived limits to the transfer of heightened transaction costs of joining up neoliberal fragmentation to strategic brokers, there are, therefore, no limits to the range of skills these newly engaged brokers will be asked to deploy. Whether all this adds up to a new partnering state that is substantively post-neoliberal remains to be seen. Plausibly, though, a complex, re-gendered re-embedding of state, community and market relations is emerging, with strategic brokers providing all sorts of legitimating, rejoining and realigning labour. In this configuration, basic neoliberal settings will persist, but in a new, itself shifting hybrid, based on expansion into previously less governmentalised modes of domestic and social engagement.

What this also shows is that wider neoliberal settings seem to require legitimation and embedding from less than neoliberal subjectivities operating in less than neoliberal local spaces and domains. What is not so clear, however, is the ability of would-be "post-neoliberal" activists and projects to reach up from these localised domains and colonise wider political and governmental projects to the point where key statutory and policy frameworks underpinning neoliberal settings are changed, and real post-neoliberal, territorial accountabilities for social outcomes are possible. For example, in New Zealand the Public Finance Act underpins a continued emphasis on contractualism and a narrow, market-contested output accountability regime. Strategic brokers are more involved in making up for the shared accountability shortcomings of the Public Finance Act than they are in designing its demise. This is not to say, however, that all this is merely co-option. As our research shows, many of these strategic brokers know exactly the kinds of unreasonable demands being placed on them, but are determined, against whatever structural constraints, to make the most of the new situation.

Finally, we argue that this case exemplifies an argument that neoliberal spaces and subjectivities are not simply imposed from above, nor is "resistance" simply a bottom-up political response to macro-level structural processes. Rather, new governmental spaces and subjects are emerging out of multiple and contested discourses and practices. Seen from this point of view, neoliberalism is likely to have many varied effects, and be subject to re-embedding contests in diverse, locally specific ways. Not only is neoliberalism a political-economic process that aspires to foster globalisation, marketisation and entrepreneurship, paradoxically it could also constitute a rallying cry for various sites of community. In this context, explicating further the contradictory spaces and subjects associated with different forms and phases of neoliberalism, both in New Zealand and more generally, would make a major theoretical and empirical contribution to contemporary debates.

Acknowledgements

This research was funded by the New Zealand Foundation for Research Science and Technology Project UOAX0233. Earlier versions were presented at a Workshop on New Welfare State Architectures, Boston, 2002 and the Annual Meeting of the American Association of Geographers, New Orleans, 2003. Our thanks to the other members of the Local Partnerships and Governance Research Group for their intellectual engagement, to Megan Courtney and Maria Butler for their research collaboration, and to the referees and editors for their generous and constructive comments.

Endnote

[1] We are very conscious our project is also contributing to the broader process of naming, categorizing and constituting local partnerships.

References

Audit Commission (1998) *A Fruitful Partnership: Effective Partnership Working.* London: Audit Commission

Brock K (2002) "State, society and the voluntary sector: Agency, ownership and responsibility." Paper presented at the Annual Canadian Political Science Association Meeting, Toronto, 29 May

Brodie J (1996a) New state forms, new political spaces. In R Boyer and D Drache (eds) *States Against Markets* (pp 383–398). London: Routledge

Brodie J (1996b) Restructuring and the new citizenship. In I Bakker (ed) *Rethinking Restructuring* (pp 126–140). Toronto: University of Toronto Press

Challis L, Fuller S, Henwood M, Klein R, Plowden W, Webb A, Whittingham P and Wistow G (1998) *Joint Approaches to Social Policy.* Cambridge: Cambridge University Press

Clarke J and Glendinning C (2002) Partnerships and the remaking of welfare governance. In C Glendinning, M Powell and K Rummery (eds) *Partnerships, New Labour and the Governance of Welfare* (pp 33–50). Bristol: The Policy Press

Clarke J and Newman J (1997) *The Managerial State: Power, Politics and Ideology in the Making of Social Welfare.* London: Sage

Community and Voluntary Sector Working Party (2001) *Communities and Government: Potential for Partnership.* Wellington: New Zealand Government

Conradson D (2002) "Negotiating value-based tensions: Voluntary welfare provision in Christchurch New Zealand." Presentation to the Geography Department, University of Auckland. Mimeo available from author

Craig D (2003) Re-territorialising health: Inclusive partnerships, joined up governance, and common accountability platforms in Thirdway New Zealand. *Policy and Politics* 31(3):335–352

Department of Prime Minister and Cabinet (2003) *Sustainable Development for New Zealand: Programme of Action*. Wellington: Department of Prime Minister and Cabinet, January

Edwards B, Goodwin M, Pemberton S and Woods M (2001) Partnerships, power and scale in rural governance. *Environment and Planning C: Government and Policy* 19:289–310

Gray J (1998) *False Dawn: The Illusions of Global Capital*. London: Granta Publications

Harriss J (2001) *Depoliticising Development: The World Bank and Social Capital*. London: The Anthem Press

Hastings A (1996) Unravelling the process of "Partnership" in urban regeneration policy. *Urban Studies* 33(2):253–268

Hochschild A (1983) *The Managed Heart*. Berkeley: University of California Press

Housing Corporation of New Zealand (1990) *Partnership in Housing: Housing Corporation Partnerships Create Housing Solutions*. Wellington: Housing Corporation of New Zealand

Hudson B, Hardy B, Henwood M and Wistow G (1999) In pursuit of interagency collaboration in the public sector. *Public Management* 1(2):235–260

James C (2002) Dialogue: Partnership the way for welfare. *New Zealand Herald* 4 April

Jessop B (2002) Liberalism, neoliberalism and urban governance: A state-theoretical perspective. *Antipode* 34(3):452–472

Keil R (2002) "Common-sense" neoliberalism: Progressive conservative urbanism in Toronto, Canada. *Antipode* 34(3):578–601

Kelsey J (2002) *At the Crossroads*. Wellington: Bridget Williams Books

Larner W (2000) Neoliberalism: Policy, ideology, governmentality. *Studies in Political Economy* 63:5–26

Larner W (2003) Guest editorial: Neoliberalism? *Environment and Planning D: Society and Space* 21(5):309–312

Larner W (2005) Neoliberalism in (regional) theory and practice: The Stronger Communities Action Fund in New Zealand. *Australian Geographical Studies* 43(1):9–18

Larner W and Butler M (2005) Governmentalities of local partnerships: The rise of a "partnering state" in New Zealand. *Studies in Political Economy* 75:85–108

Ling T (2000) Unpacking partnership: The case of health care. In J Clarke, S Gewirtz and E McLaughlin (eds) *New Managerialism, New Welfare?* (pp 82–101). London: Sage

Loomis T (2002) A framework for developing sustainable communities: A discussion paper. Wellington: Ministry of Social Development

Maharey S (2001) Social entrepreneurs media release and speech. New Zealand Government, 23 November

McClure M (1998) *A Civilised Community: A History of Social Security in New Zealand 1898–1998*. Auckland: Auckland University Press in association with the Historical Branch, Department of Internal Affairs

Ministry of Maori Affairs (1988) *Partnership Response: Policy Statement*. Wellington: Ministry of Maori Affairs

Newman J (2001) *Modernising Governance*. London: Sage

New Zealand Government (2001) *Statement of Government Intentions for an Improved Community–Government Relationship*. Wellington: Ministry of Social Development

Peck J and Tickell A (2002) Neoliberalizing space. *Antipode* 34(3):380–404

Phillips S (2001) "Striking an accord: The limits of transnational policy transfer in Canada's voluntary sector—Federal Government Framework Agreement." Paper presented to the Annual Meeting of the Canadian Political Science Association, Toronto, 29 May

Polanyi K (1957) *The Great Transformation. The Political and Economic Origins of our Time*. Boston, MA: Beacon Press

Porter D and Craig D (2004) The third way and the third world: Poverty reduction and social inclusion strategies in the rise of "inclusive" liberalism. *Review of International Political Economy* 11(2):387–423

Reich R (2001) *The Future of Success*. New York: Alfred A Knopf

Review of the Centre (2002) Report presented to the Ministers of State Services and Finance. Wellington: New Zealand Government

Rhodes R (2000) The governance narrative: Key findings and lessons from the ESRC's Whitehall Programme. *Public Administration* 78(2):345–363

Robinson D (ed) (1997) *Social Capital and Policy Development*. Wellington: Institute of Policy Studies

Roelvink G and Craig D (2005) The man in the partnering state: Regendering the social through partnership. *Studies in Political Economy* 75:109–125

Rose N (1999) Inventiveness in politics. *Economy and Society* 28(3):467–493

Salamon L (ed) (2002) *The Tools of Government: A Guide to the New Governance*. New York: Oxford University Press

Sen A (1999) *Development as Freedom*. London: Oxford University Press

Seuffert N and McGowan J (2000) *Making the Most of Contracting: Information and Exchange in Context for Community Groups*. Hamilton: University of Waikato

Social Advisory Council (1986) *Partnership: The Delivery of Social and Community Services*. Wellington: Government Printer

State Services Commission (1989) *Partnership Dialogue: A Maori Consultation Process*. Wellington: State Services Commission

Tenbensel T (2001) Health prioritisation as rationalist policy making: Problems, prognoses and prospects. *Policy and Politics* 28(3):425–440

Valverde M (1995) The mixed social economy as a Canadian tradition. *Studies in Political Economy* 47:33–60

Walsh J, Craig S and McCafferty D (eds) (1998) *Local Partnerships for Social Inclusion?* Dublin: Oak Tree Press

Wilson A and Charlton K (1997) *Making Partnerships Work: A Practical Guide for the Public, Private, Voluntary and Community Sector*. London: Joseph Rowntree Foundation

Wilson C, Hendricks A K and Smithies R (2001) "Lady Bountiful" and the "Virtual Volunteers": The changing face of social services volunteering. *Social Policy Journal of New Zealand* 17:124–146

Wolch J (1990) *The Shadow State: Government and the Voluntary Sector in Transition*. New York: The Foundation Centre

Wendy Larner is Professor of Human Geography and Sociology, School of Geographical Sciences, University of Bristol, having recently moved from the University of Auckland, Aotearoa New Zealand. She is co-editor (with William Walters) of *Global Governmentality: New Perspectives on International Rule* (Routledge 2004), and author of over 40 journal articles and book chapters. Her research interests include political economy, governmentality, economic geography and social policy.

David Craig is Senior Lecturer, Department of Sociology, University of Auckland. His research spans comparative governance, health and public policy, and international political economy. His current book (co-authored with Doug Porter) *Empires of the Mind: Poverty Reduction, Good Governance and Development Beyond Neoliberalism* will be published by Routledge in 2005.

Chapter 2

Authority and Expertise: The Professionalisation of International Development and the Ordering of Dissent

Uma Kothari

An expert helps disguise the government of men as the administration of things, thus making it possible for men to be governed as if they were things. (Adams 1979 quoted in Crewe and Harrison 1998:109)

Introduction

I discuss the successful co-optation of "alternative" approaches to international development into the mainstream neoliberal agenda of multi-lateral and bi-lateral agencies, and argue that this is enabled by the ongoing professionalisation and technicalisation of the UK development industry. I suggest here that an increasingly technocratic and tool-kit approach to development has exacerbated the depoliticisation of development and the atheoretical perspective of much development discourse. This has been achieved by limiting the effectiveness of critical voices and contesting discourses through their conscription into neoliberal discourses and practices. I focus upon how the key figure of the development "expert" acts as an agent in consolidating unilinear notions of modernising progress, construed as "the only force capable of destroying archaic superstitions and relations, at whatever social, cultural and political cost" (Escobar 1997:86). Through this agency, "experts" embody the unequal relationship between the "First" and "Third" Worlds, and between donors and aid recipients, and exemplify the process through which development is located within institutionalised practices. This production of the "professional" development expert, identified as such not solely because of the extent and form of their knowledge but often because of who they are and where they come from, legitimises and authorises their interventions by valorising their particular technical skills and reinforcing classifications of difference between, for example, the "developed" and "developing" worlds (see Bhabha 1994).

I begin with an examination of the post-war production of the development expert and the reproduction of systems of expertise and forms of authority that they articulate. To highlight the rising status and importance of the expert, I subsequently contrast the contemporary development professional with the British colonial officer, a figure who was frequently opposed to these new systems of expertise and subjectivity. Many former colonial officers who subsequently worked for the aid industry condemn post-independence development "experts" as self-designated professionals arguing that they possess limited knowledge and experience of the countries for which they advise, design and implement policies. This discussion exemplifies the continuities and divergences from colonialism to development and, more importantly, the trajectory from colonial rule to the neoliberal agenda and discourse of contemporary international development. The third section demonstrates the constraining effects of designating and channelling expertise and the subsequent co-optation of potentially critical discourses. This discussion focuses upon the creation of professionals and the exclusive forms of knowledge that surround the practice of participatory development—a popular approach that through its incorporation into mainstream, orthodox development has led to its widespread adoption in development policy and practice reflecting, in part, the continuing universalising project and strategies of neoliberalism (see Kothari and Minogue 2002). These refer primarily to the policies of economic reform, minimalist states, privatisation and principles of market-based economics and the policy instruments of, for example, the World Bank and IMF's structural adjustment programmes that enable them. But neoliberal policies further extend to, and affect, social, cultural and political issues including processes of social change and development, access to rights and justice as well as forms of individual and community dispossession (see Harvey 2003).

Post-Colonial Professionalisation of Development and the (Re)Production of Authority

Development is predicated on the assumption that some people and places are more developed than others and therefore those who are "developed" have the knowledge and expertise to help those who are not (Parpart 1995:221). These often unspoken assumptions are highly problematic but continue to prevail in development thinking and are embodied in the ideas and practices of the professional. The forms of expertise produced are developed in part by reasserting (colonial) dichotomies that distinguish between the "modern" and the "traditional", whereby the "traditional" culture, forms of social organisation, production and beliefs of the Third World are seen as outmoded and in need of being succeeded by more "modern", inevitably Western, attitudes and practices. As Escobar writes:

> Development fostered a way of conceiving of social life as a technical problem, as a matter of rational decision and management to be entrusted to that group of people—the development professionals— whose specialized knowledge allegedly qualified them for the task. Instead of seeing change as a process rooted in the interpretation of each society's history and cultural tradition ... these professionals sought to devise mechanisms and procedures to make societies fit a pre-existing model that embodied the structures and functions of modernity. (1997:91)

Escobar (1995) also maintains that "principles of authority" are in operation within development discourse which involve the role of the expert who continually identifies problems, categorises and labels them and then intervenes to resolve them. Indeed, the use of these "technical assistance experts", as they used to be known in the 1950s, is central to most development interventions (Crewe and Harrison 1998:93) and consequently, as shown below, development schemes reflect a form of cultural imperialism founded on ideas about the "professional", "expert" and "expertise". Crucially, however, these are not neutral categories but are notions reconfigured through neoliberal development imaginaries. They are taken up by prevailing ideological orthodoxies contemporaneously and ideas about professionalism, for example, have been absorbed by neoliberal thought and operationalised in development practice. Furthermore, by privileging certain groups of individuals and particular forms of knowledge, they articulate a eurocentrism that is highly gendered and racialised.

There is also a discursive practice in development that shapes "who can speak, from what points of view, with what authority, and according to what criteria of expertise; it sets the rules that must be followed for this or that problem, theory or object to emerge and be named, analysed, and eventually transformed into a policy or plan" (Escobar 1997:87). Supporting this view, Crewe and Harrison (1998) suggest that the perception of the ignorance of "local" people sometimes emerges out of their lack of familiarity with the latest development techniques, although these have often emerged out of Western fashions which are necessarily updated so rapidly that building expertise in them is always just beyond the reach of "local" development practitioners. Indeed, "experts are also able to confirm the legitimacy of their role and intervention by claiming to possess the latest and more advanced expertise" (Crewe and Harrison 1998:97). This superior knowledge "relies on constant reiteration and renewal of technical language, methods and orthodoxies" (109) and as Chambers posits, "the rate of obsolescence of development fashions and ideas has accelerated" (1993:1).

The expatriate development professional further enjoys the cultural capital acquired by being from or of the West and reproduces this on the ground through technical knowledge associated with "modern", scientific ideas. However, while they may have institutionalised practical and discursive knowledge, their experiences and approaches are inevitably subjective and contextual. Yet whilst knowledge is "constructed, reaffirmed or reworked through the social encounters, experiences and dilemmas of everyday life" (Long 2001:171), the knowledge of development professionals and the Western notions of "progress" embodied within them continue to be reinforced through the power embedded in the relationship between donor and beneficiary. Indeed, expatriate development consultants not only acquire but also continuously adapt these forms of cultural capital in order to maintain their status and legitimise their interventions. This process is enabled by the continuous (re)invention and articulation of distinct forms of professionalism, changing fads and fashions of development that require the acquisition of new forms of expertise (skills, techniques, knowledge). In this way, the separation between "expert" and "local" knowledge and an intellectual distance between donor and recipient is maintained. Thus, the exercise of power has a role in promoting, suppressing and ultimately ranking forms of knowledge. As Sibley puts it, "[T]he desire to maintain monopolies over areas of knowledge encourages ritual practices designed to protect the sacred status of established approaches to understanding" (1995:127).

It is not only significant what knowledge people possess but who possesses it. As Crewe and Harrison observe, "[t]he division between indigenous and Western or scientific knowledge is, however, based on ideas about people rather than on objective differences in knowledge or expertise" (1998:92). Beneficiaries of aid in developing countries are generally not seen as having expertise not only because their knowledge and experience is devalued but, more importantly, because the very notion of expertise is socially, culturally and geographical informed. Using examples of stove technologies, Crewe and Harrison (1998) highlight that the value of technical knowledge is predetermined by its source and the social context from which it emerges. That is, the value of knowledge is based more on the (racial, gendered, national) characteristics of people rather than about what they know (1998:96). For example, international agencies rarely fund experts from Africa, Asia and Latin America to advise the British voluntary sector on their national development work. The idea that British NGOs might learn from people from those regions is novel to many and unconvincing to some. This has led to a failure on the part of most development workers to recognise the ability of "recipients" of aid to identify the issues that concern them and to manage their own resources (Crewe and Kothari 1998).

While the colonial officer was perceived as a "legislator", development experts and professionals are presented simply as "interpreters" representing different views of change and progress (see Bauman 1989). It is evident that "experts" are not only transmitters of development ideas, language and techniques but in the process are also involved in the (re)design of development and the power relations embodied within it. Townsend, Porter and Mawdsley (2002) demonstrate this with their focus on how the transnational community of non-governmental organisations "move resources, authority and concepts from donors to recipients, and return images, information and legitimisation from recipients to donors" (832). Their research with NGDOs finds them to be powerful transmitters of the new managerialism and of development fashions, "taking buzz-words to all corners of the globe, and bringing back to the privileged of the earth images of people, of needs, of realities that attract more funding and legitimisation to donors and to NGDOs" (Townsend, Porter and Mawdsley 2002:830). This process of managing discourses of development, a hallmark and imperative of neoliberalism, has recently led to the inclusion and subsequent reshaping of potentially radical or alternative approaches that made an attempt to introduce different versions of the means and ends of development. This process of adverse incorporation (see Wood 2003) is dealt with in more detail subsequently.

The following section highlights the continuities and divergences in the transition from colonial rule to neoliberal development. The distinctions of authority, knowledge and difference that are mobilised to support a neoliberal development agenda, examined above, have led to the emergence of more formalised relationships between former colonies and colonial authorities following independence. This increasing professionalisation over time is based in part on the institutionalisation of these relationships but is also related to changing ideas about what constitutes expertise and what kinds of knowledge are deemed relevant. What counts as professional expertise in development is not primarily founded on in-depth geographic knowledge about other places and people, but is located in technical know-how. This new kind of development skill is increasingly recognised globally and reflects the universalising principles of the neoliberal agenda. In order to understand and explain this shift in notions of expertise and the ways in which the neoliberal agenda reinforces forms of global control through these processes, the following section explores the historical trajectory of the construction and articulation of knowledge and expertise during the colonial period and the period of transition to development policies and practices following independence.

From Colonial Officer to Development "Expert"

In order to provide a historical context as well as a critique of neoliberal forms of professionalism, this section explores the distinctions between the UK colonial officer who was embedded in colonial forms of rule and authority, and the development expert located within a neoliberal development discourse.

This section includes interview material from research with former UK colonial officers. Between 2001 and 2002, I interviewed 15 people who had previously worked for the UK Colonial Office, most of whom were posted as junior administrators to sub-Saharan Africa and subsequently, following independence, became engaged in the international development industry. During the course of the interviews much of my time was spent in the homes and offices of individuals who, while having spent much of their careers outside of Europe had relocated, on retirement, to the more provincial areas of Britain, and particularly the Home Counties and other rural settings in the South East. The research traced the genealogy of post-war international development through the personal testimonies of these individuals. Their reminiscences and retrospective narratives evoke forms of cultural capital, reveal how colonial administrators (and development professionals) are conduits for dominant ideas and discourses about other people and other places but, crucially, also continually negotiate and mediate these conventions in accordance with their experiences on the ground. For whilst colonial officers and development consultants are interpellated by powerful institutionalised practical and discursive knowledge, apparatuses which also provide legitimacy and a context for their specific roles, their experiences and approaches are inevitably subjective and contextual.

The distinctions between colonial authority and the development expert articulate similarities and divergences in their modes of maintaining dichotomous classifications of "modern" and "traditional", and exercising and legitimising their authority. At a fundamental level, both colonialism and development involve an engagement with institutions and ideas which originate in the West and have a global reach. Accordingly, the authoritative missions of colonial rule and development are inevitably embedded in relations of power, control and knowledge that are expressed and mobilised by the colonial administrator and the development professional, respectively. As embodied sites of power, each exercises forms of control and imparts knowledge in and amongst people from other parts of the world. More than this, however, I suggest that the transference of power heralded by the shift from colonial to development regimes marked a change in the ways in which this power and knowledge were exercised. During the colonial era, policies were legitimised and sustained in a variety of ways including the invocation of the cultural capital acquired by administrators as representatives of empire. Following the end of colonial rule, however, development interventions were increasingly authorised through notions of professionalisation. While I concur with Parpart's assertion that the process of professionalisation and the acquisition of expertise emerges and gains credence due to its embeddedness in enlightenment thought (1995:222), it was given a considerable fillip by the emergence of a post-colonial development industry, which has sustained many of the unequal power relationships between coloniser and colonised, and donor and beneficiary.

There is ample evidence that development embodies and is founded upon colonial relations (Cowen and Shenton 1996; Crush 1995). Thus, development represents, albeit in multiple and varied ways, the ongoing relationship between Britain and its (former) colonies (Dirks 1992; Goldsmith 1997; Said 1989). As Smith warns:

> it would be a mistake to conclude that ... de-colonisation marked the end of empire. It did effectively signal an end to colonialism as a specific form of empire, but imperial interest and global reach continue to the present (1994:268).

A number of different perspectives have emerged to account for this continuing relationship. There are those who argue that colonialism survives the post-colonial period in the form of economic and political relations and social and cultural representations. While Said argues that "to have been colonised was a fate with lasting, indeed grotesquely unfair results" (1989:207), Goldsmith claims that development brings the Third World into the orbit of the Western trading system in order to create an ever-expanding market for the West's goods and services and to gain a source of cheap labour and raw materials for its industries. Thus, he argues, "development is an old idea and the path along which it is leading countries of the Third World is a well-trodden one" (1997:69).

Others have commented on the similarities between colonialism and development as projects of modernity and progress, through the reassertion of dichotomies of the "modern" and the "traditional" and the "West" and the "rest" to inform the classification that justify their interventions. Equally, even though elements of both endeavour to promote forms of philanthropy and charity, they also construct and evoke representation of the "other". Said contends that "[T]hroughout the exchange between Europeans and their 'others' ... the one idea that has scarcely varied is that there is an 'us' and 'them', each quite settled, clear, unassailably self-evident" (1994:xxviii). Indeed, Nicholas

Dirks (1992) suggests that colonialism is a cultural project that created and perpetuated dichotomies through cultural classifications and representations of self and other. That is, the process of colonisation was based upon particular types of knowledge which required the classifications of "other" and "difference", superiority and inferiority in order to justify and sustain colonial power and control. These distinctions and power relations were prevalent in colonial times as:

> ... in drawing racial, sexual and class boundaries in terms of social, spatial and symbolic distance, and actually formulating these as integral to the maintenance of colonial rule, the British defined authority and legitimacy through the difference rather than commonality of rulers and "native". (Mohanty 1991:10)

This process of "othering" legitimates forms of control and inequality and is therefore not surprisingly also invoked and reproduced in contemporary development discourse. Thus the racial and gendered boundaries and distinctions, marking the power relations between colonisers and colonised, continue to be reinscribed though often subsumed within notions of expertise and professionalism (see Kothari 2002).

Mercer, Mohan and Power (2003) develop these ideas by rethinking the political geography of African development and examining the relationship between colonialism and contemporary policies towards the representations of Africa. They demonstrate how the legacy of colonialism is evident in contemporary African development through a continuing colonial imagination and articulation of "racialised knowledges" that is linked to a series of interventions and practices (420).

It must be remembered, however, that the era of colonialism, like the historical evolution of development and its ongoing formation, never embodied unchanging and homogeneous objectives and practices. As Said writes:

> Imperialism, the control of overseas territories and peoples, develops in a continuum with variously envisaged histories, current practices and policies, and with differently plotted cultural trajectories. (1989:219)

Indeed, the establishment of the Colonial Development Corporation (CDC) in 1948 marked the beginning of more structured and formal development work undertaken by colonial administrators when they were increasingly required to address, for example, community development, food production strategies and most obviously forestry and natural resources projects. That these were well under way, under the auspices of the CDC, by the late 1940s highlights how there has not been a unilateral trajectory from a colonial to a development moment but rather an intertwining of these fields, wherein heterogeneous and shifting ideologies and practices were imbricated in each other.

Brigg (2002) cautions, however, that international development strategies and practices are not inevitably an extension of colonialism. Indeed, in order to understand the specific operation and design of power through development there is a need to explore how the West maintains its authority since decolonisation, processes of globalisation, the setting up of the Bretton Woods institutions and the nature of international finance and trade have altered the environment within which development takes place. Moreover, within the development process, changing discourses of foreign aid, theories and policies have successively shaped practices as have the evolving relations between the West and its former colonies. Yet, contemporary development strategies and interventions produce unequal global relations, not solely by invoking colonial forms of rule of the past, but also through the construction of expertise. In fact, the development of tools and techniques designed and controlled by the development expert privilege forms of Western knowledge. Masquerading as universal and neutral, they pose as "acceptable" forms of authority by mobilising overarching discourses of "humanitarianism", "philanthropy" and poverty alleviation, presented in contradistinction to the exploitative colonial projects.

Lester explores this genealogy of ideas about humanitarianism and "of a modern British sense of responsibility for the plight of distant strangers" (2002:277). He suggests that this sensibility informs prescriptions aimed at the "moral and material improvement of distant subjects" and is evident in discourses of contemporary international development. Indeed, as Power notes, "development agencies build a kind of branded image for themselves and justify interventions around these" (2003:172) and that these are often constructed so as to appeal to a "global moral imperative". The extent of these feelings of guilt, obligation and moral responsibility are reflected in the narratives of former colonial officers:

> Back in this country most people don't care at all but some have this feeling of guilt with a small "g". I think, like all human endeavour, it [development aid] is a mixture of moral responsibility, an historic connection and a shade of guilt. (Former UK colonial officer)

Another commented, "I think we carry on giving aid because we feel some kind of moral responsibility for what happens over there, and if it's not too pious a word—guilt".

While there are continuities in colonial forms of control evident in development discourse and practice, these are now embodied in development, as opposed to colonial, institutions and agencies, and enabled through new or revised methods, techniques and modes of operation. Despite this apparently progressive change, ironically, many former colonial officers viewed this transformation in practice with dismay.

Changes brought about by political independence in former colonies led many of those employed in the British Colonial Office to leave Africa and Asia and find employment back in the UK. Amongst those embarking on second careers were a group of individuals who found employment in the newly emerging and rapidly expanding international development industry in the UK. A quote from one of the interviewees referring to the moment when he was required to leave the colonial service reveals this trajectory from colonialism to development:

> And I thought, right if I can no longer do this job and work out here the next best thing is to be working for the development of Kenya in the development field—after all it is the same thing. Yes, I was fed up in that it was clear that the winds of change meant you couldn't stay on forever. But, what's the point of chasing a dwindling Colonial Empire around—let's get back and get our teeth into something that will be important—helping Third World countries.

Their experiences and skills as expatriates in the colonial service were initially thought to be particularly suited to the work of international development, but later their attitudes and values towards other people in other places were considered "old fashioned" and "unprofessional". The following section reveals this shift from the more ideologically overt "civilising mission" of colonial rule and the valorisation of regional specialism, to the increasing importance of the universalised technical expertise of the development professional within the contemporary neoliberal development agenda.

In the colonies, colonial officers were immersed in the area allocated to them and subsequently many gained a very intimate knowledge of its geography and peoples, albeit often of a small physical area. Initially, all new recruits to the colonial office were given training for their forthcoming posts, although this preparation was of a very different order to contemporary forms of training devised for development professionals. They were required to attend the 12-month induction programme known as the Devonshire A course in Cambridge, in which they were educated on a broad, general range of subjects, including imperial history, language skills, judiciary and ethnology (see Kirk-Greene 2000). While they were tested on these subjects through examinations, for most, the key skills learnt were how to have the "correct" attitude and moral sensibilities necessary to work in the colonies. "Reliability", "honesty" and "good character" (in addition to sporting prowess) were valued much more highly than academic knowledge and technical skills. When they moved into the field of development following independence, these qualities and behaviours were still prevalent. However, as younger development "professionals" joined the industry, these mores were perceived to be not only less important but outdated and unprofessional. That is, the relationships that colonial administrators had with former colonies were seen to be paternalistic, highly personalised and overtly superior. Other criteria for recruitment became esteemed, placing, for instance, greater importance on technical skills and expertise than on regional knowledge and personal character.

Former colonial officers articulated a deep disappointment and suspicion of the process whereby their regional specialism was replaced by technical expertise, and a more profound resentment between the "old" and the "new". As one former colonial administrator recalls:

> In 1970 in ODA [UK Overseas Development Administration; now the Department for International Development] there was still a residue of old colonial servants—former District Commissioners or Provisional Commissioners and all the Agricultural Advisers, Engineering Advisers, and Education Advisers were all ex-colonials who had experience overseas. By 1983, the young, very intelligent, tremendously articulate had taken over but with no overseas experience. The attitude towards what was happening in the developing countries had changed. It had become more impersonal and less sympathetic.

Over time they became increasingly dismayed at what they saw as the professionalisation of the relationship between Britain and its former colonies and the valorisation of a development expert founded on criteria that denied and dismissed what they felt was their in-depth experience and knowledge of other people in other places. As one former colonial officer notes:

> The conditions where lots of people could live for a decade or two in Africa and Asia are gone. As a professional you won't be on the inside, you'll still be as a tourist, on the outside ... Most aid agencies don't want too much expertise on a single country. The senior people get worried if they can be contradicted by somebody from below who knows better. In Whitehall now, the desk officers are lucky if they even visit the countries they're handling in the files on their desks.

This reduction of in-depth knowledge of other places and people was expressed as a considerable problem within the contemporary development industry:

> There is far too much Eurocentrism in the international development system and every now and again we all agree one size doesn't fit all but then we go into the next round of debate about getting a

consensus that's going to be a one size solution. In many countries not even the size for that country fits all parts of the country.

Former colonial officers also felt that the end of empire had brought with it a social distancing from colonialism that reinforced the "expertise" and professionalism of the development consultant which was often misplaced:

> I can remember once a British High Commissioner saying to me "Why does ODA send out these terribly bright, articulate economists who don't understand what the hell is going on in my country; I don't want to see any more ... they lack any feel for the country".

Despite recent arguments advocating a more central role for the "area specialist" that draw attention to the significance of contextuality (see Parnwell 1999), the knowledge of particular geographical areas during the colonial period has largely been replaced by the specific technical expertise of the post-independence development consultant. This is manifest, for example, in the techniques and themes of conflict analysis and post-conflict reconstruction, gender analysis, rural development, environmental impact assessment and natural resource management. Although there were some colonial officers who went overseas in the forestry, agricultural and veterinary departments, many did not see themselves as experts armed with a collection of technical skills. Indeed, this form of technicalisation emerged out of a discrediting of, and subsequent apparent distancing from, colonial forms of knowledge and practice and has been increasingly mobilised and developed within a neoliberal agenda in which particular technical skills are becoming envisaged as universal and not necessarily requiring such contextual specificities. The experts who possess these techniques, thus, appear to move unproblematically between and within countries, taking with them their particular expertise, but often with limited knowledge of the different historical, social and cultural contexts in which they are required to apply it. Highlighting this issue, Green asks why are "development projects so similar in so many places?" (2003:1) and suggests that this "standardization of development globally" is in part due to new forms of managerialism in planning practices. Similarly, Townsend highlights this issue when she asks "[H]ow may we understand a community of ideas which produces such strikingly parallel local talk in such distant and dissimilar locales?" (1999:613). In an attempt to address this question, I suggest that, although ideas about development may be interpreted and articulated in numerous ways, experts are conduits and translators of a meta-language reflecting a particular view of social change and the practice of development. Therefore, the rolling out across the globe of similar sets of processes and procedures is often necessary to bring about this form of change. Thus, as Duffield (2001) argues, neoliberal global forms of control, through managing and containing the periphery, manifest and represent a form of global governance.

The personalised accounts of the implications of the end of empire, provided above, demonstrate the emergence of a new form of professionalism that is universalising through its global transmission of ideas about process, yet fails to acknowledge its cultural specificity or location. It constructs homogenising discourses of, for example, gender and development or project planning, that masquerade as universal but are, in fact, particularly Western. These processes contribute to changing development paradigms and priorities, an outcome that reflects the dominance of Western neoliberalism. Furthermore, as I have tried to demonstrate above ' ... the decisive role of neoliberal technocrats, draws explicit attention to neoliberalism as a *social* process: its diffusion is carried not simply by faceless, structural forces but also by structurally positioned agents' (Peck 2004:393).

Adverse Incorporation and the Ordering of Dissent: Participatory Approaches to Development

This section develops the arguments presented above by investigating and exemplifying the ways in which a neoliberal development process monopolises expertise and authority by professionalising and technicalising development interventions from without, thereby shaping expressions of dissent and potentially limiting critical, challenging and emancipatory approaches. Indeed, these previously excluded or marginalized discourses of opposition become enmeshed within a neoliberal developmentalist frame through incorporation. As an example, I explore the emergence of participatory approaches to development. I contend that although the intentions of many participatory advocates and practitioners are concerned with decentring the authority of the development professional, its co-optation into mainstream development discourse and practice and incorporation onto the neoliberal development agenda has ironically reinforced the centrality of Western knowledge and expertise (see Cooke and Kothari 2001).

This co-optation is enabled by the professionalisation of development following the establishment of the Bretton Woods institutions and the reproduction of authority that they articulate. And, following the "crisis" of development in the 1980s, this professionalisation then accelerates and expands to encompass alternative approaches which were previously marginal to the development mainstream.

More specifically, despite some post-war gains in social and economic development, since the 1980s there has been a widespread recognition of the failure of international development to alleviate poverty and reduce inequalities within and between regions. As Sachs writes, far from being a success:

> [T]he idea of development stands like a ruin in the intellectual landscape. Delusion and disappointment, failures and crime have been the steady companions of development and they tell a common story: it did not work. (1992:1)

Schuurman captures some of the various explanations that have been proffered for this failure. He suggests that international development reached an impasse in the 1980s because of increasing levels of poverty, exclusion and inequality, and a concomitant crisis in development thinking with the principal theories and paradigms which had dominated understandings of the world being increasingly challenged (Schuurman 1993, 2000).

What emerged out of this impasse is rather paradoxical. There was a flourishing of so-called "alternative" forms of development such as participatory approaches to development (Chambers 1995) and gender analysis (Moser 1993) that focused on the failure of development planning to address diversity and inequalities in society. These challenges highlighted the divergent needs and interests of beneficiaries of aid and critiqued inappropriate and ineffective top-down planning processes. There was also the emergence of "anti-development" and "post-development" perspectives, (see Escobar 1995; Rahnema and Bawtree 1997; Rist 1997; Sachs 1992) whose proponents went further to argue that development should be rejected "not merely on account of its results but because of its intentions, its world-view and mindset" (Pieterse 2000:175). At the same time, however, the neoliberal agenda prospered in response to the impasse, most notably through the structural adjustment programmes promoted by the World Bank and IMF. More significantly, its rise to hegemony meant that it was also profoundly effective at co-opting the "alternative" critical discourses identified above.

Accordingly, in the 1980s the World Bank and other multi- and bilateral development agencies appeared to encourage these seemingly alternative approaches incorporating concerns around issues of participation, gender, empowerment and environment onto their agenda (see World Bank, *World Development Reports*). Forms of alternative development become institutionalised and less distinct from conventional, mainstream development discourse and practice (Pieterse 1998). Following co-optation, these discourses became increasingly technicalised in order to fit into the more formalised development planning frameworks and models favoured by these organisations. This process was enabled by the relatively weak theoretical rootedness of some of these formative approaches that allowed them to be more easily encompassed. This strategy of appropriation reduced spaces of critique and dissent, since the inclusion and appropriation of ostensibly radical discourses limited the potential for any challenge from outside the mainstream to orthodox development planning and practices: "the conscription of critical discourses into the mainstream is often accompanied with a watering down of the challenges and political commentary that went with their construction" (Kothari and Minogue 2002:11). As these approaches were adopted they were embedded within a neoliberal discourse (Rist 1997) and became increasingly technicalised, subject to regimes of professionalisation which institutionalised forms of knowledge, analytical skills, tools, techniques and frameworks. These competencies were, in turn, acquired through training schemes and courses of study, producing professional "experts" ready to go into the field and apply these criteria in the practice of development. Indeed, as Francis writes, "PRA's distinctive combination of personal transformation, political empowerment and methodological practice is above all embodied in and transmitted through specialized training" (2001:79).

Interestingly, although some former colonial officers were dismayed that the importance of in-depth and local knowledge has been displaced by the increasing valorisation of technical know-how, the World Bank and other development agencies claim that participatory development is precisely about local, though not necessarily in-depth, knowledge, experience and interests. This highlights the divergent and changing understandings of what constitutes geographic and contextual knowledge. Perhaps what is being invoked here is a temporal basis of the form and depth of knowledge whereby colonial officers' knowledge was presumably gained through extensive periods in the field while that of participatory practitioners is through rapid appraisal techniques.

The development industry has thus successfully established and sustained its expertise, authority and managerial distance despite challenges from development alternatives. As Chambers suggests, professionalism maintains itself through a "repertoire of defence against accordance and threat" (1993:5), which includes assimilation whereby familiar methods are used "to modify, describe and often put some sort of number to the discordance, coding it so that it can be fitted on as an extension of the normal paradigm" (1993:6). This absorption is manifest in, for example, the gender and development approach which has largely become constrained and enmeshed in technical processes. Here, gender analytical frameworks initiated by "professionals" tend to prioritise increasing women's participation in economic processes rather than uncovering and addressing broader unequal power relations between men and women. Indeed the more political term "feminist" has largely been replaced in development speak by the more acceptable terminology of "gender".

This exemplifies how development orthodoxies seem to be more concerned with generating exclusive professional knowledge and skill, and "experts" who possess these vaunted qualities, than with alleviating poverty and addressing exclusionary processes. This is also clearly seen with the emergence of participatory approaches to development and, more specifically, with the tools and techniques of Participatory Rural Appraisal (PRA) (see Chambers 1992, 1997; Oakley 1991). Broadly,

> the aim of participatory development is to increase the involvement of socially and economically marginalized people in decision-making over their own lives. The assumption is that participatory approaches empower local people with the skills and confidence to analyse their situation, reach consensus, make decisions and take action, so as to improve their circumstances. The ultimate goal is more equitable and sustainable development. (Guijt and Shah 1998:1)

Participatory approaches emerged in an attempt to challenge top-down development planning and in the process empower recipients of aid. Indeed, as Mohan and Stokke write: "the starting point is to reject the assumption that 'experts' know best what creates the space for local knowledge to be assessed" (2000:252). But despite those who advocate for the de-professionalisation of development, such as Chambers, who asserts that development practice should "put the last first" (1993, 1997), participatory development has become increasingly professionalised through training manuals and skills workshops whereby only those trained in the preferred methods and techniques are acknowledged as authorised facilitators. Thus, the power and authority of the "outsider" or the facilitator are confirmed. Despite claims which insist that PRA originated in the "South", this approach is nearly always associated with Chambers and other expatriates, who are identified as the "experts".

Craig and Porter show how participatory approaches are new forms of control and management through the dominance of projects, professionals and organisations. Through these three instruments, they argue, "it was believed that the task of 'Development' could be turned into a series of technical (and thus politically neutral) organisational processes and bounded, manageable objectives" (1997:230). Despite the origins of PRA as an avowedly alternative approach to development which encouraged "learning reversals", there is the suggestion that it has become yet another authoritative discourse practised in ways that conceal the agency of the "outsider" or "expert" and reinforce unequal power relations (Mosse 1994).

Moreover, the process of participation is also not as transparent as it may seem. The very act of inclusion, of being drawn in as a participant, can perform the exercise of power and control over an individual. As Wood (1999) suggests, there are forms of "adverse incorporation" where the act or process of inclusion is not always to the benefit of those groups who have previously been excluded. For example, "the mere presence of women in decision making committees without a voice can be counter-productive in the sense that it can be used to legitimise a decision which is taken by the male members" (Mohanty quoted in Cornwall 2003:1330). Cohen (1985) similarly refers to insidious modes of inclusionary control which lead to a diminution in the spaces and potency of dissent through adverse incorporation. He suggests that programmes designed to bring the excluded in often result in forms of control which are more difficult to challenge as they reduce spaces of conflict and appear to be benign and liberal. Using a case study of a participatory natural resource development project in western India, Mosse also demonstrates how, as public and collective events, PRAs tend to emphasise consensus building that, given unequal social relations of, for example, gender, mean that the "perspectives and interests of the most powerful sections in a community are likely to dominate" (Mosse 1994:509). Furthermore, those who have the greatest reason to challenge and confront power relations and structures are brought/bought into the development process in ways which disempower them insofar as they are able to challenge prevailing hierarchies and inequalities, reinforcing an inclusionary control and conformity (Kothari 2001).

The process of incorporation also performs a selective function to exclude certain people and particular forms of knowledge which cannot be absorbed. The methodological tools and techniques of participatory development such as seasonal calendars, pie charts and wealth-ranking schema similarly require a purification or cleaning up of knowledge; a tidying up of people's lives through the exclusion of anything messy that does not fit in with the clean tools and ideal structures implied by participatory techniques. For example, although participatory approaches to development aim to uncover social and local issues of dominance and exclusion, women may feel unable to represent certain kinds of experiences of violence or abuse using the tools provided or indeed in public, group settings. The use of participatory techniques often requires the taking out of anything which complicates normative procedures and forms of analysis and representation, making people's lives and their social interactions linear and sterile as they fit into charts, diagrams and tables, and conform to the boundaries of the methodological tools.

A further criticism of participatory approaches lies in the rather one-sided extraction of information from local people. Development professionals are frequently unable to share ideas with "locals" to promote a more participative exchange because in order for them to express and maintain their professionalism, they need to retain authoritative distance. This may create a tense ambivalence because of the twin demands to be participative and authoritative. The difficulty in maintaining this balancing act is complex and compromised. For instance, although Chambers (1997) highlights the problematic role which combines a need to be both "insider" and "outsider", others argue that this minimises the cultural resonance that the "expert" conveys, a status which cannot simply be discarded through the adoption of a few participatory techniques. Furthermore, even when the knowledge and experiences of local people are valued (in Participatory Rural Appraisal exercises, for example), some form of development intervention is nearly always considered necessary by external funding bodies, who prescribe the imperative of employing professional "facilitators" or "moderators". In this way, previously routine, local participative activities and relationships become institutionalised and labelled within a development frame. This is confirmed by Cooke (2004) who suggests that "(I)t is an intrinsic, defining, feature of development that it provides it own self-legitimising meta-narrative which gives meaning to the experiences and actions of those it would develop, its subjects and objects" (53).

   In this section I have tried to show that while the role of development "experts" has been challenged, and attempts made to recognise the importance of local knowledge, the development expert need not fear a loss of their intellectual status nor challenges to their ontological security in the face of these recent "alternative" approaches to development. Instead, their authority and expertise have been confirmed through the appropriation, technicalisation and subsequent mainstreaming of potentially disruptive discourses of development. Critiques of PRA have tended to focus on the technical limitations of the approach which stress the need for a re-examination of the methodological tools. However, they neglect the broader picture because as Cooke (2004) argues, participatory practitioners have been "allowed in through the door precisely because there is no danger of them challenging neoliberal hegemony, and, worse, because they sustain it"(44).

Conclusion

A discursive analysis of development really only began in the 1980s (see Ferguson 1994; Sachs 1992). Nevertheless, the desire to reveal the many embedded, tenacious strands of colonial forms of knowing and representing has gained momentum and is exemplified in the approaches of, for example, Crush (1995), who illustrates the ways in which development ideology is produced and reproduced to valorise particular forms of (Western) knowledge and maintain the economic and intellectual superiority of the West. More specifically, others such as Parpart (1995) remind us of the close connection between this control over knowledge and assertions of power, and the role of the development expert. Yet paradoxically, as shown above, former colonial officers have provided a historical perspective on the emergence of professionalism and the rise of the technical expert as well as a trenchant critique which highlights the devaluing of in-depth geographic knowledge, the overly abstract analysis of local contexts and the globalisation of homogenising development processes and techniques.

I have demonstrated how development has become a technical process of intervention that maintains the legitimacy and authority of Western modernity and the dominance of the neoliberal agenda. There is clearly a need for beneficiaries of aid and more importantly communities of First World policymakers and practitioners to critique this process (Cooke 2004). Through such critical awareness, international development agencies could be persuaded to question their assumptions about expertise and the impact of their expatriate consultants and make more extensive use of existing expertise within aid-receiving countries (Crewe 1997).

Escobar offers a possible solution to the problems of institutionalisation of development practices and co-optation of alternative approaches identified above. Against searching for grand alternative models or strategies, he argues for:

> the investigation of alternative representations and practices in concrete local settings, particularly as they exist in contexts of hybridisation, collective action and political mobilization (1995:19).

Beyond these more practical challenges to the centrality of Western knowledge and expertise, there is a fundamental issue here that relates to the limitations of spaces available to locate development outside this technocratic frame. While there are ongoing critiques of development practice, many of these are restricted to challenging orthodox practices and techniques which can ultimately only lead to limited methodological revisionism instead of to a more wholesale questioning of the discourse. For example, it is common to see challenges to the mainstream followed by a list of recommendations for better practice. This form of critique operates within the discursive and practical norms of the development process, and tends to confirm the centrality of the professional and the technocratic process. Any adoption of such constrained recommendations is done with the belief that, with some tinkering around with the tool-kit, the problems of development will be more appropriately addressed. As Crush reminds us, to move outside of the managerial, technical, professionalised and expert-led field and frame of development, however, has become increasingly difficult as:

> The (development) machine is global in its reach, encompassing departments and bureaucracies in colonial and post-colonial states throughout the world, Western aid agencies, multilateral organisations, the sprawling global network of NGOs (non-governmental organisations), experts and private consultants, private sector organisations such as banks and companies that marshal the rhetoric of development, and the plethora of development studies programmes in institutes of learning worldwide. (1995:6)

The question that remains, therefore, is how can critical voices be effective within a neoliberal development agenda?

Acknowledgements
Some sections draw on the findings of a life history project with former colonial officers ("From colonialism to development: Continuities and divergences", funded by the University of Manchester). I would like to thank Tim Edensor, Andries du Toit, Nina Laurie, Liz Bondi and three anonymous referees for their insightful comments and those who were interviewed and whose reflections are anonymously referred to.

References

Bauman Z (1989) *Legislators and Interpreters*. Cambridge: Polity Press

Bhabha H K (1994) *The Location of Culture*. London: Routledge

Brigg M (2002) Post-development, Foucault and the colonisation metaphor. *Third World Quarterly* 3(3):421–436

Chambers R (1992) Rural appraisal: Rapid, relaxed and participatory. IDS Discussion Paper 311. Brighton: University of Sussex

Chambers R (1993) *Challenging the Professions*. London: Intermediate Technology Publications

Chambers R (1995) *Poverty and Livelihoods: Whose Reality Counts?* Sussex: IDS

Chambers R (1997) *Whose Reality Counts? Putting the Last First*. London: Intermediate Technology

Cohen S (1985) *Visions of Social Control*. Cambridge: Polity Press

Cooke B (2004) Rules of thumb for participatory change agents. In S Hickey and G Mohan (eds) *From Tyranny to Transformation? Exploring New Approaches to Participation* (pp 42–55). London: Zed Books

Cooke B and Kothari U (eds) (2001) *Participation: The New Tyranny?* London: Zed Books

Cornwall A (2003) Whose voices? Whose choices? Reflections on gender and participatory development. *World Development* 31(8):1325–1342

Cowen M P and Shenton R W (1996) *Doctrines of Development*. London: Routledge

Craig D and Porter D (1997) Framing participation: Development projects, professionals and organisations. *Development in Practice* 7(3):229–236

Crewe E (1997) "Expertise and identity in international consultancy." Paper presented at Research Consultancy Conference, University of Warwick, 18 June

Crewe E and Harrison E (1998) *Whose Development?* London: Zed Books

Crewe E and Kothari U (1998) "'The local culture is the problem': Racism in the international aid industry." Unpublished paper

Crush J (ed) (1995) *Power of Development*. London: Routledge

Dirks N B (ed) (1992) *Colonialism and Culture*. Ann Arbor, MI: University of Michigan Press

Duffield M (2001) Governing the Borderlands: Decoding the power of aid. *Disasters* 25(4):308–320

Escobar A (1995) *Encountering Development: The Making and Unmaking of the Third World*. Princeton, NJ: Princeton University Press

Escobar A (1997) The making and unmaking of the Third World through development. In M Rahnema and V Bawtree (eds) *The Post Development Reader* (pp 85–93). London: Zed Books

Ferguson J (1994) *The Anti-Politics Machine*. Minneapolis, MN: University of Minnesota Press

Francis P (2001) Participatory development at the World Bank: The primacy of process. In B Cooke and U Kothari (eds) *Participation: The New Tyranny?* (pp 72–87). London: Zed Books

Goldsmith E (1997) Development as colonialism. *The Ecologist* 27(2):69–77

Green M (2003) Globalizing development: Policy franchising through participatory project management in "non-places". *Critique of Anthropology* 23(1):1–21

Guijt I and Shah G (eds) (1998) *The Myth of Community: Gender Issues in Participatory Development*. London: Intermediate Technology

Harvey D (2003) *The New Imperialism*. Oxford: Oxford University Press

Kirk-Greene A (2000) *Britain's Imperial Administrators, 1858–1966*. Basingstoke: Macmillan

Kothari U (2001) Power, knowledge and social control in participatory development. In B Cooke and U Kothari (eds) *Participation the New Tyranny* (pp 139–152). London: Zed Books

Kothari U (2002) Feminist and postcolonial challenges to development. In U Kothari and M Minogue (eds) *Development Theory and Practice: Critical Perspectives* (pp 35–51). Basingstoke: Palgrave

Kothari U and Minogue M (2002) Critical perspectives on development: An introduction. In U Kothari and M Minogue (eds) *Development Theory and Practice: Critical Perspectives* (pp 1–15). Basingstoke: Palgrave

Lester A (2002) Obtaining the "due observance of justice": The geographies of colonial humanitarianism. *Environment and Planning D: Society and Space* 20: 277–293

Long N (2001) *Development Sociology: Actor Perspectives*. London: Routledge

Mercer C, Mohan G and Power M (2003) Towards a critical political geography of African development. *Geoforum* 34:419–436

Mohan G and Stokke K (2000) Participatory development and empowerment: The dangers of localism. *Third World Quarterly* 21(2):247–268

Mohanty C (1991) Under western eyes: Feminist scholarship and colonial discourse. In C Mohanty, A Russo and L Torres (eds) *Third Word Women and the Politics of Feminism* (pp 52–80). Bloomington: Indiana University Press

Moser C (1993) *Gender Planning and Development: Theory, Practice and Training*. London: Routledge

Mosse D (1994) Authority, gender and knowledge: Theoretical reflections on the practice of participatory rural appraisal. *Development and Change* 25:497–526

Oakley P (1991) *Projects With People: The Practice of Participation in Rural Development*. Geneva: ILO

Parnwell M (1999) Between theory and practice: The area specialist and the study of development. In D Simon and A Narman (eds) *Development as Theory and Practice* (pp 76–94). Harlow: Longman

Parpart J (1995) Deconstructing the development "expert". In M Marchand and J Parpart (eds) *Feminism, Postmodernism and Development* (pp 221–243). London: Routledge

Peck J (2004) Geography and public policy: Constructions of neo-liberalism. *Progress in Human Geography* 28(3):392–405

Pieterse J N (1998) My paradigm or yours? Alternative development, post-development, reflexive development. *Development and Change* 29(2):343–373

Pieterse J N (2000) After post-development. *Third World Quarterly* 21(2):171–191

Power M (2003) *Rethinking Development Geographies*. London: Routledge

Rahnema M and Bawtree V (eds) (1997) *The Post Development Reader*. London: 2ed

Rist G (1997) *The History of Development: From Western Origins to Global Faith.* London: Zed Books

Sachs W (ed) (1992) *The Development Dictionary: A Guide to Knowledge as Power.* London: Zed Books

Said E (1989) Representing the colonized: Anthropology's interlocutors. *Critical Inquiry* 15:205–225

Said E (1994) *Culture and Imperialism*. London: Vintage

Schuurman F J (1993) *Beyond the Impasse: New Directions in Development Theory.* London: Zed Books

Schuurman F J (2000) Paradigms lost, paradigms gained? *Third World Quarterly* 21(1):7–20

Sibley D (1995) *Geographies of Exclusion*. London: Routledge

Smith N (1994) Introduction: Postcolonial geographies. In A Godlewska and N Smith (eds) *Geography and Empire* (pp 268–269). Oxford: Blackwell

Townsend J (1999) Are non-governmental organizations working in development a transnational community? *Journal of International Development* 11:613–623

Townsend J, Porter G and Mawdsley E (2002) The role of the transnational community of non-government organizations: Governance or poverty reduction? *Journal of International Development* 14:829–839

Wood G (1999) *Concepts and Themes: Landscaping Social Development*. London: DFID

Wood G (2003) Staying secure, staying poor: The Faustian bargain. *World Development* 32(3):455–471

World Bank (annual) *World Development Reports*. Washington DC: World Bank

Uma Kothari is a Senior Lecturer at the Institute for Development Policy and Management, University of Manchester. She teaches social development and history and theories of development. Her research interests include processes of migration, colonialism, postcolonialism and development and chronic poverty and livelihood strategies. She is currently carrying out research into global street peddlers in Europe and on the branded clothes industry in Mauritius. Her edited books include *Participation: The New Tyranny?* (2001), *Development Theory and Practice: Critical Perspectives* (2002) and *A Radical History of Development Studies* (forthcoming).

Chapter 3

Dropping Out or Signing Up? The Professionalisation of Youth Travel

Kate Simpson

Introduction

The rise of the gap year has cemented the cult and commercial status of travel for much of Britain's youth and brought youth travel to the attention of the state, educationalists, employers and the tourist industry alike. Such attention has resulted in a revolution in the values associated with youth travel, producing an increasingly corporate focus and professional, self-governing, careerist persona for participants. Here, I argue that the rise of the gap year has professionalised and formalised practices of youth travel, bringing them into contact with neoliberal understandings of education and citizenship, where emphasis is placed on young people's acquisition of global knowledge as governable subjects with market potential.

An estimated 200,000 British people aged 18–25 annually take a gap year.[1] Gap years can involve any manner of activities, though typically they include periods of work, either paid or voluntary, and often some form of travel. The practice of the gap year has expanded considerably in the last ten years, with a corresponding rise in its public and institutional profile. It is no longer a sub-set of the tourist industry pursued by a disparate minority of young people. Rather, it has opened up to mass participation, and popular scrutiny. As a result, pressure has been exerted by actors both within and outside the industry to professionalise gap year activities and practices.

Traditionally a gap year represented a break from formal education or employment in order to find time to engage in "extra-ordinary" experiences. However, as I shall argue, gap years are now becoming increasingly incorporated into formal educational and employment structures and institutions. While young people have often been side-lined in neoliberal literatures and critiques, the economic realisation of the gap year is occurring in a context where neoliberal values are increasingly being applied to young people's travel, leisure and educational practices. I argue that while young people are being encouraged to "broaden their horizons" and become better citizens through participating in gap years, this occurs in the context of neoliberal forms of self-regulatory citizenship (Dean 1999). The types of citizenship encouraged through the gap year give primacy to the ability of the individual to compete in social and employment market places.

I concentrate on structured gap year programmes that offer volunteer-tourism activities specifically based in the Third World. While such programmes represent only a part of the gap year market, accounting for an estimated 10,000 participants a year, they are highly visible to the public and play an important role in shaping popular understanding of youth travel. For example, in the year 2000 Prince William took a gap year and received front-page newspaper coverage (for example, see Hardman 2000; Jobson 2000; Kerr 2000). Although his 12-month "gap" included time in Europe, it was his period in Chile with Raleigh International that attracted media and public attention (for example, see Jobson 2000; Kerr 2000; Vidal 2000; Wilson 2002). Gap year programmes such as those of Raleigh International offer participants the opportunity to visit and encounter geographically distant others with the promise that through such encounters their "horizons will be broadened" and knowledge of others enhanced (for examples, see YOG 2001; gap-year.com 2002; World Challenge Expeditions 2002). Below, I illustrate how the historical and contemporary processes associated with colonialism, and the geographies of uneven development that constrain and condition "broad horizons" knowledges of others, appear to be unproblematic for the UK gap year industry. This situation contrasts sharply with similar programmes in other countries, notably Canada, the USA and Australia, which tend to occur at different points in the life course and function in significantly different ways. Crucially, US and Canadian international volunteer-tourism programmes generally form part of structured college courses rather than acting independently of formal education. While influenced by market forces (student willingness/ability to pay and the accessibility of suitable destinations) unlike UK programmes, they are shaped more by educational institutions than commercial companies.[2] They therefore include a more considered education dimension than gap years, often prioritising pedagogies that aim to critically examine the historical and socio-economic basis of uneven development.

The research I draw on is from a larger study conducted for my PhD thesis (Simpson 2005), and includes several data sources. Interviews and participant observation were conducted with two groups of gap year participants in South America. I spent six weeks in 2001 with the first group, which included 14 participants, and three months with the second group, comprising 17 participants. All of the participants were engaged in structured volunteer-based gap year programmes run by an organisation that I have conducted research with for a number of years. In addition, data were also produced through interviews with the gap year industry and a discourse analysis of the industry's grey literature and web-based promotional materials.[3] I also examined material from a range of companies, media sources and institutions that have been significant commentators on the gap year.[4]

The next section details the processes that have professionalised gap year practices and outlines the ways in which a gap year industry has come to colonise previously informal practices of youth travel. I argue that the gap year industry has actively sought legitimisation from state and commercial institutions. The following section draws on examples from volunteer-tourism gap year programmes based in Latin America; demonstrating that the industry produces particular geographies in which to locate its practices. Through an examination of the industry's ability to market itself as operating in spaces that are simultaneously dangerous and safe, I argue that the gap year industry is able to create a particular geography for its participants to visit, and claim knowledge of. In the next section I explore issues of knowledge production within gap year programmes, and argue that gap year experiences allow participants to claim authoritative knowledges of distant others, thereby reinforcing patterns of global uneven and unequal development.

The Professionalisation of the Gap Year

Prince William's arrival in Chile represented the pinnacle of institutional acceptability for the gap year. No longer are gap years for rebels, dropouts and "people with nothing better to do"; now they are for hopeful professionals and future kings. Institutional acceptability of the gap year has been achieved through a combination of popular enthusiasm, and the realisation of the potential economic value of youth travel. An industry has evolved around gap year practices which functions to formalise, popularise and to some degree police the industry's activities. Fundamental to these processes has been the emergence of a set of marketable values that can be accepted by institutions, desired by parents, and bought by young people. In the following, I first explore the formalisation of the gap year, before going on to examine its growing institutional acceptability. These two processes combined have worked to professionalise the gap year.

Moving into the neoliberal market place has required the gap year industry to develop a set of definable and marketable commodities. Such commodities have concentrated on offering individualised forms of cultural and corporate capital. Drawing on Bourdieu's concept of cultural capital and Urry's (1990) application of this to the field of travel, corporate capital in the gap year represents an extension of incorporated or embodied forms of cultural capital. Cultural capital is held by individuals in the form of experiences and education (Hayes 1997; Robbins 2000), yet has specific value to the corporate workplace. Taking a gap year supposedly offers opportunities to enhance one's access to both social spaces and employment. Thus, commodities such as "broad horizons", "personal development", "leadership and teamwork skills" have been marketed and sold to potential participants. For example, Venture Co, which provides three-month volunteer-tourism programmes in South America and India, lists the commodities offered in the following terms:

> Does the idea of travel to far off destinations appeal to you? How about the adventure of joining an expedition into the world's greatest mountain ranges? And I expect you'd like to help a disadvantaged community and acquire new skills while working on an aid project … At the same time you're probably thinking about how your gap year will fit into the broader picture, will it be something to impress future employers and how will it look on your CV? (Venture Co 2002)

Venture Co offers opportunities that range from the corporate capital of an enhanced CV to the promise that one will acquire new skills while helping a disadvantaged community. In so doing, Venture Co neatly summarises the gap year industry's key commodities; commodities that are not only becoming more readily recognised by those outside the industry, but are increasingly being presented as necessities for success in both corporate and social spaces. For example, World Challenge, one of the larger commercial providers of gap year programmes, opens their brochure: "Journey of A Life Time", with the statement that their programmes will:

> enable you to learn invaluable life skills, as well as introduce you to wider cultures and the genuine challenges of life survival. For people who want to succeed in life, there is no greater graduation. (World Challenge Expeditions 2001:1)

World Challenge is effectively packaging their programmes as a necessity for young people. Furthermore, a language of "graduation" and "success" ties the gap year into education. This process of making the gap year part of, rather than distinct from, formal education and employment institutions is fundamental to its professionalisation and institutional recognition. As World Challenge implies, a gap year has become a requirement for success. It is now a part of one's progression to employability, as necessary in the UK as "A" levels and as inevitable as a degree.

Alluded to in both of the statements above from World Challenge and Venture Co is the fact that gap year industry commodities are not solely targeted at developing corporate compatibility, but also intend to offer cultural capital. The gap year offers young people the cultural capital of experience with its incumbent associations with achieving "broad horizons". Third World travel experiences act as cultural capital, giving one something to display to peers and, according to the journalist quoted below, a way in which to claim new friends:

> It is also hard not to become more interesting after a year of travel. During those first few terrifying days at university, no matter how often people tell you their totally cool and totally identical stories about trekking through Nepal on acid, they're still more fun to talk to than those—how young they seem! who are having the conversation about what "A" levels they got. (Merrit 2000:2)

The above quotation expresses clear expectations about who will be interesting, and who will not. A person risks cultural impoverishment if going to university (and into other arenas) without the capital of Third World travel. In this way the gap year is creating a level of social stratification, where cultural capital acts like economic capital to become a mechanism of inclusion and exclusion (Kaur and Hutnyk 1999). By taking a gap year young people are able to acquire both identity and capital. As the gap year industry's primary products, these are marketed to young people, parents, employers and educators alike. The following quotation by the YOG, an industry organisation for gap year providers, illustrates this point well: "A year out can say as much, if not more about you as an individual as any set of exam results ever can!" (YOG 2001). Fundamentally, what the gap year industry sells in a neoliberal market place is difference, be it difference from one's peers or job market competitors.

Indicative of the recent move towards professionalisation, the emergence of organisations such as the YOG has contributed to the promotion of a defined and bounded notion of the gap year. Formed in 1998 by 20 of the self-identified key players in the gap year market, the YOG has a specific mandate:

> The Year Out Group is an association of leading year out organisations that was formed in 1998 to promote the concept and benefits of well-structured year out programmes, to promote models of good practice and to help young people and their advisers in selecting suitable and worthwhile projects. (YOG 2003)

The group has now grown to around 30 members and has played a significant role in seeking and publicising institutional support for the gap year. Its formation demonstrates the emergence of a distinct corporate identity around the gap year, and the apparent need to establish boundaries for inclusion and exclusion within that identity. The YOG specifically state that they work to promote structured gap years. Such a statement is a direct rejection of gap years that involve purely independent travel or work, as this form does not support industry-provided packages. This theme will be returned to later, specifically in the context of the institutional legitimation of the gap year; however, here it is important to note that being the provider of structured gap years represents a criterion for inclusion and exclusion that the industry wishes to establish and police.

The emergence of the YOG reflects the growing range of independent and predominantly commercial promoters that are becoming a key part of the gap year industry. Despite an often-assumed relationship between the gap year and the charity and NGO sectors, the majority of YOG's membership consists of commercial companies, reiterating the gap year's position in the tourism market place. The emergence of companies such as gapyear.com and gap-year.com, and the publication of guidebooks to the gap year by, for example, Lonely Planet (see Hindle 2003) demonstrate how promoting, and to some degree monitoring/regulating, the gap year industry is, in itself, a commercially viable profession. A growing number of "added value" providers are also being established. For example, the organisation "Objective" offers safety-training programmes run by former SAS army officers which claim to: "Maximise the experience of your gap year by minimising risk avoid unnecessary hassle, cope with the unexpected, stay healthy, keep kit safe" (Objective 2004). As an organisation, Objective is responding not only to the growth of the gap year market, but also its formalisation and the corresponding need to professionalise its practices. In a similar manner, but targeting a different aspect of the market, for a fee, "Gap Profile" offers the opportunity to gain a "City and Guilds Profile of Achievement" gap year qualification. This is not a qualification in a particular skill, rather it is a generic qualification, one that apparently could be taken by any gap year participant on any programme. The perceived need for qualifications to bear testimony to the value of the experience, no matter how participants choose to spend their time, illustrates the gap year's evolving corporate compatibility and focus on professionalisation. Furthermore, as the gap year becomes increasingly bound to certain values and esteemed in specific ways, a hierarchy of gap year experiences emerges. So, as those participants with a formal qualification become more highly valued than those without, the gap year, like school grades, university location or type of degree studied, can act to stratify young people. With the introduction of a qualification, comes the potential to fail a gap year. Thus no longer can the gap year be separated from the mechanisms of formal, assessed education and employment, rather it seems to have become an extension of those same developmentalist tools.

As the gap year has been formalised and established in the public imagination, so too has it received significant institutional recognition. In July 2000 the issue of gap years was raised in the House of Lords during a debate on voluntary service for young people. During this debate Baroness Warwick of Undercliff, the chief executive of the Committee of Vice-Chancellors (now Universities UK) and also the chair of Voluntary Service Overseas (VSO), expressed her support for the gap year:

> For those thinking of applying to university—again I must declare an interest as chief executive of the Committee of Vice-Chancellors and Principals—it is essential that they know that a gap year experience, so long as it is well structured, will be warmly welcomed. (United Kingdom Parliament 2000:column 1574)

Baroness Warwick's comments were reiterated by other peers (see Lord Lucas and Baroness Andrews quoted in United Kingdom Parliament 2000). However, despite such enthusiasm for the gap year, it is unclear upon what evidence or research such endorsements are based. Indeed, to date there has been almost no academic research on the subject.[5]

Beyond debate in the House of Lords, state support for the gap year in the UK has also come directly from government ministers, most notably Jack Straw, the Foreign Secretary:

> Taking a gap year is a great opportunity for young people to broaden their horizons, making them more mature and responsible citizens. Our society can only benefit from travel which promotes character, confidence, decision-making skills. (Hogg 2001:1)

This statement was apparently made for gapyear.com and is used prominently by many providers and promoters of gap years (for example, see Lancaster University Department of Geography 2002; the leap 2003). As with the comments made in the House of Lords, it is unclear upon what evidence Mr Straw bases his confidence in the gap year. What Mr Straw offers in this and other statements endorsing the gap year is an increasingly defined notion of what can and should be gained from a gap year, while also identifying its perceived value to the state. In this way, the gap year fits well with government agendas promoting volunteering amongst young people[6] and citizenship education. However, what forms of citizenship are people in positions of influence like Jack Straw encouraging through the gap year? So far we have seen that official statements expressing support for the gap year predominately focus on the individualised advantages that it offers, thereby endorsing the development of an active, self-regulating, competitive citizen.

As well as support from institutions and figures of state, the gap year has received endorsement from the educational establishment. Tony Higgins, the Chief Executive of the UK's University & College Admission Service (UCAS), in 2001 stated:

> UCAS believes that students who take a well-planned structured year out are more likely to be satisfied with, and complete, their chosen course. The benefits of a well-structured year out are now widely recognised by universities and colleges and cannot fail to stand you in good stead in later life. (YOG 2001)

Baroness Diana Warwick, this time in her role as chair of Universities UK, has also endorsed the gap year from the perspective of universities. The following quotation is taken from the Universities UK website, and formed part of a speech given at the National Council for Voluntary Organisation (NCVO) conference in 2001:

> Gap years can help address the pressing need to improve skills of graduates entering the workplace. Universities generally like to take students who have done a gap year because they are more mature and a step ahead of the rest. (Universities UK 2001)

Baroness Warwick is effectively offering legitimation from the entire UK university system. As with other commentators, she repeats the theme of maturity, though also mentions the principle of competitive advantage and structure. Indeed, the principle of structure appears in the majority of establishment endorsements offered for the gap year. Jack Straw mentioned structure in his statement to gapyear.com, similarly Tony Higgins from UCAS stresses the need for a "well planned structured year-out" (YOG 2001); while for the YOG, promoting structured gap years is a key part of their mandate (YOG 2001). Structure, in the context in which all the above advocates use it, implies planning, organisation and ultimately the consumption of industry-produced packages. This represents a move away from the association of youth travel with the "hippie drifter", a figure who sought freedom and mobility through travel as a rejection of Western market-driven consumerism (Ateljevic nd). The promotion of the gap year as a structured experience fits into a broader agenda of making the gap year a market-compatible commodity. Through the need for structure comes, in part, the need for an industry to provide such structured experiences. Furthermore, a hierarchy of gap year experiences can be developed with those experiences that demonstrate structure being valued (by the state and educational organisations) above those that do not. No longer does one simply take a year off from formal education/employment; now one takes a "gap", with its bound notions of value and purpose.

To summarise, the rise in public and institutional recognition of the gap year has produced an increasingly bound and recognisable product. This product represents a transformation of the gap year from a symbol of hedonistic youth travel by individuals and groups of young people into a training ground for future professionals. Simultaneously, this has made the gap year not only institutionally acceptable, but also market compatible. So, the mythical values of structure, maturity and the oft-mentioned "broad horizons" have become products for which there is a commercial market, and no shortage of sellers.

Where in the World? The Contradictory Geography of the Gap Year

International gap year programmes operate in a particular geography, which frames not just *where* participants travel to, but also *how* they travel. The professionalisation of the gap year, and its evolving market orientation, has produced a definable geography of the gap year. That is, it has produced spaces that are constructed through a particular set of imaginations, which prescribe where gap year programmes occur and the activities in which they engage. There are many dimensions to the imaginations that construct gap year spaces. Historical process and perspectives (most notably, colonialism and traditions such as the Grand Tour, as well as missionary and volunteer work) have acted to shape possible gap year geographies. As the industry seeks to establish itself as professional, it has increasingly been required to manage the perceived risks of its activities. Yet, simultaneously, the industry has needed to recognise that to some degree danger is a desired element of its programmes. In the following discussion I first offer a brief guide to the geography of the gap year, concentrating on its historically located nature, before going on to examine the contradictory conceptualisations of danger and safety and their role in constructing gap year geographies. I argue that the simultaneous and potentially contradictory marketing of safety and danger is central to neoliberal professionalisation.

While the term "gap year" may be relatively new, the practice itself has strong historical roots, which continue to inform both how and where gap year programmes occur. Historical practices exert an influence on the geography of the modern gap year. Colonialism is of particular interest because of its strategic and lasting impact on both the possibilities and rationale for travel. Colonialism is not just a conquest of territory and resources but also a conquest of the way in which the world has become known; a construction of ideas as much as a construction of States. In *Orientalism: Western Conceptions of the Orient*, Edward Said (1978) argued that the Orient is not a geographical fact but rather a historical and cultural creation. This creation reflected a distinct set of power relations and cultural imperatives, which told more about the state of Europe than it did about the nature of the area deemed to be the Orient. Geography is therefore not a simple matter of imagination, but rather a conscious construction which articulates, legitimates and maintains power relations between regions:

> Orientalism … is not an airy European fantasy about the Orient, but a created body of theory and practice in which, for many generations, there has been a considerable material investment. (Said 1978:6)

It is this investment that makes Orientalism ideologically robust and part of teachable wisdom (Said 1978). Said's understanding of place as politically and strategically constructed can be extended to the colonial process in general. The need to legitimate colonialism demanded a gaze in which colonisation became natural and even desirable. European colonialism itself has been largely dismantled and deservedly critiqued; however, the colonial gaze lingers on. As a discourse, colonialism, like the discourse of development that succeeded it, "created a space in which only certain things could be said or even imagined" (Escobar 1995:39). This process helped produce a set of norms that continue to inform the way global relations are understood and practised. As I argue below, in turn, these processes have helped shape a geography of the gap year.

The gap year industry expresses both the desire to distance its practices from those of colonialism while also making direct reference to its historical roots. For example, in the opening to the Latin American section of their brochure, the company i-to-i remind participants of their travelling ancestry:

> Botanists have delved into the Amazonian jungles to pluck plants, explorers have canoed out of sight, and archaeologists have explored the burial rites of the Incas. Now it is your turn to explore Latin America for yourself. (i-to-i 2002:10)

The historical motivations for travel are therefore not a forgotten legacy. Rather they remain evocative and powerful and can be called upon to inspire contemporary travellers. As a result, the geography of the gap year draws direct linage from the geographies constructed through and by colonialism.

Colonialism effectively centred history on a Western view of the world, defining all-else in opposition and creating an endless logic of binaries (McClintock 1995). Dichotomies between civilised/uncivilised, Christian/un-Christian, First/Third World, coloniser/colonised were created not just to define the difference between the Western (colonising) self and the foreign (colonised) other, but also to naturalise and legitimate colonialism. The creation of dichotomies between self and other may not be a process unique or new to colonialism, but the dichotomies of that era continue to populate understandings of others and indeed continue to be mobilised. Binaries and dichotomies between self and other are a defining feature in the presentation of gap year geographies, and in this way produce geographies that are consistent with the colonial constructions of others noted by both Said (1978) and McClintock (1995). Homogenous descriptions of groups of people and cultures are relied upon to produce evocative and recognisable imagery. The three quotations below are taken from different gap year organisations and offer descriptions of Brazil, Paraguay and Bolivia, respectively:

> This tropical paradise ignites the Western imagination like no other South American country, and the people of Brazil delight visitors with their energy and joy. (Travellers Worldwide 2003a)

> Often chaotic and sometimes infuriating, it is a beautiful country where the people are unfailingly charming and welcome GAP volunteers into their homes. (GAP Activity Projects 2003)

> With a generally shy and gracious population, Bolivia is one of the safest Latin American countries to visit. (Travellers Worldwide 2003b)

All three of the above statements seek to summarise entire nations of people in simple pairs of descriptors. This process of essentialising others serves the purpose of creating simple, recognisable categories through which such others can become "known", as I illustrate in the following discussion.

In the first of the above quotations, Travellers Worldwide makes a direct reference to the Western imagination, which is effectively what all the above statements aim to appeal to. The need to create a simple geography, one that offers the opportunity for consumption, is integral to the global map created by the gap year industry. It is the availability of prescribed cultural experiences, and indicators of their successful consumption, that in part defines the geography of the gap year. This approach to geographical construction is constant with the characteristics of Said's Orientalism:

> The Orient was almost a European invention, and had been since antiquity a place of romance, exotic beings, haunting memories and landscapes, remarkable experiences. (Said 1978:1)

In a similar manner, the Gap Year industry creates a space populated by the existence of consumable experiences of others. So, whether it is the "energy and joy" in Brazil, the invitations into Paraguayan homes, or the "shy graciousness" of Bolivians, a gap year traveller knows what to expect and how to consume the experience. Through these essentialised, textual representations, which are usually supported by evocative visual images, travellers are offered a known geography. That is, they are provided with expectations of the nature of their destinations, with no suggestion that these may not be universal. Thus, a geography idealised for the traveller is constructed. Based on the above statements, travellers can expect spaces that are a "delight to visitors", "charming and welcoming" and, finally, "safe". Such geographies are not offered as fractured or partial, but rather as the essential nature of the places and peoples to be visited.

The geography of the gap year is certainly worthy of more detailed attention;[7] however, here I will concentrate on one particular aspect of this geography, namely the industry's paradoxical relationship with issues of danger and risk. Industry operators need to prove that gap years are safe in order to recruit participants. Yet, on the other hand, danger is also a marketable commodity, one that many young participants themselves actively seek. Here I am arguing that the existence of dangers in travelling, in part, legitimises the development of an industry around the gap year. As a result of perceived dangers, the industry can sell safety. Gap year providers need to convince parents and themselves that participants will survive their programmes, whilst simultaneously allowing participants a sense that survival will at least be a struggle. Consequently, the role played by danger in gap years is ambiguous.

Central to some of the ambiguity around danger is the difference between perceived and actual risk. The gap year industry offers many activities marketed as dangerous, with bungee jumping serving as the archetypal example. However, such activities are probably safer than crossing any average road in the capital cities of popular destinations such as Ecuador or Peru. It is the availability of universalistic and simplistic geographies that makes the marketing of such partial geographical imaginations of danger possible. These geographies are exemplified in the statement below, which was made by the parent of a gap year student and quoted in a recently published report on the gap year:

> The world like ancient Gaul, is divided into three parts (well it is for gap year parents like me). The first part has food that can be eaten and hospitals that don't require you to bring your own plasma. This includes North America, Western Europe and Australia/New Zealand. The second part has none of the above but is gentle and

civilized. This is India. The third part is like the second, except with violence complimentary. Here we're talking at least 80% of South America. Madeline, my 17 year old daughter, set off for Guatemala, a country which seemed to me (and I may be doing it an injustice), to have civil war like Scotland has weather. If it isn't raining now, just wait 20 minutes. (Michael Tobert, gap year parent, quoted in Hogg 2001:12–13)

The parent quoted above sums up whole continents under the neat labels of "dangerous", "safe" or "gentle", reducing the entire world to three categories and effectively offering a re-imagination of the politicized categories of First, Second and Third Worlds. While the basis of such a process of categorisation is questionable, it is important to note that this statement was published in a report produced by gapyear.com, which, as an organisation, actively seeks to promote gap years. On the subsequent page of the report the author asks the question "Are gap years safe?" and concludes thus:

We believe that in the future this barrier [the perception of danger] will naturally fall and the issue of safety will assume its correct place, namely in discussions about leaving the home and venturing out as a young adult. (Hogg 2001:14)

Deciphering quite what the author means by this statement is something of a challenge, however the context is relatively clear. Danger is being presented as a present but, crucially, manageable condition of taking a gap year, and as discussed further on, if danger is present then safety becomes a sellable commodity.

Returning to the earlier quotation from a gap year parent, parental perception of a difficult or dangerous country may well increase the allure of going there. A sense of danger is an integral part of a gap year experience for many participants. The ability to survive the experience and successfully negotiate risks and fears are all part of establishing one's credibility, and acquiring the life skills supposedly learnt. When discussing with participants in Peru and Ecuador why they chose particular destinations, issues of risk, difficulty and danger were often expressed. It is important to highlight, however, that what is being discussed is perceived risk and perceived danger. Indeed, in many cases participants recognised the prominence of perception and labelling in defining where was considered dangerous. The following conversation was a follow up to an earlier comment made by Peter,[8] where he described South America as "kind of dangerous":

Kate: So why does it [South America] feel kind of dangerous? [asked in response to an earlier comment by Peter]

Peter: because it is always hyped up in the newspapers.

Debbie: you never hear the good things.

Peter: Yeah actually some parts of Colombia now are dangerous, but the rest of the country, because I was talking to a Colombian chef the other day and he said it is not that bad, it is actually very nice, but people just think that Colombia is dangerous. And now they think Argentina is really dangerous but it is not at all.

Debbie: They are all really labelled, probably they are not like their labels at all but no one has really explored it enough to change those labels.

Jane: It is Third World so people think that is dangerous.

In this conversation, it is acknowledged that a dangerous image is probably just a question of labelling and misinformation by the media. Yet, despite recognising this, the participants still reproduce an image of South America as dangerous. Despite the dangerous label, none of the participants had researched the reality of this issue any further before arriving in Ecuador (where they were at the time of the interview), suggesting that they did not perceive such dangers as real or likely to affect them. Instead, it seems that danger was all part of making Ecuador and Peru desirable gap year destinations for them. Thus dangers, and the ability to survive them, can be an intrinsic part of establishing the cultural capital of travel. According to Phillips (1999) and Sorensen (2003) danger confers authenticity on travel experiences so that suffering and managing not to spend money become key markers that backpackers, in particular, use to attribute value to their experiences.

Given the cultural status, value and appeal of danger to partici-pants, the gap year industry is in the complicated position of both selling danger and selling safety. Earlier in the conversation quoted above, it was mentioned that it was better to go to South America "with someone who knows where they are going". Thus while danger gives value and desirability to a destination, the safety and security of going "with someone" is a key part of the product bought. Though danger and risk may all be integral parts of a gap year experience there is little discussion within the industry of the nature of these dangers. Gap year organisations remain equally vague on the dangers of their programmes, preferring instead to stress the safety precau-tions that they can offer. For example, Teaching and Projects Abroad, a large provider of gap year placements, emphasise that:

Before we go anywhere countries must be politically stable and safe. If they are not, we don't go. We are in constant contact with the Foreign Office regarding stability and safety and, of course, we have the added security of overseas staff. (Teaching & Projects Abroad 2002)

While violence, coups, terrorists and civil war may be the predominant image of danger, the real risk is more likely to lie in tap water, bald bus tyres and drunk drivers. These risks are out of the control of most gap year organisations, and beyond the spectrum of worry for most 18-year-old participants. Consequently, all programmes involve those risks and dangers that, like bungee jumping, are controllable. Gap year providers may be happy to have their participants perceive their destination countries as dangerous, but it is vital that, as professional organisations, they are seen to run safe programmes, and that they market this to the parents of their potential clients. In fact, as we have seen, selling safety is a key product in the gap year market and integral to its geography.

Selling Knowledge, Becoming Expert
The discussion above has indicated that a gap year is a period of exploring geographies of danger, cultures, others, self and above all difference. One of the purposes of a gap year is to seek out difference, to leave the ordinary in search of the extra-ordinary. The value of the gap year is premised, to a large degree, on the presumed relationship between encountering difference and knowing difference. In this section, I examine two aspects of the relationship between gap years and knowledge production. First, I offer a critique of the way the industry sells education without any specific mechanism for its delivery. Second, I examine how gap year experiences position travelling participants as experts. I argue that, despite the apparent professionalisation of the gap year industry, so far its gaze has proved myopic and has yet to be focused on the industry's basic practices.

Earlier, I examined various statements from important figures in state, education and employment; in the majority of these commentaries reference was made to what participants would learn through taking a gap year. The notion of "broad horizons", as expressed by Jack Straw, encapsulates the idea that learning automatically occurs through travel. At present, the primary mechanism through which the majority of gap year organisations presume participants learn about others is through the experience of contact. Such a learning model is encapsulated in Allport's 1954 "Contact Hypothesis" (Pettigrew 1998), in which Allport advocated that contact between different social groups would reduce prejudice and increase tolerance (Amir and Ben-Ari 1985; Pettigrew 1998; Wittig and Grant-Thompson 1998). The assumption was that experience alone (in the form of contact) would be enough to cause a change in values. However, over recent years the Contact Hypothesis has received much criticism, at the heart of which has been a questioning of the presumed positive nature of contact, and also of the way in which experience is processed.

Allport's Contact Hypothesis is based upon the assumption that contact automatically deconstructs false stereotypes and prejudice. However, Allport specified four preconditions for such contact. Namely, that there would be equal status between the contact groups, that there were common goals for achievement, that the groups would need to co-operate, and finally, that there was authority support for contact. This last condition translates into some form of shared value system between groups (Pettigrew 1998). These criteria are relatively taxing, particularly the last, and there is little evidence of their application within gap year programmes. Consequently, the situation is one where mere contact, under any set of conditions, is assumed to produce positive relationship outcomes. While such contact may be beneficial in the relationships between gap year participants from the developed world, in terms of explaining the relationships between Third World visitors and hosts, it appears deeply flawed. The assumption that contact alone breaks down stereotypes directly contradicts research suggesting that far from challenging pre-held views, contact experiences may in fact accentuate deep-seated attitudes (Amir and Ben-Ari 1985; Pettigrew 1998). Stereotypes, in the form of generalisations and simplifications about groups of others, can be deeply entrenched, established over prolonged periods of time, and, consequently, robust (Nederveen-Pieterse 1995). To assume that a short period of contact with the stereotyped other will automatically contradict, and hence unseat, such stereotypes is, at best, naive. The gap year industry's reliance on contact as a source of learning about others needs to be challenged, in terms of the nature of knowledges it might produce and also its validity as an educational strategy. The point I wish to make here is that a reliance on contact is the product not of a deliberate educational strategy, but the default setting when no such strategy exists.

In addition to the apparent reliance on contact, gap year experiences appear premised on the principle that linking experiences across time and space is unproblematic. In the comment below the director of a major gap year provider describes the potential for participants to act in the future in more empathetic ways to peoples across the world as the "most important" thing his organisation offers:

Well the most important thing we do is something that we don't advertise ... We have sent the best part of 10,000 people, who are middle-class young people, many of whom will have significant jobs in the years to come and they will have lived in a Third World country, they will have had that experience of the developing world and not just of the beaches of Gambia, not just a bit of backpacking but they will actually have lived, and worked in a Third World country. And I think, actually, that is the most important factor, that there is a generation now that are going through, because of us, a generation that are going to go through and run banks and run big companies and what not, for whom the Third World is not strange and out there and who will have friends in the Third World. That I think is the prime most important thing ... I mean how much better it might have been if all the ummm all the people who are middle and high management of Shell had spent some time in West Africa for example, an idealist example, but how differently they would have treated the Ibo people in Nigeria? (Author's interview, UK organisation's headquarters 2001)

While there are multiple assumptions apparent in the above comments, of relevance here is the vagueness of the time scale implied. Social action is presented not as an issue for everyone in their everyday encounters, but as an issue for the few, and for the future. So while much of the gap year industry claims to promote an agenda of social responsibility, it is unclear who is seen as the actors within this agenda. With such assertions, rather than focusing on their own participants, organisations are concentrating on generic and unknown actors who hold identifiable power in the future. Gap year organisations are, in effect, abdicating any direct responsibility for converting experience into action in either the short or long term. They assume an emphasis on macro over micro-level changes, so that action becomes the responsibility of a few powerful individuals, rather than of the powerful masses of the developed world.

A further perspective from which to critique the gap year's reliance on contact is a pedagogical one. A reliance on contact to stimulate learning is also a reliance on experience as an educational process. That is, experience is not treated as part of an educational process, but as an education in and of itself. Experiential education is a well-established pedagogy, however its mobilisation in many gap year programmes represents a misunderstanding of its complexities. As an educational concept, experiential education fits within various pedagogical traditions, including social justice and the work of theorists such as Paulo Freire and John Dewey. According to experiential education theorists, experience is more than just a set of physical interactions, instead, it is part of a process of interpretation and critical reflection (Adams 1997). By comparison, in the gap year, the concept of experience has been simplified and transformed from a pedagogical process to a method. So that experience alone, in the sense of social interaction, is promoted as an educational process in its own right. Consequently, as with Allport's Contact Hypothesis, the processes through which participants learn about others remain ignored. In contrast to this approach, recent research on cross-cultural interaction and service learning projects has argued strongly for the management of the various processes involved in inter-group contact (Adams 1997; Bell 1997; Crabtree 1998; Pettigrew 1998). Such processes include learning about one another, generating effective links, and inter-group reappraisal (Pettigrew 1998). These principles are further supported by the work of groups such as the Association for Experiential Education, which emphasise the need for experience to be part of a cycle of action and reflection (Krnas and Roarke 1994). However, despite evidence from both research and practice current in other educational forums, such active processing is woefully missing from gap year programmes. Critically, the adoption of an educational approach based on the presumed value of contact and the value of experience is in fact a result of the almost total lack of educational strategy within the majority of UK gap year programmes. Despite the professionalism of the industry in terms of its marketing and packaging, this gaze seems not to have been focused on one of its key products, namely "broadening horizons".

I now turn to the second point concerning the partiality of the gap year industry's professional gaze by focusing on the construction of experts. Here, I have concentrated solely on international volunteer-tourism programmes which involve doing development work. The gap year industry's relationship with development is complex and beyond the scope of this contribution;[9] relevant to the argument here, however, is how gap year programmes are creating a new generation of development experts. Gap year programmes for volunteers are premised on the usefulness of such volunteers. Situations are presented in which the international volunteer can offer help, advice, support and generally be needed. For example, Teaching & Projects Abroad open the Mongolia section of their brochure with the statement: "a culture older than Genghis Kahn needs you!" (Teaching & Projects Abroad 2003:18). This statement, made seemingly without irony, implies that Mongolia is struggling for want of a few British teenagers. Meanwhile Venture Co is keen to stress that: "We have carefully selected the projects that present the opportunity for you to be of genuine value to an indigenous community and to give something back" (Venture Co 2002). A point that Student Partnership Worldwide (SPW) similarly makes with their promise that: "SPW will not send you where you are not needed. You will not be doing a job that a local could do better than you" (Student Partnership Worldwide 2002).

Whatever "genuine value" or "needs" participants will meet, are never clearly identified in the publicity literature from these organisations. What is created, however, are situations and spaces in which the gap year volunteer will be needed and will be able to provide some external expert assistance. Volunteer-tourism places travellers in the position of expert or at least as knowledgeable by locating them in placements as teachers, builders, medical workers etc. Often these are identities and positions not available to the same individuals "at home". The freedom from qualifications can be used as an enticing part of such programmes. For example, Travellers Worldwide, an organisation that offers placements in 16 countries spread across the globe, emphasises in bold type on the opening page of their website: "You don't need any formal qualifications" (Travellers Worldwide 2003b). The freedom from qualifications makes gap year programmes accessible, and provides spaces in which participants can experiment with possible future professional identities.[10] This process has become a major selling point for the gap year industry, which is able to market placements on the basis of the opportunities they offer for professional and CV advancement.

Creating spaces in which the travelling participant can experiment with an expert identity also creates a set of social power relations that frame the encounters between hosts and visitors. The traveller is able to experiment with a new identity, while also being presented to their hosts as an expert, a process that is particularly pertinent given the inequalities through which tourism to the Third World inherently operates (Hutnyk 1996). In creating apparent experts, the gap year industry risks not only permitting practices for which participants are not held accountable, but also establishing exploitive relationships between travellers and hosts. This risk is exemplified in the quotation below in which a volunteer with Teaching & Projects Abroad manages to de-humanise ill Ghanaians into textbooks for his or her own learning:

> The practical experience I got was very rewarding. You can see everything and do see everything. A single patient in Ghana will often have many different conditions to advanced states, which make them textbook examples. Even though I had no experience, just a good deal of interest, I was allowed to be present in operations and to assist in the delivery of babies. (Unnamed participant quoted in Teaching & Projects Abroad 2002:5)

Though perhaps extreme, the above quote is revealing, articulating a relationship between traveller and host that is, at the very least, troubling. The traveller is presented with an expert identity, in this case medical worker, and is then encouraged to experiment with this identity *on* a group of people.

The gap year industry may be seeking an increasingly professional persona, but at present this seems to have produced a highly myopic gaze. Through programmes participants are presumed to learn about others; to acquire "broad horizons". However, the mechanisms through which such learning is to be engendered remain largely ignored. Deliberate educational strategies remain wanting, leaving the industry dependent on assumptions about the value of contact and the inevitability of learning by experience. Such a lack of a pedagogical perspective becomes even more problematic when the social and geographical frameworks in which participants travel are considered. The uncritical adoption of the position of expert, and with it the practices of experimentation, frame the contact encounters between hosts and visitors within powerful inequalities. These relationships produce the world in which gap year participants can travel and claim knowledge about. Without critical reflection, and with the authoritative power granted to knowledge produced through the supposed authenticity of first-hand travel experiences (Heald 2003), this world becomes a known and powerful reality.

Concluding Comments

Over the last ten years the gap year has evolved from a symbol of rebellion and an escape from the formal institutions of education and employment in the UK into a bastion of those same structures. This evolution has demanded an increasingly professional face for its practices, which has resulted in the establishment of the YOG and a growing rhetoric about what a gap year can and should be. As a result, structured Third World travel experiences are playing an important role in defining "good" gap years. The professionalisation of the gap year has received vocal support from a range of actors, including state representatives interested in promoting particular types of (global) UK citizens. Chiming with a concentration on neoliberal self-regulating citizenship, the growing gap year industry has focused on personal CV development by providing tailored programmes and providing new support services, especially for those travelling to Third World destinations. The increasing professionalisation and diversity of the gap year industry means that paradoxically it has been able to market both safety and danger successfully to its audiences while remaining unengaged with and unreflexive about the colonised and colonising geographies that it reproduces in the process.

The professionalisation of the gap year is proving to be highly myopic. Despite the fact that one of its primary claims is that it offers opportunities for education and global learning, across the industry there appears to be little strategy for the actual delivery of these goals. Consequently, the industry has left itself reliant on outdated and pedagogically questionable methodologies. If the gap year is to evolve from an eccentric form of adventure tourism into an experience that offers geographically disparate peoples an opportunity to encounter and learn about one another, then the professional gaze needs to be extended beyond marketing and rhetoric and onto the practices of the programmes that the industry operates.

Endnotes
[1] Author's interview: Richard Oliver of the Year Out Group (YOG) (2001).
[2] Although some institutions work with commercial companies, universities usually retain control over curricula design and course credit systems.
[3] I conducted interviews with senior members of five gap year organisations, and analysed materials from 20 gap year providers and a number of support organisations. All the gap year providers analysed are members of the YOG.
[4] These include companies such as the gapyear.com and Objective, who act to promote and support gap years, the University and College Admissions System (UCAS), Universities UK, the House of Lords, as well as a wide range of popular media reports and articles.
[5] While cultural geography research has focused on identity formation among independent travellers in countries which have become important gap year destinations (see, for example, Desforges' 1998 work on Peru), the gap year industry itself has come under little academic scrutiny. What research that there has been has tended to be produced by undergraduates or has come from within the gap year industry (for example, see Hogg 2001).
[6] Between 2001 and 2004 the government have committed to spending £300 million to promote volunteering amongst young people (National Centre for Volunteering 2003).
[7] For a more detailed discussion of the geography of the gap year see Chapter 5 in my PhD thesis 'Broad Horizons? Geographies and Pedagogies of the Gap Year', University of Newcastle upon Tyne.
[8] All research participants' names have been changed.
[9] For more details on the relationship between development and the gap year see (for a discussion of some of these issues, see Simpson 2004).
[10] The freedom from the need for formal qualifications and the ability to experiment with new identities can actually now be turned into a qualification. As discussed earlier, it is possible to receive a City & Guild gap year qualification, which I would argue could be seen as part of the gap year's creation of experts.

References
Adams M (1997) Pedagogical frameworks for social justice. In M Adams, L A Bell and P Griffin (eds) *Teaching for Diversity and Social Justice* (pp 30–43). London: Routledge
Amir Y and Ben-Ari R (1985) International tourism, ethnic contact, and attitude change. *Journal of Social Issues* 41(3):105–115
Ateljevic I (nd) "Theoretical encounters: A review of backpacker literature." Unpublished paper
Bell L A (1997) Theoretical foundations for social justice education. In M Adams, L A Bell and P Griffin (eds) *Teaching for Diversity and Social Justice* (pp 3–15). London: Routledge
Crabtree R D (1998) Mutual empowerment in cross-cultural participatory development and service learning: Lessons in communication and social justice in El Salvador and Nicaragua. *Journal of Applied Communication Research* 2:182–209
Dean M (1999) *Governmentality: Power and Rule in Modern Society*. London: Sage

Desforges L (1998) Checking out the planet. In T Skelton and G Valentine (eds) *Cool Places: Geographies of Youth Cultures* (pp 175–192). London: Routledge

Escobar A (1995) *Encountering Development: The Making and Unmaking of the Third World*. West Sussex: Princeton University Press

GAP Activity Projects (2003) Country overview, http://www.gap.org.uk/uwhere/uwhere.html (last accessed 18 October 2003)

gap-year.com (2002) Volunteer abroad, http://www.gap-year.com/volunteeringabroad.asp (last accessed 30 April 2003)

Hardman R (2000) Prince has rough ride in Patagonia. *The Daily Telegraph* 11 December 2000:1–3

Hayes E (1997) The form of capital, University of Pennsylvania, http://www.english.upenn.edu/~jenglish/Courses/hayes-pap.html (last accessed 24 April 2003)

Heald S (2003) "Finding fun without innocence." Paper presented at Association of America Geographers Annual Conference, New Orleans

Hindle C (2003) *The Gap Year Book: The Definitive Guide to Planning and Taking a Year Out*. London: Lonely Planet

Hogg C (2001) *The 2001 UK Gap Year Report*. The Gap Year Company

Hutnyk J (1996) *The Rumour of Calcutta: Tourism, Charity and the Poverty of representation*. London: Zed Books

i-to-i (2002) *Volunteer & Work Abroad*. Leeds: i-to-i.

Jobson R (2000) Wills reigns as Prince of many parts. *Daily Express* 1, 2–5

Kaur R and Hutnyk J (eds) (1999). *Travel Worlds: Journeys in Contemporary Cultural Politics*. London: Zed Books

Kerr J (2000) Wills' royal flush. *The Mirror* 11 December:1, 8–9

Krnas J P and Roarke S M (1994) Learning through travel. *The Journal of Experiential Education* 17(3):20–28

Lancaster University Department of Geography (2002) Thinking of taking a gap year? http://geography.lancs.ac.uk/posters/gap%20years.pdf (last accessed 30 October 2003)

McClintock A (1995) *Imperial Leather: Race, Gender and Sexuality in the Colonial Contest*. London: Routledge

Merrit S (2000) Have a nice year . . . , http://www.observer.co.uk/review/story/0,6903,356244,00.html (last accessed 9 July 2002)

National Centre for Volunteering (2003) Speech by Fiona McTaggart MP, http://www.volunteering.org.uk/centre/mctaggarttxt.htm (last accessed 30 October 2003)

Nederveen-Pieterse J (1995) *White on Black: Images of Africa and Blacks in Western Popular Culture*. London: Yale University Press

Objective (2004) Objective gap safety, http://www.objectivegapyear.com/(last accessed 15 April 2004)

Pettigrew T F (1998) Intergroup contact theory. *Annual Review of Psychology* 49:65–85

Phillips P (1999) Tourists, terrorists death and value. In R Kaur and J Hutnyk (eds) *Travel Worlds: Journeys in Contemporary Cultural Politics* (pp). London: Zed Books

Robbins D (2000) *Bourdieu & Culture*. London: Sage

Said E (1978) *Orientalism: Western Conceptions of the Orient*. London: Penguin Books

Simpson K (2004) Doing development: The gap year, volunteer tourists and a popular practice of development. *Journal of International Development* 16(5):681–692

Simpson K (2005) "Broad horizons: Geographies and pedagogies of the gap year." Unpublished PhD thesis, University of Newcastle

Sorensen A (2003) Backpacker ethnography. *Annals of Tourism Research* 30(4):847–867

Student Partnership Worldwide (2002) Why SPW? http://www.spw.org/whyspw.htm (last accessed 4 November 2002)

Teaching & Projects Abroad (2002) frequently asked questions, http:www.teaching-abroad.co.uk/faq.htm (last accessed 20 August 2002)

Teaching & Projects Abroad (2003) *Teaching & Projects Abroad*. West Sussex

the leap (2003) feedback, http://www.theleap.co.uk/feedback.shtml (last accessed 30 October 2003)

Travellers Worldwide (2003a) Brazil, http://www.travellersworldwide.com/12-brazil/12-brazil-about.htm (last accessed 18 October 2003)

Travellers Worldwide (2003b) Home page, http://www.travellersworldwide.com/index.htm (last accessed 12 October 2003)

United Kingdom Parliament (2000) Voluntary service for young people, House of Lords, http://www.parliament.the-stationery-office.co.uk/pa/1d1999000/1dhansard/v.../00705-27.ht (last accessed 22 October 2003)

Universities UK (2001) National Council of Voluntary Organisations, http://www.universitiesuk.ac.uk/speeches/show.asp?sp=30 (last accessed 21 October 2003)

Urry J (1990) *The Tourist Gaze*. London: Sage

Venture Co (2002) Ventures, choose your venture, Inca venture, http://www.ventureco-worldwide.com/inca.htm (last accessed 30 October 2002)

Vidal J (2000) Raleigh ho! *The Guardian* 9 October:4–5

Wilson P (2002) Where William goes, others follow. *The Daily Telegraph* 20 July

Wittig M A and Grant-Thompson S (1998) The utility of Allport's conditions of intergroup contact for predicting perceptions of improved racial attitudes and beliefs. *Journal of Social Issues* 54(4):795–812

World Challenge Expeditions (2001) *Journeys of a Lifetime*. London

World Challenge Expeditions (2002) *Education for Life*. London

Year Out Group (YOG) (2001) Home page, http://www.yearoutgroup.org/ (last accessed 10 July 2001)

Year Out Group (YOG) (2003) About us, http://www.yearoutgroup.org/about_yog.htm (last accessed 28 October 2003)

Kate Simpson worked in the gap year industry for a number of years before starting her PhD at the University of Newcastle, UK, which she was awarded in 2005.

Chapter 4

Ethnodevelopment: Social Movements, Creating Experts and Professionalising Indigenous Knowledge in Ecuador

Nina Laurie, Robert Andolina and Sarah Radcliffe

Introduction

Professionalisation in development is increasingly under scrutiny by critics of development's consolidation as a global industry. For some, the development industry has become professionalised to such an extent that it is difficult to think outside its terms of reference (see Escobar 1995). Such critics argue that the professionalisation of a development language makes it almost impossible for actors (individuals, communities, states and strategic alliances of interest groups) to envisage futures that are not bound up in some form of development imaginary. Thus, development is increasingly being analysed as a particular form of modernity (Watts 2003). We explore how contemporary interests in neoliberal social inclusion approaches are currently shaping new knowledges and experts. Rather than focusing on the colonisation of development imaginaries, however, our analysis emphasises struggles over knowledge production and established cultures and traditions in new forms of governance, associated with neoliberal development. Concentrating on the relationship between neoliberalism and governmentality, we emphasise how notions of self-regulating citizenship, combined with increased national and international recognition of indigenous collective rights, is opening up opportunities for contests over the ways in which political decision making and terrains of development are managed and by whom. Specifically, we examine whether current forms of development professionalisation are generating spaces for creative thinking and action by indigenous social movements and/or are being used by those actors to re-work the power relations of development and promote other modes of knowing.

Indigenous actors in Andean Latin America have mobilised to counter the impoverishing and individualising effects of neoliberal reforms, both nationally and transnationally. The Andean countries of Ecuador and Bolivia, among others in the region (see case studies in Perreault and Martin 2005), have adopted many neoliberal measures, including fiscal austerity, privatisation, promotion of non-traditional exports, encouragement of foreign investment, and tariff reductions, and changes to labor protection (Conaghan, Malloy and Abugattas 1990; Huber and Solt 2004). Efforts to establish democracy, transparent and accountable forms of rule, under the neoliberal "good governance" agendas have set the parameters for the political context for neoliberalism's implementation (Kohl 2002). The speed and depth of neoliberal restructuring were publicly and politically contentious (Corkhill and Cubbitt 1988; Hey and Klak 1999), although governments and international financial institution representatives presented them as benign, any problems being blamed on their incompleteness (Walton 2004).

By undercutting the foundation of nationalist political economies of corporatist forms of distribution and representation, neoliberal reforms have re-worked the interactions between state and citizens, not least the ways in which indigenous groups make claims on the state and on diverse development actors. Neoliberal regimes not only favour individuals (as entrepreneurs and property owners) over collective subjects, but fiscal cutbacks reduce or remove subsidies, price guarantees and credits upon which indigenous and rural livelihoods were previously based, albeit precariously (Yashar 1999). Across many Latin American countries with large indigenous populations, such as Ecuador, Bolivia, Guatemala and Mexico, the dismantling of rural development programmes in the 1980s and 1990s provided the incentive for indigenous movements to protest (Yashar 1998:31). New rights for ethnic-racial groups, established under the new democratic constitutions of the 1990s, failed to deliver meaningful security and opportunities (Yashar 1999:87). In this context, the politicisation of ethnic cleavages (Yashar 1998) occurs under neoliberal forms of governance that police ethnic–racial borders and rights, and reduce socio-economic rights (Hale 2002).

In the Andean countries of Ecuador and Bolivia, indigenous people have mobilised to contest harsh neoliberal stabilisation and to propose alternatives to radical restructuring (Collins 2000; Pacari 1996). Neoliberal measures to open markets in land, water, and new commodities, and to promote non-traditional exports (such as flowers and shrimps in Ecuador), have profound impacts on rural well-being, thereby impacting most on already impoverished indigenous and land-less/near landless groups. Indigenous responses to such pressures include alternative law proposals, nationwide protests, coalition building with other social actors, and strategic essentialism (see Pacari 1996). Indigenous engagement with the cultural politics of neoliberalism has generated new ways of presenting indigenous cultures, knowledges and forms of organisation, often within transnational, national and local spheres (Brysk 2000; Collins 2000; Comaroff and Comaroff 2001; Valdivia 2005).

Understanding development institutions in dynamic relation to transnational advocacy networks (Keck and Sikkink 1998; Sikkink 1991), we focus on indigenous social movements and development in the Andes. In particular, we examine the case of Ecuador where highly organised indigenous movements have been engaged in transnational development networks for more than a decade.[1] Important in shaping understandings of culturally appropriate forms of development, these networks have become influential sites for debating and fixing the meanings and tools of "development-with-identity" in both the Andean region and the international donor community more generally. Development-with-identity embraces a wide set of understandings and divergent views about how to make development sensitive to Indian needs. It has been established in a number of different Andean locations, resulting from intersecting state, social movement and NGO efforts to re-work indigenous livelihoods and income security. Often resting upon complex multicultural and multiethnic practice and dialogue that involves indigenous, *mestizo*, African-Andeans and whites, development-with-identity treats indigenous culture as a flexible and dynamic resource, as the basis for creative thinking outside the standard "box" of development solutions (Radcliffe, Laurie and Andolina 2005).

While terms like development-with-identity and ethnodevelopment pre-date the rise of neoliberal development policies, their use was originally confined to a small set of indigenous activists and specialist NGO and donor actors. However, discontent over the social impacts of structural adjustment policies in the 1990s brought such approaches to the fore in social development policy. Indians became visible not only because of their political mobilisation and international networking, but also due to the multilateral requirement for indigenous participation and attention to social difference within beneficiary groups. Advocates for change in Andean education ministries and donor organisations pressed for new inclusionary policies, arguing that harsh neoliberal adjustment increases inequality (Oliart 2005).

We understand neoliberalism to be a particular hegemonic form of regularisation of knowledge and the social relations that enhance the market and individualism. Contests over the roll-out of such forms of neoliberalism in development are particularly evident in social policy making, where the agency of the human targets of development is a central issue. In broad terms, social development policies include strengthening institutions and civil society organisations; the social inclusion of previously marginal groups; recognition of social diversity (ie gender, ethnicity, age, cultural and economic characteristics) and the participation of all stakeholders in project decision-making and execution. Social development, therefore, represents a key terrain for challenging understandings of regularisation and struggles over the role of different development actors in shaping knowledge and expertise. Under neoliberal approaches, social development pays particular attention to previously marginal groups like indigenous people because their exclusion from development is believed to carry unwarranted costs (Garland 2000). Thus social development's long-standing interest in participatory approaches is increasingly being framed by the new managerialism and audit cultures associated with neoliberal development (Mawdsley, Townsend and Porter 2002; Townsend, Porter and Mawdsley 2002). These cultures involve indigenous stakeholders not only in the design and implementation of development projects but also in monitoring administrative efficiency and good governance. This occurs in contexts where notions of development expertise are actively contested. We argue that while neoliberalism is increasingly setting the social development agenda, in some contexts this occurs in ways that open up spaces for indigenous challenges to, and participation in, local and regional policy implementation.

As donor organisations have attempted to address indigenous issues, policy initiatives have been shaped by new forms of thinking. In particular since the mid-1990s, the concept of social capital has become influential in neoliberal social development. Although the concept has a long intellectual history and diverse definitions (Hyden 1997), in the development field social capital is defined broadly as the social glue or "norms and social relations embedded in the social structures of society that enable people to coordinate action and achieve desired goals" (Narayan 1999). While development-with-identity ideas predate the recent interest in social capital, the concept has become central to the formulation of a specific understanding of ethnodevelopment policy that focuses on bringing Indian populations out of poverty. Whereas some versions of development-with-identity engage with empowerment, racism and institutional strengthening, the understanding that has become predominant in donor rhetoric is one rooted in narrow understandings of social capital and culture which sideline such concerns.[2] Thus elsewhere we argue that ethnodevelopment policy is emerging as more limiting than wider development-with-identity understandings in its interpretations of indigenous development (Radcliffe, Laurie and Andolina 2005). Ethnodevelopment interprets culture and indigenous identity in ways that make it compatible with neoliberal social policy but potentially restrict indigenous agency, seeing indigenous culture mainly as a means of allocating resources and recognising beneficiary groups in development projects. In this respect, ethnodevelopment operates in the context of Latin American neoliberal multiculturalism through which the dividing lines between racial–cultural groups are structured and policed (Comaroff and Comaroff 2001). As applied in countries such as Guatemala, Ecuador and Bolivia, neoliberal multiculturalism provides rigid categories and criteria for membership by which the distinction between non-indigenous and indigenous groups can be claimed and maintained (Hale 2002).[3]

While other authors have highlighted the ambivalent ways in which orthodox development programmes and ideas are negotiated and reworked by indigenous organisations in their efforts to be authors of their own development,[4] drawing on work from a wider project[5] (see Andolina, Laurie and Radcliffe 2005), we seek specifically to highlight the power relations involved in knowledge production in the context of contests over emerging notions of ethnodevelopment. We examine power not only through the roles and norms of institutions, but also in relation to how governmentality[6] informs understandings of development and vice versa. Focusing on the "episteme of government" (Dean 1999:31), we analyse the forms of thought, knowledge, expertise and calculation employed in governing through neoliberal ethnodevelopment. Concentrating on Ecuadorian indigenous social movement's involvement in ethnodevelopment professionalisation, we argue that the negotiations that occur in and through training programs are, in practice, struggles over how such courses will be used to facilitate one or another mode of governing people and spaces. These modes are distinguished by how they define and treat ethnic distinctiveness under ethnodevelopment and configure relations of power between different ethnic groups.

Drawing on Michael Watts' notion of governable spaces of indigeneity (Watts 2003:24), our analysis focuses on the extent to which the institutionalisation of indigenous professionalisation challenges state forms of governmentality in relation to education. Rather than understanding indigenous identities in terms of pre-given ethnic identities, Watts (2003:24) illustrates how indigeneity is constructed through complex and unstable processes of identification based upon diverse historical genealogies. Drawing on Foucauldian understandings of governmentality and notions of governable space (Rose 1999), Watts argues that spaces of indigeneity are governed through complex processes that involve contests over the invention and re-invention of tradition and local knowledge and processes of representation in relation to culture, territory and resources. Referring to the case of Nigeria he contends that:

particular "populations" have been constructed as indigenous; this construction ... has emerged from the nationalist struggle as customary rights were added to a discourse of citizenship. But the process received enormous energy as indigeneity as a political category garnered international support ... The emergence in Nigeria of a national debate over resource control ... is precisely a product of indigenous claims-making on the state, a process by which ethnic identifications must be discursively and politically produced ... One of the striking aspects of the governable spaces of indigeneity as they emerged in the Delta is that they became vehicles for political claims, typically articulated as the need for a local government, or in some cases a state. (Watts 2003:24)

Like Watts, we see governable spaces as not only comprising indigenous peoples but also other actors, crucially the state. However, in our approach we consider that the state has more agency in constituting governable spaces of indigeneity than Watts suggests. Historically, in the Andean case, governable spaces have not only been forged as states have responded to indigenous claims, but the state has also taken a direct role in the formation of such spaces through its own racial projects. These projects include *indigenismo*[7] and, as we argue, its current support for neoliberal multicultural development. As noted by Deborah Yashar, "neoliberalism ... has become synonymous with the culpable state and has enabled the indigenous movements to target the state for retribution, justice and guarantees" (1998:36). Whereas previous discussions of governable spaces of indigeneity have been concerned with local space and local knowledge (albeit in some cases "with an eye to" national and international politics; Watts 2003:24), we are arguing for an analytical framework that takes into account complex geographies and multiple scales. We ask to what extent governable spaces of indigeneity are currently being established in Ecuador through multiple scales and overlapping geographies via ethnodevelopment professionalisation?

In the remainder of this contribution, first we discuss the emergence of new development expertise under ethnodevelopment. Next, examining the relationship between popular education, indigenous politics and training, we argue that popular education for indigenous people is becoming more formal and informed by neoliberal concerns with good governance. Third we focus on the politics of indigenous knowledge and argue that, as donors are becoming more interested in the generation of indigenous development expertise, indigenous knowledge is becoming professionalised in a variety of ways which generate contests over governable space when indigenous movements attempt to challenge fixed-space representations of indigenous knowledge. We see indigenous knowledge as more than concepts, conceptualising it additionally in terms of issues of resources, institutions and social relations. In the final section we analyse the extent to which the institutionalisation of ethnodevelopment in Ecuador creates spaces that allow indigenous movements to both engage with the state and to bypass it in order to achieve development-with-identity goals.

Ethnodevelopment: Changing Development Experts and Expertise

Arguing that reality has been colonised by the discourse of development, post-development writers like Arturo Escobar stress how development experts fail to acknowledge the continued inability of development approaches to deliver results that lessen inequality and reverse deteriorations in living conditions. Although critical of the emphasis on the singular character and oppressive claustrophobic closure of the development project in Escobar's work, Michael Watts (2003:13) also highlights development's frequent failures in securing rule and producing governable subjects and spaces. For earlier development critics such as Robert Chambers (1983, 1992) and Michael Edwards (1989), experts themselves are part of these failures because the popular knowledges that enable people to design, implement and monitor their own work are devalued as experts are created. A system of education and training which relies on experts will never be able to deliver change, Edwards claims, "because the attitudes of the expert prevent people from thinking for themselves" (1989:119).

While these arguments are thought provoking, such conceptualisation of experts is now somewhat dated. In contrast to a development industry populated by expatriate consultants, in recent years, the shift towards neoliberal social development models has placed more emphasis on stakeholder participation and developing human and social capital that is "indigenous" to a particular area. As active subjects in neoliberal development, these actors are expected to be self-governing, self-motivated and focused on de-centralised managerial efficiency. While there is growing diversity in the location of development professionalisation, support for training indigenous people as development experts in the Andes is highly transnational (Laurie, Andolina and Radcliffe 2003). As a result, new indigenous expert elites are emerging from the ranks of the social movements and becoming important advocates in transnational development and human rights circuits (Brysk 2000; Lloyd 1998).

There is clearly a need to investigate the new elites emerging as the identities of those seen as development experts change under neoliberal development. However, James Scott (1998) also reminds us of the imperative to analyse how certain forms of knowledge become narrowed, turned into everyday practices and routinised in development. He analyses how particular forms of knowledge become institutionalised as "normal" through practice, while Uma Kothari (2005) examines how what is accepted as "normal" development knowledge varies over time. She argues that, as development paradigms change, the construction and validation of experts through the knowledges they possess also shifts. Her study indicates how British colonialism prized colonial officer's in-depth knowledge of a local space, territory and socio-cultural economic context. By contrast, contemporary development workers are generalists, valued by the development industry (donors, INGOs [international NGOs], states and activists) for the generic tools they can apply anywhere. Therefore, in contemporary development paradigms local specialist knowledge detracts from development expertise, raising questions about how indigenous knowledge and actors are seen and valued.

Below we examine the expertise associated with indigenous development needs and agendas by focusing on the knowledges and experts emerging in the Andes. We argue that the current popularity of ethnodevelopment as a paradigm not only reflects donor interests in enhancing indigenous social capital under neoliberal visions of development, but is also explained by its ability to respond to the development-with-identity demands of indigenous social movements and key advocates working within NGOs, government and multilateral institutions. Indigenous movements have long demanded culturally appropriate education that reflects indigenous everyday realities and practical needs. For indigenous movements, culturally appropriate professionalisation recognises indigenous values and knowledges and seeks to strengthen indigenous political structures, organisations and leadership. The provision of this type of professionalisation equips indigenous communities to generate their own development projects based on their knowledge of their reality without having to rely on outside experts and technicians.[8] The context for training ethnodevelopment experts therefore differs from that described by Edwards (1989). The transnational professionalisation spaces we are concerned with here are indigenous training schools operated by indigenous organisations to promote leadership skills. We argue that these spaces comprise locations in which indigenous movements can engage in, shape and sometimes contest neoliberal development and notions of governable space and subjects.

Andean Popular Education and Indigenous Movements
Described as a world *"sin letras"* (without letters) (Oliart 1999), the Andes are characterised by a large number of people with little or no

formal schooling and by irregular contact with written texts. Such contexts have prompted extensive work in popular education. Building on the radical pedagogies of Paulo Freire that challenge students and teachers to empower themselves to promote democracy, equality and generate social change (1970, 1998), popular education has long envisaged educational alternatives in Andean America and questioned the notorious socialising of indigenous people into a discriminatory nation (Luykx 1999; Puiggrós 1991). In contrast to schooling and formal qualifications, alternative visions permit a greater focus on the specific needs of communities where literacy is not merely a goal of education but also a political tool for everyday life. Linked to NGO promotion of the Freire model as part of agricultural extension work, popular education has played an important role in Andean development (Gianotten and de Wit 1985). However, until recently the approach did not distinguish between meeting the class-based needs of indigenous peasants and strengthening indigenous culture and indigenous peoples' political voice (Kane 2001).

Popular education has recently started to focus more explicitly on indigenous concerns, while programs are becoming more formal as part of regularising training under enthnodevelopment. As a result, it is no longer necessarily the case that popular education is more informal than university courses. Many teachers move seamlessly between delivering popular training and university courses[9] and the professionalisation and institutionalisation of transnational ethnodevelopment networks mean that training programmes are now becoming more academically formal. For example, in Ecuador the ECUARUNARI[10] training school for women, a three-year programme, awards a diploma, has exams and requires course work as well as assessed participation in class. In addition, many training courses run curricula that are more flexible than university programs, comprising distance learning, workshops, seminars and short residential courses. Given the gendered nature of the double/triple burden in community, domestic and paid work, flexible training programs are often more appealing to women. In some cases, women have opted for the ECUARUNARI women's training programme after finding that their needs were not met by standard university education (*Pachamama* 2000). These training programmes therefore resemble formal educational spaces but, unlike state-sponsored education, their curricula are shaped by the agendas of indigenous movements. These agendas involve engaging with the latest development thinking while seeking to strengthen indigenous identity and organising power through curricula that cover old and new topics as well as deploying empowering Freire-type teaching methods.[11]

Whereas NGO-led grassroots popular education in the 1970s largely concentrated on technical training in agriculture/production, the remit of new indigenous training courses is broader. They reflect

INSTRUCTOR: Companero Miguel Angel Carlosama

TEMA: LIDERAZGO POLITICO "SITUACION ACTUAL DEL MOVIMIENTO INDIGENA Y
SU PROYECTO POLITICO"

Primero hacemos un análisis de coyuntura desde 1980 a 1998

A NIVEL INTERNACIONAL

OPORTUNIDADES	POR QUE
Premio nobel de la Paz Rigoberta Menchu	Es una índigena
Levantamiento indígena Chiapas - México	Se rebelan por oir a los indígenas
Discusión de la declaración universal de los derechos de los pueblos indios - ONU	Se esta hablando a nivel nacional
Vicepresidente indio en Bolivia	Es un indígena
Visita del Paps Juan Pablo II a Cuba	Hay muchas oporunidades para pueblos
Avance de la ciencia y tecnologia	Se la puede utilizar para nuestro bien
Toma de la Embajada en Peru por el MRTA	Para hacer oir nuestros derechos
Relaciones entre movimientos sociales	Hay mas unión entre nosotras
Se encuentra el cadáver del Che Guevara	Ayuda a unir a nuestros pueblos
El premio que recibio Luis Macas	Es indígena
Patiucipación de las mujeres en China	Para tratar de los derechos de las mujeres
Caida del muro de Berlín	Caída del socialismo
Consejo de Co-ordinacóion de Mujeres Indígenas del Ecuaranard - APN	15

Figure 1: Rigoberta Menchu appears as an international role model for indigenous leaders in training programs. Source: Training course handbook (ECUARUNARI 1998)

social development interests in strengthening civil society, promoting strong citizenship and leadership training, as well as fortifying the role of poor and indigenous communities (and particularly the poorest members within communities, who are often women) in decentralised development planning. Illustrating these interests, the first seminar in the ECUARUNARI programme for indigenous women and young people comprised familiar topics such as local sustainable development (ECUARUNARI 1998), yet the project management and evaluation modules contained "a focus on participation, gender, culture and ecology" thereby linking into contemporary gender mainstreaming approaches in social development (see Radcliffe, Laurie and Andolina 2004). Other modules covering established topics like political and organisational leadership, and involving consciousness raising for leaders, were followed by a new element comprising in-depth analyses of local, national and international contexts for indigenous leadership. Despite the new orientation, the teaching methods remained interactive and problem solving, maintaining a clear Freire-type structure for sessions focused on debating the historical genealogies of indigenous movements. One session on the international context for women's leadership provided a chronology (1980–98) of the key international activities and events that created political opportunities for indigenous movements (Figure 1). Indicating an extroverted sense of place, the seminar method was explained as follows:

> This workshop seminar should bring indigenous women closer to a knowledge and understanding of politics. [It does this] through a methodology that stimulates debate from the different positions and political tendencies that the different social actors maintain in the national and international situation with regard to the political project of indigenous people and the state. In this way, this module uses life histories of the great historical leaders and aboriginal peoples in order to recoup oral traditions and the role played by women in indigenous uprisings. (ECUARUNARI 1998:15)

By focusing on the history and international context for indigenous identification, this course represents a building block in establishing a governable space of indigeneity over which the indigenous movement has control. Internationally renowned indigenous leaders are represented as role models in such narratives and Rigoberta Menchú, in particular, often represents a transnational icon in contemporary indigenous leadership training.[12] Historical figures are also celebrated as illustrated by the ECUARUNARI program, which takes the name of Dolores Caguano, who fought to obtain education for indigenous people in the Andean highlands in the nineteenth century (*Pachamama* 2000).[13]

By re-working long-established expectations of tradition and modernity, indigenous organisations establish claims, engaging in struggles over governable spaces of indigeneity (on the Andes, see Kleymeyer 1996; also Watts 2003). A professionalisation programme operated by another Ecuadorian indigenous movement, FENOCIN,[14] clearly demonstrates such politics. In a module on nutrition and traditional medicine, understandings of medical plants are re-cast by also adopting an extroverted sense of place which seeks to break down dichotomies of Western and indigenous knowledge as Elena Ipaz of FENOCIN explains:

> We have a lot of knowledge about traditional medicine among our
> compañeras and from our ancestors ... Many times we don't value
> what we have because we have the [Western] medicines to hand. But
> combined with Western medicine we could change not just Ecuador
> but also the world, as we have seen with the plant *Uña del gato* which
> is a medicinal plant.[15]

Establishing governable spaces in these cases therefore seems to
rest on an intimate relationship between professionalisation and
indigenous agency through re-working authoritative histories and
knowledges.

Links between activism and professionalisation are further cemented by experiences of indigenous political action being incorporated
into the professionalisation curricula of university programmes.
According to Catherine Walsh, a module director at the Andina
University in Quito, indigenous leaders and advocates feature as
guest speakers in order to ensure that academic programs relate to
the everyday struggles of indigenous movements.

> I taught the conflicts class in a way that meant I could bring in lots of
> outside people. Those people ranged from folks that worked with
> COICA [pan Amazonian indigenous organisation], folks involved in
> Afro-American and Afro-Ecuadorian movements, involved in a
> more legal perspective, on collective rights or legislative projects
> that impact indigenous peoples, environmental concerns, confronta-
> tion with oil companies ... The intention of inviting most of the
> speakers was to have people that are immersed in day to day
> struggles, conflicts.[16]

Embodying what elsewhere we have called the "transnational curriculum on indigenous professionalisation" (Laurie, Andolina and
Radcliffe 2003:482), this particular university teacher used activist
experiences in Ecuador as the material for classes she also taught
on a university indigenous professionalisation programme in
Cochabamba, Bolivia. One of her sessions focused on analysing
the success of protest tactics such as marches and road blocks in
indigenous and peasant mass mobilisation in the two countries. A
video made by the Ecuadorian indigenous confederation CONAIE
(Confederación de Nacionalidades Indígenas del Ecuador) was
shown to promote discussion among the student body comprising
representatives from Bolivian pro-indigenous NGOs, indigenous
leaders, and advocates working in relevant government departments. These classroom discussions occurred during the Bolivian
municipal elections in 1999 when several students were standing
for public office. They also coincided with the start of mass mobilisations against water privatisation in Cochabamba (see Laurie,

Andolina and Radcliffe 2002). A number of students were important actors in the Committee of Defence for Water, subsequently
reconstituted as the Coordinator for the Defence of Water and
Life which led to the now internationally famous, Cochabamba
water wars in April 2000. Thus, professionalisation, in this particular case, fed into wider activist debate across national boundaries about the governance of the neoliberal market place where
indigenous expertise, political strategy and tactics were mobilised
by citizens questioning the rights of newly privatised companies
(see Laurie, Andolina and Radcliffe 2005a). In such contexts,
sharing knowledge about forms of contestation is shaping governance models by considering debates about how to generate new
ways of working in relation to development and education across
borders and into a wider area. In emphasising such relationships
and networks, our analysis points to the importance of new geographies of knowledge production under ethnodevelopment that
emphasise the existence of governable spaces of indigeneity that
are not confined within local boundaries.

Professionalisation: Spatialising and Scaling Indigenous Knowledge

The production of new indigenous activist expertise through indigenous professionalisation involves a contested process of re-scaling and
re-evaluating indigenous knowledge. Over the last two decades there
has been a revolution in how indigenous knowledge is circulated and
valued (Silitoe 1998). On the one hand, advances in international
human rights, the recognition of indigenous peoples in international
law and greater interest from donor agencies, NGOs, and the corporate world have contributed to its higher profile in development. On
the other hand, the emergence of indigenous knowledge as a key
element in indigenous movement discourse has also allowed the
creation and strengthening of certain transnational linkages, to such
an extent, that donors, indigenous movements, NGOs and states alike
agree that respect for indigenous knowledge is central to fulfilling
development-with-identity agendas. As we discuss below, however,
these diverse actors do not necessarily agree about how this knowledge should be represented, particularly in relation to space and
scale. Such discrepancies are important, as they represent struggles
over controlling governable space.

In the emerging academic literature on indigenous knowledge,
most definitions are linked to natural resource management, knowledge about a specific territory and/or knowledge held by a particular
group who are assumed to live in a bounded geographical space.[17]
Thus, definitions of indigenous knowledge often follow fixed

space-related understandings of the indigenous subject, where the emphasis is on survival mechanisms and the role of information about a territory and its environment in community reproduction. In contrast, indigenous protest over legislative reform has meant that policy understandings of indigenous knowledge have been success-fully shaped by indigenous movements' emphases on modes of think-ing. Such approaches focus on the diverse *ways* of knowing and processes of learning, rather than on the acquisition of specific knowl-edge bases themselves. Indigenous knowledge is thus defined in social-cultural, relational terms by indigenous movements engaged in political struggle over education, rather than by spatial parameters that fix particular knowledges in specific places. Indigenous activism around such interpretations of knowledge production has successfully influenced state education policies in Ecuador to the extent that reform laws directly engage with the logics, frameworks and epistemologies of different ethnic groups. Ecuador's Program of Bilingual Intercultural Education,[18] passed in 1989, is characterised by a critique of the Spanish model of education through the promotion of Andean notions and ancestral forms of thinking and learning (Rival 1996:409).

As donors also become interested in the role of indigenous knowl-edge in generating new development expertise, knowledge production is becoming more professionalised, opening up the terrain for more struggles over controlling the governable spaces of knowledge produc-tion. Recognising indigenous knowledge as key to the enhancement of indigenous social capital, donor organisations involved in ethno-development scale indigenous knowledge at the local level through large-scale programmes that aim to disseminate specific indigenous knowledges. For example, the World Bank's "Indigenous Knowledge for Development" programme, UNESCO's "Best Practice of Indigenous Knowledge" and UNDP's "Indigenous Knowledge Program"[19] initiatives all seek to transfer indigenous knowledge for adaptation to other contexts.[20] In this way, indigenous knowledge is only seen to have more general importance when experiences or "best practices" move from one *local* place to another.

Central to such large-scale transnational initiatives is the idea that local indigenous knowledge must first be professionalised (ordered and systematised) so that it can be circulated and shared. Representations of indigenous knowledge as inherently oral and local provide the motiva-tion for developing systematisation mechanisms, reflecting donor concerns that the full commercial potential of indigenous knowledge could remain untapped or, with the rise of genetic patenting, be taken out of the hands of indigenous communities (Lander 2001). Large-scale systematisation programmes are also re-enforced by donor support for the local (re)production of indigenous knowledge. This support includes funding spaces of dialogue between community members, local authorities and national/international development partners and facilitating local communities in forming research agendas and establishing networks that help practitioners and communities exchange knowledge about local practices (Gorjestani 2000). Therefore, local indigenous knowledge production, in many cases, is intimately bound up in transnational development discourses and networks, even though the definitions of indigenous knowledge, and power positions held by network actors, may be diverse.

Such initiatives to increase the systematisation and institutionalisation of information flows in transnational development networks, however, do not necessarily empower Third World network members. Townsend, Porter and Mawdsley (2002) argue that international funding mechanisms usually require specific types of monitoring based on burdensome report writing cultures that constrain Southern NGOs in their attempts to insert ideas onto donor agendas. In the case of NGOs with pro-indigenous and explicitly politicised agendas, monitoring and evaluation processes can produce contests over the control of governable space by becoming conduits for the introduction of new paradigms, whether or not there are desired by local and national organisations. For example, an evaluation of the Bolivian NGO CENDA[21] by a consultant working for an international funder caused resentment in the NGO because of an emphasis on social capital.[22] Such incidences reflect the implicit ways in which indigenous knowledge is being drawn into donors' neoliberal discourses and institutionalised through transnational monitoring and evaluation networks. While the distinctions between "indigenous" and "Western" knowledge is often blurred by indigenous movements, as in the case of the FENOCIN module of tradition medicine mentioned above, indigenous movements also sometimes draw on this binary as part of a political platform. In order to gain control over how their knowledge is represented and valued in development, indigenous leaders emphasise how indigenous knowledge has been downgraded by colonisation and the practices of "scientific" knowledge which see it as empirical and local. Luis Macas, a prominent leader in the Ecuadorian indigenous confederation CONAIE, says:

> I believe that our knowledge has unfortunately been left out of scientific recognition. For all the results that it has obtained through thousands of years in many aspects our knowledge definitely does not have the same scientific value. I think that's precisely why we should revalue it; give it its own value, its own authenticity, the scientific value it should have. This should not only be cast simply as empirical knowledge. (Interview, Luis Macas, CONAIE, Quito, May 2000)

Macas's vision of indigenous knowledge questions its scaling at the local level, challenging established geographies of knowledge production that draw a sharp distinction between (local) indigenous knowledge and the construction of an international knowledge system. Macas's position questions the approach of academics such as Warren (1991) who suggest that:

> (i)ndigenous knowledge contrasts with the international knowledge system generated by universities, research institutions and private firms. It refers to the knowledge of indigenous peoples as well as any other defined community. It is the basis for local-level decision making in agriculture, health care, food preparation, education, natural-resource management, and a host of other activities in rural communities. (Warren 1991, cited in "what is indigenous knowledge?" at http: www.worldbank.org/afr/ik/basic.htm)

Indigenous leaders like Macas therefore challenge definitions of indigenous knowledge that see it as unique to a given culture or society and only local, rather than also universal.

In scaling indigenous knowledge beyond the local level, indigenous activists are repositioning themselves in relation to development. By claiming that their knowledge speaks both to, and beyond, their reality, they are assuming a governing position (Dean 1999). They are establishing an episteme of government where indigenous knowledge is central and "normal", with general rather than empirical development application. With these claims, indigenous movements are establishing a form of development identification whereby indigenous people are not only actors and agents in ethnodevelopment but also experts. In the following section we examine the extent to which indigenous engagements with different forms of institutionalisation are creating opportunities to promote indigenous knowledge and modes of knowing.

Institutionalising Professionalisation: Hybrid Development Institutions in Ecuador

The strong focus on activism in many professionalisation programmes has been facilitated by the range of hybrid development institutions[23] emerging from development-with-identity networks. Forged through the transnational alliances and higher profile of indigenous movements post 1992 and coinciding with donor interest in social inclusion agendas, the position of these institutions in relation to development agenda setting has been strengthened in recent years. As a result, an NGO sector of fused grassroots and academic interests operating transnationally helps set the agendas of new courses designed to meet the training needs of indigenous leaders, activists and advocates. For example, both the ECUARUNARI and FENOCIN training courses mentioned above are involved in exchanges, conferences and other activities with Latin American countries including Bolivia and Brazil and take part in Latin America-wide Forums (*Pachamama* 2000).[24] These networks draw in transnational actors and engage indigenous movements in responding to the development industry's demand for social development personnel sensitive to indigenous issues. At the same time, indigenous movements themselves look for professionalisation geared towards strengthening the protagonist role of indigenous movements in multicultural neoliberal state formation, where new decentralisation laws and land reform have opened up opportunities for the recognition of indigenous rights, including collective rights, to resources and decision making power (Laurie et al 2002). As a result, indigenous movements envision professionalisation as a way of strengthening their bargaining position in negotiations over law making and development implementation.[25]

   In the following discussion we explore the ways in which these professionalisation agendas are played out in Ecuador.[26] While strong transnational linkages exist within professionalisation circuits (see Laurie, Andolina and Radcliffe 2003), below we focus on contests over establishing governable spaces at a national level, in order to understand the influence that different institutional settings have on indigenous social movements' involvement in professionalisation. We focus on the role of hybrid development institutions by contrasting the professionalisation approaches of PRODEPINE (the Development Project for Indigenous and Black Peoples of Ecuador) and CODENPE (National Development Council of Nationalities and Peoples of Ecuador). We argue that PRODEPINE's focus on supporting professionalisation through the mainstream university system aims to enhance the human capital of individual indigenous professionals but provides limited opportunities for establishing alternative governable spaces. By contrast, our analysis of CODENPE illustrates how hybrid development organisations facilitate the creation of counter spaces (Lefebvre 1991:63) by promoting alternative forms of indigenous training.

Governable Space and By-passing the State

PRODEPINE and to a greater extent CODENPE are populated by staff in key positions with backgrounds in indigenous advocacy and activism (see Figure 2). Financed themselves by transnational donors (eg the World Bank), the government and indigenous movements, these institutions, in turn, fund and support indigenous professionalisation in a variety of ways. PRODEPINE provides more than 700 scholarships for indigenous Ecuadorians to study in established university programs[27] and engages directly with the World Bank's vision of ethnodevelopment. Through professionalisation it aims to promote critical diversity in order to avoid mechanistic development outcomes:

> They [The World Bank] have accepted all the suggestions we have raised because we have achieved things with their support that have focused attention at the level of communities' needs. Imagine if all we did was to train people in development questions, this would need to get sorted out urgently, would it not? Because before you knew it we would be producing a very developmentalist generation, with a narrow vision. So the fact that we have diversified the career [options] will allow the level and criteria of [future] opinions to be more diverse. This will allow us to make the process richer. (Interview, Ariruma Kowii, PRODEPINE, Quito, March 2000)

PRODEPINE's program has so far been successful, with low drop-out rates and an increased demand for scholarships from indigenous movements.[28] Yet, mainstreaming indigenous students into established universities is not straightforward. While PRODEPINE seeks to strengthen the position of indigenous students in relation to the discriminatory education environments that many encounter, its offer of foundation and access programmes to improve writing skills of indigenous and black university students is often rejected by students who do not want to be seen as "different".[29] Attempts to lessen the power of institutionalised racism in the classroom meet with difficulties because funders have little direct control over the classroom experiences of indigenous students. As the person in charge of administering PRODEPINE scholarships in La Salesiana University argues, in these contexts professionalisation can become a site for reproducing intolerance:

- Identifies as Quichua born in Cañari
- Worked as a lecturer in Catholic University from 1984 to 1986 as a researcher in Quichua language and as promoter of literacy training in Ecuador
- Founded a distance learning centre (Corporacion Educativa MAC), where he acted as rector, researcher, and promoter, and learned computer and textbook production skills to apply to bilingual education
- Directed a project by the Ecuadorian NGO ESQUEL Foundation in the Amazon region. Decided he needed knowledge about the environment and biodiversity
- Left behind bilingual education to work in development natural resource conservation as of the end of 1992, studying geography
- Since 1998 has worked in CODENPE. This work was initially in participatory development planning, now directing the Identity and Culture Department to implement an intercultural development program

Figure 2: An example of the career trajectory of ethnodevelopment professionals. Biography: Isidoro Quinde, leading figure in the CODENPE

When we began this semester we wanted to institutionalise the baptism of the new students [an initiation ceremony]. The first baptism had taken place with the young people who are now in their fourth semester, who organised the event and are predominantly white *mestizos*. Now we had started a new semester I told them to get together with the third semester cohort to agree on how to organise the welcome for the [incoming] pre-university students. The result was that they couldn't agree with each other. The junior cohort are mainly indigenous (*indios*) and the older class are mainly white. They couldn't agree and so some said that they were not going to agree to participate in the indigenous student's event because they would [do a ceremony] to clean [the soul] with alcohol and hallucinogenic indigenous leaves and they don't share such traditions. The others, the white *mestizos*, were going to break an egg and throw liquid over the heads of the indigenous students. So the indigenous students said no [to this], that they would feel aggrieved by this and that it was making a joke of them. So [at first] it seemed like a superficial thing but deep down you realise [as a teacher] that there really is intolerance, one towards the other.[30]

In the light of such examples it appears that, rather than representing an opportunity to question the values that govern formal educational spaces, mainstreaming indigenous students into existing university programmes can create division which leaves students (including the *mestizo* majority) untouched by the intercultural experience.

Aware of the tensions around mainstreaming indigenous students into existing university structures, CODENPE is heavily involved in supporting indigenous movement initiatives to establish training outside the established university system in Ecuador via CONAIE's proposal for an Indigenous University. While focused on providing university training for indigenous leaders, CONAIE's proposal for an Indigenous University differs from traditional models of higher education by emphasising decentralised and flexible forms of course delivery. Programmes comprise part-time study based on distance learning, practical sessions and occasional workshops, with an academic calendar organised around the agricultural cycle. Plans for the Indigenous University were first discussed in 1988 as part of the Ecuadorian Indigenous Movement's demand for intercultural, bilingual education. The proposal was resurrected in 1994 when data from a CONAIE study indicated that less than 1% of indigenous people go to university in Ecuador;[31] however, Congress failed to grant the proposal legal status by refusing to recognise it as a state university in 1996. At first glance, this decision seems surprising, given the Ecuadorian state's formal support for Andean forms of thinking, as expressed in the 1989 Program of Bilingual Intercultural Education mentioned above. However CONAIE's proposal represents a number of challenges to state forms of governmentality to which we now turn.

Departing from the usual practice of course delivery by professional teaching staff nominated by university rectors representing state authorities, CONAIE's proposal calls into question the state's jurisdiction over higher education. Granting the proposal public university status would mean that a semi-autonomous, indigenous only university, working to different curricula and an alternative calendar would become established outside of the state's direct governing control. Added to this, the explicit political mission of the Indigenous University could represent a problem for the state. As expressed by one of its key advocates, Luis Macas, an ex-president of CONAIE, the aim of the university is to systematise the experience of indigenous movements' struggles against state reform in order to strengthen indigenous organisation:

> The experiences that the indigenous movement had during the struggles [against state reforms] have not necessarily been systematised. So everything that went on has not been organised. It has not been systematised. So one of the things that the Indigenous University has to do is to provide follow-up (*seguimiento*). These studies will serve to nourish the indigenous movement.[32]

Given this agenda, it is perhaps therefore unsurprising that the state was unwilling to grant approval. In Michael Watt's (2003:24) terms, it was being asked to approve a "governable space of indigeneity" which, in effect, would lead to it relinquishing a governing role in order to take up a legitimating one. That is, this situation would reduce the decision-making power and scope of the state over potentially critical voices.

Examining governing processes in this way casts an interesting light on the role that CODENPE, as a hybrid development institution, played in continuing to garner support for the Indigenous University proposal.[33] As a hybrid development institution, CODENPE receives funding from the government and is therefore able to facilitate engagement with the state, while also providing the independence to bypass it in certain contexts. Its direct link with transnational funders committed to ethnodevelopment creates a certain level of autonomy that allows it to adopt a critical stance vis-à-vis state practices, discourses and institutions where they impinge on indigenous development. In turn, this situation can generate counter spaces (Lefebvre 1991:63) that set up possible pathways towards alternative forms of governmentality (in this case in relation to education). The outcomes of this particular development encounter around professionalisation nevertheless remain ambiguous because while CODENPE provides a means of maintaining open communication between the state and indigenous movements, these same channels also potentially provide opportunities to facilitate state monitoring of the university project as it develops in the future. The struggles over establishing control over the governable spaces of indigenous professionalisation in Ecuador therefore seem unlikely to be resolved quickly.

Conclusion

We have addressed the connections between indigenous social movements and the emergence of development experts and knowledges under ethnodevelopment. Specifically, we have examined the ways in which processes of professionalisation shape these connections, knowledges and expert identities. Our understanding of governmentality in the context of indigenous politics and development has drawn on Watts' (2003) analysis of the invention and re-invention of traditional and local knowledge in the Ogoni struggle in Nigeria. In attempting to unpick the complex relationship between governmentality and development, Watts (2003:24) argues that the "governable spaces of indigeneity" become vehicles for political claims focused on local government and the state. Our research goes further to suggest that governable spaces of indigeneity are more multiscalar and involve complex and overlapping geographies. Demands for local autonomy *are* reflected in the emphasis that Andean indigenous social movements place on training indigenous leaders capable of engaging in current multicultural neoliberal decentralisation and producing their own development plans. However, the governable spaces they produce are not confined to the local and national scale. They also operate through transnational networks, institutionalised in a range of hybrid development institutions that coalesce around culturally based understandings of knowledge production and development practice. While a pan-ethnic solidarity movement is only in the making in Nigeria (Watts 2003:24), pan-ethnic, transnational networking among indigenous movements in the Andes is well established (Brysk 2000). The governable spaces and professionalisation processes that help maintain these networks therefore cut across all scales, including the international.

Although the relationships established between indigenous movements, (I)NGOs and donors through indigenous professionalisation have provided spaces to engage in and contest multicultural neoliberalism in the Andes, the local, national, regional and transnational actors involved in these governable spaces remain uncomfortable allies. Linking cultural issues with popular education raises expectations among donors, indigenous people and (I)NGOs about the type of politics, interactions, power relations and spaces associated with professionalisation. These multiscalar expectations are at times incompatible with each other and tensions around ethnodevelopment become evident. We argue that professionalisation plays a crucial role in shaping the long-term success of ethnodevelopment networks, which will stand or fall by their ability to shift the power relations of knowledge production, decision making and policy implementation.

Acknowledgements

We are indebted to our activist, educator and policy-making colleagues who spent time sharing their experiences and to the anonymous referees; together, they helped shape the arguments here. Research was funded by the ESRC (#L214 25 2023: "Now we are all Indians? Transnational Indigenous Communities in Ecuador and Bolivia").

Endnotes

[1] 1992 is seen as an important moment for Latin American indigenous movements. Local and national organisations were strengthened by mobilising through international alliances to protest against Spain's Quincentenary celebrations of Columbus's arrival in the Americas.

[2] In saying this, we also recognise that the narrowing of definitions of ethnodevelopment and social capital was part of a contested process within donor organisations and their networks of advisors during the 1990s (see Bebbington et al 2003).

[3] Although also focusing on the ways in which neoliberal policies are increasingly engaging with multicultural agendas, our approach differs from Charles Hale's discussion of neoliberal multiculturalism, in that it recognises indigenous people's and other social actors' (including anthropologists employed by bilateral and multilateral agencies) active role in shaping contemporary development, and wider racial projects.

[4] See, for example, Bebbington (1996, 2000), Kleymeyer (1996) and Perreault (2003).

[5] This work draws on more than 170 interviews conducted with indigenous leaders, advocates, trainers, donors and government representatives in Bolivia and Ecuador between 1999 and 2000. All interviews were taped and transcribed. It also involved extensive participant observation in a wide range of meetings and events associated with indigenous development. This included participant observation in professionalisation classes in Bolivia (June–December 1999, December 2000 and March 2001), as well as a questionnaire survey with more than 80 students engaged in university professionalisation programs in Ecuador.

[6] Devised by Michel Foucault, governmentaility means "rationality of government" according to conceptualisations of the territorial or human space to be governed, and of appropriate modes of governing.

[7] In the twentieth century *indigenismo* celebrated pre-Conquest achievements and the potential contribution of assimilated Indians into modern nationalism and development.

[8] Interview, Vicenta Chuma, ECUARUNARI leader in charge of women's programme, May 2000, Quito, Ecuador. Interview, Elena Ipaz, FENOCIN, May 2000, Quito, Ecuador.

[9] Interviews in Ecuador with Catherine Walsh (Andina University, Quito, Ecuador, February 2000), and in Bolivia with Fernando Garces (CENDA, Cochabamba,

Bolivia, November 1999), Pablo Regalsky (CEIDIS, Cochabamba, Bolivia, December 1999), Pamela Calla (PROEIBANDES, Cochabamba, December 1999).

[10] Confederación de Pueblos de la Nacionalidad Quichua del Ecuador: Federation of Peoples of the Quichua Nationality of Ecuador (an abbreviation of the Quichua term *Ecuador Runacunapac Riccharimuy*, which means Ecuadorian Awakening Men). This is a highland organisation.

[11] Such methods focus on participative learning and dialogue in workshops where the boundaries between the learner and the teacher are blurred.

[12] Figure 1 highlights the importance of her Nobel Peace Prize award in inspiring indigenous activism more generally.

[13] Interview, Vicenta Chuma, ECUARUNARI, Quito, Ecuador, May2000.

[14] National Federation of Indigenous Peasant Organizations.

[15] Interview, Elena Ipaz, FENOCIN, Quito, Ecuador, May 2000.

[16] Interview, Catherine Walsh, Interculturalism programme director of Andina University, Quito, Ecuador, February 2000.

[17] See, for example, Warren (1991) and Grenier (1998).

[18] DINEIB—*Programa de Educación Bilingue Intercultural*.

[19] Jointly funded by the IDRC in Canada (interview A Pero, Indigenous People's Focus Point, UNDP, New York).

[20] See UNESCO (2002) and World Bank (2002).

[21] Center for Andean Communication and Development.

[22] Personal communication, María Teresa Hosse, director of CENDA, and Pablo Regalsky, founding member.

[23] Hybrid institutions of development comprise organisations working with development agencies and quasi-governmental departments and often collaborate with private sector companies and NGOs (Radcliffe 2001).

[24] Interviews, Vilma Suarez and Elena Ipaz, FENOCIN, May 2000; Vicenta Chuma, ECUARUNARI, May 2000.

[25] Interview, Luis Macas, CONAIE, Quito, Ecuador, May 2000.

[26] For a discussion of these issues in relation to the case of Bolivia, see Laurie, Andolina and Radcliffe (2005b).

[27] These include programs in community development planning and communication in a range of public and private universities offering undergraduate and postgraduate qualifications (see Laurie, Andolina and Radcliffe 2003).

[28] Interview, Ariruma Kowii, PRODEPINE, Quito, Ecuador, March 2000.

[29] Interview, Ana Maria Varea, La Salesiana University, in charge of PRODEPINE scholarships, Quito, Ecuador, May 2000.

[30] Interview, Ana Maria Varea, La Salesiana University, Quito, Ecuador, May 2000.

[31] Interview, Luis Macas, CONAIE and key proponent of the Indigenous University.

[32] Interview, Luis Macas, ex-president CONAIE, Quito, Ecuador, May 2000.

[33] At the time of writing, the proposal is again under consideration by the state. If unsuccessful, CODENPE is committed to helping to launch the university with the support of academic exchanges with Northern European and North American universities which will endorse programmes (Laurie, Andolina and Radcliffe 2003).

References

Andolina R, Laurie N and Radcliffe S A (2005) *Multi-ethnic Transnationalism: Indigenous Development in the Andes*. Durham: Duke University Press (forthcoming)

Bebbington A (1996) Movements, modernisation and markets: Indigenous organisations and indigenous strategies in Ecuador. In R Peet and M Watts (eds) *Liberation*

Ecologies. Environment, Development, Social Movements (pp 86–109). London: Routledge

Bebbington A (2000) Re-encountering development: Livelihoods transitions and place transformations in the Andes. *Annals of the Association of American Geographers* 9(3):495–520

Bebbington A, Guggenheim S, Olson E and Woodcock M (2003) Exploring social capital debates at the World Bank. *Journal of Development Studies* 40(5):33–64

Brysk A (2000) *From Tribal Village to Global Village: Indian Rights and International Relations in Latin America.* Stanford: Stanford University Press

Chambers R (1983) *Rural Development: Putting the Last First.* Harlow: Longman

Chambers R (1992) Rural appraisal, rapid, relaxed and participatory. IDS Discussion Paper 311. Institute of Development Studies, Sussex University

Collins J (2000) A sense of possibility: Ecuador's indigenous movement takes center stage. *NACLA Report on the Americas* 33(5):40–49

Comaroff J and Comaroff J E (2001) *Millennial Capitalism and the Culture of Neoliberalism.* London: Duke University Press

Conaghan C, Malloy J and Abugattas L (1990) Business and "the boys": The politics of neoliberalism in the Central Andes. *Latin American Research Review* 25:3–30

Corkhill D and Cubbitt D (1988) *Ecuador: Fragile Democracy.* London: Latin American Bureau

Dean M (1999) *Governmentality: Power and Rule in Modern Society.* London: Sage

ECUARUNARI (1998) Consejo de coordinación de mujeres del ECUARUNARI, I seminario taller de la escuela de formación de mujeres lideres del ECUARUNARI, Baños, 3–5 April 1998

Edwards M (1989) The irrelevance of development studies. *Third World Quarterly* 11:116–135

Escobar A (1995) *Encountering Development. The Making and Unmaking of the Third World.* Princeton, NJ: Princeton University Press

Freire P (1970) *Pedagogy of the Oppressed.* New York: Continuum

Friere P (1998) *Pedagogy of Freedom, Ethics, Democracy and Civil Courage.* Oxford: Rowman and Littlefield Publishers

Garland A (2000) The politics and administration of social development in Latin America. In J Tulchin and A Garland (eds) *Social Development in Latin America* (pp 1–14). Boulder, CO: Lynne Reinner

Gianotten V and de Wit T (1985) *Organización campesina: el objectivo político de la educación popular y la investigación participativa.* Amsterdam: Centrum voor Studie en Documentatie van Latinjns America

Gorjestani N (2000) "Cultural diversity in the 21st century: The role of indigenous knowledge in development." Paper presented at World Bank Global Knowledge Fair, Kuala Lumpur, 7–10 March 2000

Grenier L (1998) *Working with Indigenous Knowledge: A Guide for Researchers.* Ottawa: IDRC

Hale C R (2002) Does multiculturalism menace? Governance, cultural rights and the politics of identity in Guatemala. *Journal of Latin American Studies* 34(3):485–524

Hey J and Klak T (1999) From protectionism to neoliberalism: Ecuador across 4 administrations (1981–1996). *Studies in Comparative International Development* Fall:66–97.

Huber E and Solt E (2004) Successes and failures in neoliberalism. *Latin American Research Review* 39(3):1250–1264

Hyden G (1997) Civil society, social capital and development: Dissection of a complex discourse. *Studies in Comparative International Development* 32(1):3–30

Kane L (2001) *Popular Education and Social Change in Latin America*. London: Latin American Bureau

Keck M and Sikkink K (1998) *Activism Beyond Borders*. Ithaca: Cornell University Press

Kleymeyer C (1996) Cultural tradition and community-based conservation. *Grassroots Development* 20(1):27–35

Kohl B (2002) Stabilising neoliberalism in Bolivia: Popular participation and privatization. *Political Geography* 21:449–472

Kothari U (2005) Authority and expertise: The professionalisation of international development and the ordering of dissent. *Antipode* 37(3):(this issue)

Lander E (2001) Los derechos de propiedad intelectual en la geopolítica del saber de la sociedad global del conocimiento. *Revista del Centro Andino de Estudios Internacional Internacionales* 2:79–112

Laurie N, Andolina R and Radcliffe S (2002) The new excluded "indigenous"? The implications of multi-ethnic policies for water reform in Bolivia. In R Seider (ed) *Multiculturalism in Latin America Indigenous Rights, Diversity and Democracy* (pp 252–276). London: Palgrave

Laurie N, Andolina R and Radcliffe S (2003) Indigenous professionalization: Transnational social reproduction in the Andes. *Antipode* 35(3):463–491

Laurie N, Andolina R and Radcliffe S (2005a) Neo-liberalisms, transnational water politics and indigenous people. In R Andolina, N Laurie and S A Radcliffe (eds) *Multi-ethnic Transnationalism: Indigenous Development in the Andes* (pp). Durham: Duke University Press (forthcoming)

Laurie N, Andolina R and Radcliffe S (2005b) Expertise in transnational development: The professionalization of transnational actors and knowledge. In R Andolina, N Laurie and S A Radcliffe *Multi-ethnic Transnationalism: Indigenous Development in the Andes* (pp). Durham: Duke University Press (forthcoming)

Lefebvre H (1991) *The Production of Space*. Oxford: Blackwell

Lloyd J (1998) "The politics of indigenous identity in Ecuador and the emergence of transnational discourses of power and subversion." Unpublished PhD thesis, University of Liverpool

Luykx A (1999) *The Citizen Factory: Schooling and Cultural Production in Bolivia*. New York: State University of New York Press

Mawdsley E, Townsend J and Porter R (2002) *Knowledge, Power and Development Agendas: NGOs North and South*. Oxford: INTRAC

Narayan D (1999) *Bonds and Bridges: Social Capital and Poverty*. Washington DC: World Bank, Poverty Group

Oliart P (1999) Leer y Escribir en un mundo sin letras. Reflexiones sobre la globalización y la educación en la sierra rural. In C De Gregori and G Portocarrero (eds) *Cultura y Globalización* (pp 203–224). Lima: Red para el desarrollo de la ciencias sociales en el Perú

Oliart P (2005) "Education and Identity in Peru". Unpublished PhD thesis, University of Newcastle

Pacari N (1996) Taking on the neoliberal agenda. *NACLA Report on the Americas* 29(5):23–32

Pachamama (2000) Boletín de las mujeres de la Confederación de Pueblos de la Nacionalidad Kichwa del Ecuador (ECUARUNARI) Quito, April 2000. Special issue on La Escuela de Formación de Mujeres de ECUARUNARI

Perreault T (2003) "A people with our own identity": Toward a cultural politics of development in Ecuadorian Amazonia. *Environment and Planning D: Society and Space* 21:583–606

Perreault T and Martin P (eds) (2005) Special issue on geographies of neoliberalism in Latin America. *Environment and Planning A* 37(2):191–329

Puiggrós A (1999) *Neoliberalism and Education in the Americas.* Boulder, CO: Westview Press

Radcliffe S (2001) Development, the state and transnational political connections: State and subject formation in Latin America. *Global Networks* 1(1):19–36

Radcliffe S, Laurie N and Andolina R (2004) The transnationalization of gender and re-imagining Andean indigenous development. *Signs* 29(2):387–416

Radcliffe S, Laurie N and Andolina R (2005) Development with identity: Social capital and culture. In R Andolina, N Laurie and S A Radcliffe (eds) *Multi-ethnic Transnationalism: Indigenous Development in the Andes* (pp). Durham: Duke University Press (forthcoming)

Rival L (1996) *Hijos del Sol, Padres del Jaguar. Los Huaorani de Ayer y Hoy.* Quito: Abya-Yala

Rose N (1999) *Powers of Freedom: Reframing Political Thought.* London: Cambridge University Press

Scott J (1998) *Seeing Like a State: How Certain Schemes to Improve the Human Condition have Failed.* New Haven, CT: Yale University Press

Sikkink K (1991) *Ideas and Institutions: Developmentalism in Brazil and Argentina.* Ithaca: Cornell University Press

Silitoe P (1998) The development of indigenous knowledge. *Current Anthropology* 39(2):223–356

Townsend J G, Porter R and Mawdsley E (2002) The role of the transnational community of non-governmental organizations: Governance or poverty reduction? *Journal of International Development* 14(6):829–839

UNESCO (2002) Best practices on indigenous knowledge, http://www.unesco.org/most/bpindi last accessed 4 April 2005

Valdivia G (2005) On indigeneity, change and representation in the Northeastern Ecuadorian Amazon. *Environment and Planning A* 37(2):285–303

Walton M (2004) Neoliberalism in Latin America: Good, bad or incomplete? *Latin American Research Review* 39(3):165–183

Warren M D (1991) Using indigenous knowledge in agricultural development. World Bank Discussion Paper 127

Watts M (2003) Development and governmentality. *Singapore Journal of Tropical Geography* 24(1):6–34

World Bank (2002) Indigenous knowledge for development, http://www.worldbank.org/afr/ik last accessed 4 April 2005

Yashar D (1998) Contesting citizenship: Indigenous movements and democracy in Latin America. *Comparative Politics* 31(1):23–41

Yashar D (1999) Democracy, indigenous movements and the postliberal challenge in Latin America. *World Politics* 52(1):76–104

Nina Laurie is Professor of Development and the environment in the School of Geography, Politics and Sociology at University of Newcastle, UK. She focuses on Latin American development with interests in gender, indigenous issues and water politics in the Andes. She works collaboratively with colleagues at CESU, San Simón University, Bolivia and together with Robert Andolina and Sarah Radcliffe she is author of *Multi-ethnic Transnationalism: Indigenous Development in the Andes* (Duke, forthcoming).

Robert Andolina is currently Assistant Professor in Political Science at Seattle University, USA. He has researched and written extensively on indigenous movement politics in the Andes of Latin America, and is author of "The sovereign and its shadow: Constituent assembly and indigenous movement in Ecuador" in *Journal of Latin American Studies*.

Sarah Radcliffe teaches geography at the University of Cambridge, UK. Her interests include social and spatial dynamics of development in Ecuador and Peru, and postcolonial and feminist theory. Her books include *Viva: Women and Popular Protest in Latin America*; *Re-making the Nation: Place, Identity and Politics in Latin America*; and *Culture and Development in a Globalising World: Geographies, Actors and Paradigms* (Routledge, in preparation).

Chapter 5

Working the Spaces of Neoliberal Subjectivity: Psychotherapeutic Technologies, Professionalisation and Counselling

Liz Bondi

An analysis is presented of how a particular psychotherapeutic practice, namely voluntary sector counselling, contributes to and resists neoliberal forms of governance. The politics of psychotherapeutic discourses, including those associated with counselling, has attracted sharp and hostile criticism from a number of social scientists. For example, sociologist Frank Furedi (2003) has recently lambasted what he describes as the "cultivation of vulnerability" by self-serving counsellors and therapists, while political scientist James Nolan (1998) decries the insinuation of therapeutic ideas into diverse aspects of policy-making and state regulation. Both follow a well-established tradition that interprets psychotherapies as inherently individualising, psychologising and de-politicising (Lasch 1980; Rieff 1966; Sennett 1977; Turkle 1979). Yet many of those positioned within psychotherapeutic practices portray themselves as politically engaged, and argue that the practices in which they are embedded contain politically subversive possibilities (Eichenbaum and Orbach 1982; Kovel 1988; Parker 2003).

My aim is not to arbitrate between these competing claims but to argue for a more ambivalent reframing that is neither condemnatory nor celebratory of the politics of counselling. My attachment to this ambivalent position is influenced by my insider position—I am a voluntary sector counsellor as well as an academic geographer—and I might therefore be described as an apologist, attempting to defend a politically dubious practice. But, as critics have persuasively argued, psychotherapeutic discourses are so pervasive that they leave none of our lives untouched (Furedi 2003; Nolan 1998; Parker 1997). Consequently, it seems to me important to avoid what Nikolas Rose (1990:257) has described as "the paranoid visions of some social analysts", in which psychotherapies are represented as relentlessly malign, and to consider instead what the appeal of particular psychotherapies might tell us about political life in neoliberal regimes, without resorting to more or less sophisticated variants of "false consciousness".

In order to contribute to this task, I explore how counsellors working in the particular context of the Scottish voluntary sector represent what they do, and I analyse their accounts in relation to debates about neoliberalism. In so doing I am not suggesting that the lens of neoliberalism is the only way of approaching the politics of counselling. Instead I deploy one particular set of theoretical resources to illuminate some of the issues at stake in debates about counselling. I argue that counselling embodies and contains considerable ambivalence that is perhaps typical of what Wendy Larner (2000:14) has called the "messy actualities" of strategies of neoliberal subject formation, at the heart of which lies a deeply ambivalent engagement with processes of professionalisation. In order to develop my argument I briefly outline connections between neoliberalism, psychotherapies and professionalisation, drawing strongly but not exclusively on Rose's (1990) equivocal account. Against this background I explore accounts of counselling offered by voluntary sector counsellors in Scotland, focusing initially on practitioners' use of the idea of empowerment to describe what they do, and then considering how this idea intersects with processes of, and debates about, the professionalisation of counselling. My account is also informed by my own embeddedness within the practice, and especially my involvement in Scottish and British organisations that have, since the mid-1970s, evolved into "professional bodies" that provide (voluntary) ethical and regulatory frameworks for counselling.

Neoliberalism, Subjectivity and the Contradictions of Autonomy

As Jamie Peck and Adam Tickell comment, "neoliberalism seems to be everywhere" (2002:38). Originating as a political commitment to free-market economic theory, neoliberalism has become a discourse of market or quasi-market relationships that has had enormous success in colonising economic and cultural life in innumerable contexts, albeit in a wide variety of ways. A key symptom and condition of the rise of neoliberalism has been its capacity to co-exist with apparently contradictory political ideas. Thus, in the 1980s, Margaret Thatcher in the UK and Ronald Reagan in the USA both wove together neoliberal economics and highly authoritarian social policies grounded in anything but free-market thinking, to generate "New Right" politics (Levitas 1986). At much the same time, the Labour government in New Zealand drew on neoliberal thinking to initiate economic restructuring within a broadly left-liberal model (Larner 2000), anticipating comparable reshapings of social democratic politics in other contexts. Across the political spectrum, social policies soon became subject to the logic of neoliberal thinking too. Neoliberalism thus proved itself to be a flexible beast, capable of being marshalled in relation to both economic and social policies, and capable of hybridising with both authoritarian and social democratic ideas. Wendy Larner (2000) has persuasively argued that it is most usefully understood using the Foucauldian concept of governmentality. As a form of governmentality, neoliberalism works by installing a concept of the human subject as an autonomous, individualised, self-directing, decision-making agent at the heart of policy-making. In so far as this vision of the human subject is recognised and assimilated, people are recruited into neoliberal forms of governmentality, even if they also, simultaneously, seek to resist some of its effects.

The model of human subjectivity associated with neoliberal governmentality is deeply problematic, especially in its association with the production of highly individualised consumer-citizens. But neoliberal subjectivity does not inevitably generate subjects oriented solely to the narcissistic gratification of individual desires via market opportunities. Indeed aspects of neoliberal subjectivity hold attractions for political activists because activism depends, at least to some extent, on belief in the existence of forms of subjectivity that enable people to make choices about their lives. And yet this entails "buying into" aspects of the very model of subjectivity that critics of neoliberal governmentality seek to contest. The need to work "within and against" systems of governance has long been recognised by political activists and theorists (London Edinburgh Weekend Return Group 1979). For example, feminists have repeatedly drawn attention to the limitations and necessity of autonomous agency as a basis for emancipatory politics. As Catriona Mackenzie and Natalie Stoljar put it:

> Although the ideal of autonomy once seemed to hold out much promise ... [it] is now generally regarded by feminist theorists with suspicion ... While feminist critiques of autonomy have identified serious theoretical and political problems ... the notion of autonomy is vital to feminist attempts to understand oppression, subjection and agency. (2000:3)

Engaging with the conundrum from a Foucauldian perspective, Judith Butler (1997) describes "the subject" as "the effect of power in recoil" (6) and argues that "in the act of opposing subordination, the subject reiterates its subjection" (11). In other words, this account insists that there is no innocent or external vantage point from which to exercise the agency required to contest a model of subjectivity that insists upon the idea that subjects are capable of self-governance. Thus, the "[n]eo-liberal strategies of rule, found in diverse realms including workplaces, educational institutions and health and welfare agencies, [which] encourage people to see themselves as individualized and active subjects responsible for enhancing their own well-being" (Larner 2000:13) are not the outcome of the top-down imposition of neoliberal political ideology, but are often, at least in part, the expression of successful campaigns to decentralise decision-making and partially democratise bureaucratic organisations.

One of the most widely cited Foucauldian writers on governmentality, Nikolas Rose (1985), has drawn particular attention to the role of disciplines within what he calls the "psy-complex" in producing highly individualised, self-monitoring, self-governing and subjectively oriented subjects. Through this interpretative lens, Rose (1990) analyses the role of psychological theory and practice in World War II, the incorporation of psychological ideas about human resources and group dynamics into industry, the reframing of child-rearing and family life in terms of psychology, and the "the nature and implications of the proliferation of psychotherapies" (xii). His account traces the rise of "technologies of subjectivity" (8), which he acknowledges vary widely and sometimes mobilise radically inconsistent philosophical bases. Indeed he argues that "the diversity and heterogeneity of psychology has been one of the keys to its continued inventiveness … and wide-ranging social applicability" (Rose 1990:10–11). Across this diversity Rose identifies and emphasises overarching commonalities in their effects, especially their role in producing "intensely subjective beings", and modern societies that accord a central role to the "subjective aspects of the lives of individuals as they conduct their commerce with the world, with others and with themselves" (1990:3).

Of the various technologies of subjectivity Rose explores, psychotherapies most fully epitomise the logic of neoliberal subjectivity in the priority accorded to individual liberty. Psychotherapeutic discourses therefore constitute influential vehicles through which neoliberal governance is dispersed and achieved. Careful to acknowledge their ambiguities, Rose argues that:

> [psychotherapeutic] technologies for the government of the soul operate not through crushing subjectivity in the interests of control and profit, but by seeking to align political, social and institutional goals with individual pleasures and desires, and with the happiness and fulfilment of the self. Their power lies in their capacity to offer means by which the regulation of selves—by others and by ourselves—can be made consonant with contemporary political principles, moral ideals, and constitutional exigencies. They are, precisely, therapies of freedom. (1990:257)

As Rose acknowledges, his account relies primarily on textual sources, and he draws particular attention to the need for further studies of psychotherapeutic technologies, which, he notes "have been little examined, analyses tending to rely upon the programmatic representations contained in textbooks and case histories" (1990:246). There is a strong emphasis on inter-personal relationships in these practices, primarily in the form of face-to-face, or co-present, relationships between clients and practitioners. It is therefore important to consider the possibility that the practices at stake elude their textual representation in important ways. I begin to take up this challenge by exploring practitioners' in-depth reflections on the practice of counselling. But before engaging with this evidence, one further concept—that of professionalisation—needs to be introduced.

Recent decades have witnessed the proliferation of claims to professional status, broadly in parallel with the rise of neoliberalism. Four decades ago, Howard Wilensky (1964) predicted "the professionalisation of everyone", and, notwithstanding the widespread erosion of public trust in professionals over the ensuing decades (O'Neill 2002; Schön 1983), the attractions of professional status do not appear to have waned significantly. Professional status is of particular relevance to debates about neoliberal governmentality, because professions can usefully be described as technologies for governing "at a distance" (Fournier 1999). Professional status confers autonomy on practitioners who are deemed to have internalised and to embody the knowledge and the conduct required for professional practice. In so doing it recruits practitioners into modes of action that express autonomous, decision-making agency, at the same time as submitting to disciplinary mechanisms. Wendy Larner describes neoliberalism as "both a political discourse about the nature of rule and a set of practices that facilitate the governing of individuals from a distance" (2000:6). The widespread extension of professionalisation can therefore be understood as symptomatic of assimilation into neoliberal forms of governmentality and as emblematic of the contradictory character of neoliberal subjectivity.

Nikolas Rose (1990:11) assumes that psychological "experts in the management of the self" are, by definition, professionals. While he explores intense conflict between different interests within this domain, he argues that they all mobilise the discipline of psychology—itself riven by dispute—to defend their own authority. For example, he delineates contestation over the role of the legal system in child welfare in the 1970s in terms of social workers, who invoke psychological ideas in favour of statutory powers of coercion, pitted against an alliance of psychoanalysts and paediatricians, who seek to restrict the role of the law and "to 'restore' the family its 'rights' to autonomy and privacy" again by appealing to the presumed authority of psychological ideas (1990:207). The psychological knowledges to which psychotherapies appeal are equally diverse, but, more importantly, psychotherapies also problematise professional expertise, generating successive attempts to eschew, as well as to embrace, professional status. Adam Phillips (1995:xiii) has described the psychoanalyst as "among other things, a figure for the ironies of competence", and has argued that Freud's idea of the unconscious radically destabilises the psychoanalyst's own claims to expertise. One expression of this problematic relationship to professional status was the uneven development of "lay psychoanalysis" in the early twentieth century. Sigmund Freud ([1926] 1959) gave his support to the development of "lay psychoanalysis", which enabled those without professional (medical) qualifications to train as psychoanalysts, and claimed for psychoanalysis a position independent of the structures of professions. This was crucial to the entry of women into psychoanalysis at the time, and in the longer term laid the foundations for tension and contestation between psychoanalysis and the medical specialism of psychiatry. But "lay psychoanalysis" remained a European phenomenon, while in North America psychoanalysis was fully assimilated into, and access to training was controlled by, the medical profession (Schwartz 1999). More recently, the emergence of practices called "counselling" enunciates and enacts some discursive distancing from the "psy" disciplines. As I have argued elsewhere (Bondi 2003a; Bondi with Fewell 2003), the development of counselling in the voluntary sector, where it sought to mobilise the ordinary relationship skills of volunteers, expressed another attempt to secure distance from, and to further problematise, professional authority.

The complex relationship between psychotherapies and professional status does not undermine Rose's overarching claims, but it adds further emphasis to the contradictoriness of forms of subjectivity associated with neoliberalism. This is important in relation to political strategies, which, necessarily, have to work with the highly ambiguous tensions that might, but will not necessarily, enable politically progressive spaces to be cultivated in the context of hegemonic and plural neoliberalism (Peck and Tickell 2002). Against this background I turn to consider counsellors' own accounts of what they do, commenting first on the character of the evidence on which I draw.

A Note on the Empirical Research

The evidence discussed comes primarily from transcripts of in-depth interviews conducted with approximately 100 practitioners involved in voluntary sector counselling in Scotland. Interviewees were recruited by invitations distributed via a diverse range of agencies situated in two cities and two rural areas. Interviews were conducted in a variety of locations negotiated between interviewee and interviewer, with the majority taking place in the premises of agencies through which participants had been recruited. Having opted in to the research project, the terms of participants' involvement continued to be open for negotiation: they were asked to give consent to be tape-recorded and were sent transcripts for approval (or not) before any material was analysed. While none objected to being tape-recorded or withdrew from the project after being interviewed, some participants used the opportunity to review the transcript to request that sections be deleted and/or to ask further questions about the protection of their identities.

The transcripts generated by the research represent counselling through the voices of a wide range of practitioners, but, as textualised accounts, they remain removed from the practice itself. Countering this, the interviews actively mobilised the insider positioning of the research team, which consisted of four members, under my leadership. Two members of this team were themselves counselling trainers and experienced practitioners. Although they conducted only a small minority of the interviews, they were closely involved in the design of the interview schedule, team discussion of the fieldwork in progress, and analysis of the transcripts. A third member of the team, myself, was also a practising counsellor, and the fourth member had undertaken an introductory training in counselling skills. The interviews elicited exchanges that we could recognise as bearing similarities to those that circulate among practitioners in a variety of contexts (for example, in informal conversations within agencies and at counselling conferences). Moreover, we conceptualised the interview itself as an encounter that mobilises some features of psychotherapeutic practices: one person is invited to speak in their own words and at their own pace while the other listens carefully, responds empathically and respectfully, and works to facilitate self-exploration and reflection (Bondi 2003b). It therefore invokes closely related technologies of subject formation.

Psychotherapies can be understood as working at the boundaries of representation. The explorations that take place between clients and practitioners seek to bring experiences that clients perceive as troubling, distressing or problematic into a shared symbolic domain, where they can be worked with in ways that aim to generate new meanings and perceptions. In so doing, experiences or emotions may be "named", that is represented discursively; equally, however, limits on representability may be acknowledged. There are parallels between these processes and what took place in the in-depth interviews discussed here, which can be understood as moments of translation at the interface between the spaces of psychotherapeutic work and the wider context within which psychotherapies are situated.

Subjectivity and Empowerment

This section explores practitioners' appeals to empowerment, which is a very widespread motif within their descriptions of the aims of counselling. The following quotations provide a few illustrations:

> We try to empower women; that's part of our ethos—to empower women and help women have a voice. (Isabel, practitioner at a women-only agency)

> I think it's about empowering people ... that's something that I would like to think counselling can help people do—to feel empowered. (Harry)

> [Counselling is about] letting people help themselves and letting them have their power bases either back or found. (Helen)

The rhetoric of client empowerment positions counsellors as facilitators or enablers, and clients as agents of change. Thus, Rachel says "we are there to enable the client to explore, to do the work that he or she would like to do", while Andrew describes himself as being there "to facilitate change—to empower the person to do it". Practitioners emphasise that the client is the one who decides what, if any, changes they wish to make in their lives. Thus, empowerment is construed as enabling decision-making as well as enabling the implementation of change, as Karen elaborates:

> It's a process of talking/listening whereby the individual who wants to take part in counselling can empower themselves to change their situation if that's what they want.

In these ways, clients are positioned as the active, directing and choice-making party in their encounters with counsellors.

According to Nikolas Rose, empowerment can be understood as a technology of subjectivity that recruits people into active self-management and fosters neoliberal forms of (individual) freedom:

> The beauty of empowerment is that it appears to reject the logics of patronizing dependency that infused earlier welfare modes of expertise. Subjects are to do the work on themselves, not in the name of conformity, but to make them free. (1999:268)

Counselling would appear to epitomise this technology. The paradox entailed in the obligation to be free sometimes becomes evident in practitioners' accounts as they struggle to explain what it means to enable, facilitate or empower. Thus, Andrew combines an emphasis on facilitation with the particular aim of "bringing out" underlying problems or difficulties:

It's to empower the person and facilitate them to—perhaps they've
not been thinking about it, but perhaps to facilitate them to bring
out really what the problem, the difficulty is.

Helen corrects her own description by shifting action from the
counsellor to the client, and then insisting that counselling is never
coercive:

it's definitely about letting people help themselves and giving them,
not giving them, letting them have their power bases either back or
found ... it's letting them help themselves, assuming that they have
come with that view in mind, and if they're not wanting to help
themselves there's nothing you can do that's going to help, so there's
no manipulation involved, no persuasion, no coercion, absolutely
nothing like that.

Andrew and Helen were both training when the interviews were
conducted, and the work they undertake to insist that the client is the
agent of change may be viewed as an expression of their relative lack
of experience in representing counselling to others. One of the effects
of training is to reduce practitioners' investment in the choices their
clients make. Reflecting on how his views of counselling changed
during training, John describes the process thus:

I really believe in what counselling can achieve, but I've not got the
same need or want [as I used to] for a client or clients to do loads of
personal development, or to overcome lots of past hurts or whatever. I think before I had a much stronger sense that that is what the
work is ... To me that feels like a bit of foreign language now, you
know. I don't actually see it quite like that any more. I still believe all
these things are possible, but I see my role much more as providing a
space for someone to use and going with what they bring to it.

This discussion of counsellors' appeal to client empowerment sup-
ports the argument that, like other psychotherapies, counselling
fosters the autonomy and self-direction associated with neoliberal
subject formation. It also suggests that under the surface of the
language of empowering clients, practitioners subtly but actively
recruit clients into a discourse of individual freedom and choice.
However, these accounts also provide evidence of commitment to
resist some features of this version of subjectivity, especially its appeal
to the bounded, self-made individual of liberal theory. In what follows
I illustrate two aspects of this resistance, concerned with collective
subjectivities and relational concepts of self, respectively.

The great majority of the voluntary sector agencies for whom these
practitioners work (some paid, some as volunteers) do not charge clients
for counselling sessions, although some solicit donations. Information
about the socio-economic status of clients is limited, but many of those

interviewed emphasise their commitment to make counselling available to disadvantaged and excluded groups. For example, Daphne says:

> I suppose what I'm interested in [is working with] people who in one way or another are more likely to be excluded from having access to counselling, whether it's people who are poor or people who would be regarded in a certain way and get referred to psychiatrists.

In such contexts, practitioners tend to interpret empowerment as flowing outwards from individual clients to those around them, as Patricia suggests:

> If by somebody coming to see me they can begin to find some peace, some resolution or contentment within themselves that makes them feel better about approaching life, then that must affect the people that they're around, and so on.

Some articulate a commitment to empowering people whose capacity for effective agency has been eroded by inequalities and oppressions, presenting counselling as a precursor to political action, as Kenneth elaborates:

> The task of counselling is to enable people to make decisions about their own life, to take control of their own life, to be the person that they want to be. There's nothing flabby about that. And if they're living in a slum dwelling, or if they're living in a violent relationship, or if they're living where they're exploited by stress and long hours, whatever it is, if you're really enabling the person to be themselves, they will take these issues up.

Accounts of this kind insist that the subjects empowered through counselling are not simply or solely self-oriented citizen-consumers, but that they understand themselves as belonging to collectives. This is a potentially crucial point of resistance to the individualisation associated with neoliberal subjectivity.

Counsellors tend to emphasise the importance of people's connections with others as a central concern of counselling work (also see Bondi 2003a). For example, when asked to comment on criticisms of counselling as fostering self-oriented individualism, Zoë said:

> I suppose there is a criticism that some people get quite addicted to individual counselling, and … it actually breaks up relationships … I don't know whether I'm just sitting on the wall about this but I feel that good counselling wouldn't do that. It would actually address people's lives as a whole, and in terms of helping people with their individual issues it would also help them grow within the context of their wider life rather than against it.

Whether or not counselling works in the way Zoë claims, her argument indicates that the language of empowerment on which voluntary sector counsellors draw is not unambiguously aligned with the highly autonomous agent of liberal and neoliberal theory. Although these counsellors focus on the effects of counselling for individuals, they do not imagine these people in isolation from others. They do not necessarily assume that empowering individuals is about supporting them to prioritise their own needs over others, because they assume that most people's needs are fundamentally relational. The point is elaborated by Kenneth, who acknowledges that there is a grain of truth in critiques of counselling as narcissistic, but interprets any such tendency as a temporary phase in a process that enables people to redefine or reposition themselves in relation to others:

> [the counselling] may have to go through a phase where the person is enabled to put themselves first, and to satisfy their own needs which perhaps previously hadn't been satisfied, which may have a kind of selfish shell to it of some kind. But ... hopefully it would lead on to something more than that. Because at the end of the day ... to be comfortable with your life, unless you are really an exception (and there are exceptions), your life will be better if you can relate to other people, if you can find your place in a group, if you can be identified with something that gives your life meaning.

A similar line of argument is developed by other counsellors, including Kirsty, whose own experience of counselling training had precipitated the end of her marriage:

> Interviewer: One of the things people from outside the counselling world criticise counselling for is that people become more self-centred, in a way that can damage relationships ... It's like the rest of the world go hang because this is what I want—that kind of image. And I wonder how—you know, because part of your story is actually about being freed up from the social expectations about marriages lasting ... So I'm wondering what your –
>
> Kirsty: It doesn't feel like—oh, it can all go hang, you know. It doesn't feel like that at all because I was very, very anxious, and if my husband had said, "oh no, I think that we should do something different" then I would have been open to that ... [It was never like] I'm gonna do this, no matter what anybody else thinks ... There was something about just being honest with people, and allowing them to be honest with me, and allowing them to say "no, I don't like this" and "I'm not happy with this" or whatever ... So it's not about just being selfish and getting my own way. It's about being honest and saying, you know, if I don't like this, then what do we do about it? And if I want to do something and somebody else doesn't like it, then what do we do about that?

The evidence I have presented in this section suggests that voluntary sector counsellors think of what they do in ways that can be understood as actively contributing to neoliberal versions of subject formation. But they also contest or resist certain features of the politics of neoliberalism, notably its relentless production of highly individuated consumers, which is countered through appeals to collective and relational dimensions of subjectivity. This suggests that, while voluntary sector counselling may be one of the technologies of autonomy through which neoliberal governmentality operates, it is equally one that has the potential to exploit the contradictoriness of these technologies. As such it contains political possibilities as well as political dangers for those seeking to counter the most problematic and divisive effects of neoliberalism. Indeed, the history of counselling suggests that it shares with neoliberalism the capacity to range across diverse political perspectives. For example, among the first organisations to take up counselling in the UK were Marriage Guidance Councils, which developed in response to inter-war and post-war concern that the institution of marriage was breaking down (Lewis, Clark and Morgan 1992). Religious leaders concerned to uphold traditional norms of family life were among those who supported such developments, but the Councils also garnered support from much more libertarian interests committed to social and institutional changes in the form and status of marriage (Lewis, Clark and Morgan 1992). The shift from offering "marriage guidance" to "marriage counselling" (in the late 1940s and early 1950s) and then to "relationship counselling" (in the 1980s) helped to hold together this coalition of interests across persistent and considerable internal tensions. In recent decades, the ambiguous politics of counselling has also been played out through debates about its professionalisation to which I now turn.

Professionalisation and Governance at a Distance

I have argued elsewhere (Bondi 2004) that the development of voluntary sector counselling services in the UK during the third quarter of the twentieth century was inspired in part by efforts to counter the relations of authority conventionally associated with professional–client interactions. Indeed, for some it was an overtly "anti-professional thing" (Peter, quoted in Bondi 2004). But by the fourth quarter of the twentieth century, counselling was itself caught up with processes of professionalisation. These processes have been evident in three main ways, namely (1) the development of systems of voluntary self-regulation into which the bulk of practitioners have been assimilated (Bondi, Fewell and Kirkwood 2003); (2) the "academicisation" of training programmes through either the external academic validation of training qualifications by universities, or the wholesale transfer of training programmes into institutions of higher education;

and (3) the growth of labour market opportunities for counsellors, signalling the institutionalisation of the specific occupation of "counsellor" within the paid workforce. Debate about professionalisation has further intensified in recent years because of the possibility of statutory regulation, which would give legal underpinning to (a unified system of) self-regulation and legally enforceable protection of title for practitioners.

For many practices subject to professionalisation, including counselling, there are both costs and benefits flowing from such developments. I have explored voluntary sector counsellors' views of professionalisation in greater depth elsewhere (Bondi 2004), and here I simply summarise the key pros and cons they identify. They generally approve of professionalisation in so far as it raises standards of practice, provides effective protection for members of the public (who are often at their most vulnerable when seeking or referred for counselling), and enhances the status of counselling. On the other hand, they express misgivings about professionalisation in so far as it reduces access to training, which has become more academic and more costly for trainees themselves; undermines important features of client–practitioner relationships by fostering legitimation by credentials rather than by quality of practice; and encourages over-reliance on relatively inflexible, impersonal frameworks, which purport to protect clients but which may, in fact, merely protect incompetent practitioners. Against the background of such debate I want to consider how professionalisation impacts upon the contradictoriness of neoliberal subjectivity to which counselling contributes.

Professional status, whether legally underwritten or not, acknowledges the capacity of individual practitioners to govern themselves— to exercise professional autonomy—without close supervision and monitoring. Professional codes of ethics for counsellors place considerable emphasis on client autonomy: the British Association for Counselling and Psychotherapy (2002) identifies autonomy as one of six fundamental ethical principles of counselling (alongside fidelity, beneficence, non-maleficence, justice and self-respect). Professional status thus accords counsellors with autonomy in their responsibility for respecting and fostering the autonomy of their clients. The professionalisation of counselling can therefore be understood as entailing the double mobilisation of technologies of autonomy, thereby tending to intensify the paradoxical demand on subjects to become increasingly self-determining.

Professional autonomy is conferred on individual practitioners by bodies that represent the profession as a whole. It therefore invokes a collective as well as individual capacity for self-governance. Full membership of a professional body typically requires successful completion of a recognised qualification, together with evidence of satisfactory practice under some kind of provisional license. After full membership is granted, professional bodies typically hold individual practitioners accountable through complaints procedures, which set out mechanisms through which members of the public may allege breaches of professional ethics or codes of conduct, and the sanctions that may be applied if complaints are upheld. Professional bodies may also require practitioners to undertake, and report upon, post-qualification practice and training (continuing professional practice), as is the case for professional bodies for counselling in the UK. These various mechanisms incorporate practitioners into a strict disciplinary framework, which, alongside its collective level of operation, individualises responsibility for maintaining discipline.

Some of the practitioners whose accounts are discussed here have been involved in counselling since the third quarter of the twentieth century, that is since before the current wave of professionalisation. These people were among those who pioneered the development and delivery of counselling training by voluntary sector organisations, which offered training to people free of charge in return for their commitment to work for a few hours per week as unpaid volunteer counsellors. They describe such work in terms of disseminating values associated with counselling to a wider population beyond the individuals actually receiving the training or the counselling. For one respondent counselling is "the salt" that draws out "flavour":

> Thomas: So there was a sense in which we would be [offering counselling training to] a lot with people who would go on from there to other things. So ... I suppose you could say [that] training [was] being offered for people who might use it in a kind of volunteer capacity. This business of the salt, you know (laughing), it was all part and parcel of that ...
>
> Interviewer: So when you say the salt, it's like you understood what you were doing as something that would just—the flavour would just percolate through?
>
> Thomas: That's right, it begins to affect things."

Another described himself as committed to creating "barefoot counsellors" and as being inspired by "a social commitment ... to unlock and deploy the talents within the community, for helping and care" (Peter).

These practitioners, together with others, especially those involved in the recruitment and management of volunteer counsellors, express particular concern about the individualising effects of professionalisation. In articulating their misgivings they make use of phrases and metaphors that describe processes of categorisation, segmentation and numerical calculation, as the following quotations illustrate:

[professionalisation] forces people into boxes. (Vanessa)

it stays in tight [instead of counselling skills flowing outwards into the wider community]. (Veronica)

evaluating the service ... becomes about numbers and that's definitely creeping into the voluntary sector more and more. (Daphne)

These descriptions suggest the operation of technologies of calculation, which are integral to processes of governmentality. Nikolas Rose (1990:7) has argued that the psychological sciences have played a key role in "rendering subjectivity calculable", suggesting that psychiatric diagnosis and intelligence testing are two paradigms for such calculation. Counsellors do not apply either of these paradigms and are typically more interested in the experiential consequences of acquiring diagnostic or other forms of categorisation than in generating comparable systems or paradigms. But professionalisation increases the exposure of counselling to technologies of calculation. By attaching data to subjects these technologies are influential vehicles of individualisation. Consequently, practitioners tend to fear that professionalisation militates against the more collective and relational approaches to subjectivity described in the preceding section, through which counselling retains the capacity to resist some features of neoliberal subject formation.

For many practitioners, the professionalisation of counselling is unstoppable. Some consider that the form professionalisation will take is inevitable, with the effects of technologies of calculation being fundamentally damaging. In Peter's words, the result of professionalisation for counselling will be that:

it will fossilise, just like other professions fossilise. And after it there'll be another wave of people who call themselves befrienders or something like that. And there'll be cowboy chaos in that area for a while, and then ... [that] will begin to ... [professionalise] and it will fossilise too, and then there'll be another [...] vehicle for unlocking the talents of the population.

However, even within such accounts there are pointers towards forms of professionalisation that might be less individualising. Indeed for all Peter's pessimism about the inevitably "fossilising" effects of professionalisation, he also argues for systems of self-regulation that invest responsibility and accountability in organisations that offer counselling services rather than solely in individual practitioners. This is perhaps the most easily available means by which some of the consequences of professionalisation can be resisted. It entails the development of what, in Scotland, is called a "recognition scheme for organisations", which provides professional recognition to a service rather than to individual practitioners. Although this scheme "buys into" the possibility of "governance at a distance" associated with neoliberal subjectivity in general and professionalisation in particular, it mitigates some of the most intensely individualising qualities of neoliberal governmentality.

Conclusion

Neoliberal subject formation is politically paradoxical. Understood as a form of governmentality, neoliberalism ironically obliges us to be free. This is, of course, the dubious freedom of the free market, but it is also the freedom that makes it possible for human subjects to participate in their own governance rather than submitting to domination (Rose 1999). The paradox of freedom is that it does not come easily: we need to be "made free" in order to participate in the freedoms available. Underpinning the freedom that renders us governable is an expansive subjectivity that inculcates within us myriad capacities to exercise self-governance. On Nikolas Rose's (1990) account, psychotherapies are influential technologies through which the capacity for autonomy is fostered. I have explored how psychotherapeutic practitioners in one particular context understand what they do, and analysed their accounts in relation to the complex politics of neoliberalism. I have argued that the rhetoric of empowerment to which voluntary sector counsellors appeal exemplifies how the practice insists upon, and recruits subjects into, self-governance. But I have also argued that the autonomy invoked through the language of empowerment is not unremittingly individualising. Further, while the processes of professionalisation to which counselling is currently subject tend to intensify its individualising tendencies, I have also drawn attention to moments of resistance. The scope for resistance may seem puny and marginal relative to the broad impetus of counselling as a psychologising, subjectifying, individualising and professionalising technology. But given its pervasive influence it is important to be able to think about politically effective ways of engaging with it, rather than arguing directly against it as a practice that is necessarily complicit with neoliberalism. As I have suggested, like psychotherapies more generally, counselling has attracted activists who consider their practice to be politically relevant. However contestable their accounts, it is, surely, important to engage in dialogue with such practitioners. Occupying a position embedded within the domain of counselling myself, this contribution is a step in my own working out of confusing and ambiguous political arguments.

Acknowledgements
I have drawn on research funded by the Economic and Social Research Council (R000239059) whose research is gratefully

acknowledged. My thanks also to all the practitioners who participated in interviews or supported the research in other ways, and to my
co-researchers Arnar Árnason, Judith Fewell and Colin Kirkwood.
Comments on an earlier draft offered by Erica Burman, Michael
Gallagher, Nina Laurie, and three anonymous referees were much
appreciated, and although I have not been able to respond to all of
them, in different ways they have helped me to think more carefully
about the issues at stake.

References

Bondi L (2003a) A situated practice for resituating selves: Trainee counsellors and the
    promise of counselling. *Environment and Planning A* 35:853–870
Bondi L (2003b) Empathy and identification: Conceptual resources for feminist field-
    work. *ACME: International Journal of Critical Geography* 2:64–76
Bondi L (2004) "A double-edged sword"? The professionalisation of counselling in
    the United Kingdom. *Health and Place* 10:319–328
Bondi L with Fewell J (2003) "Unlocking the cage door": The spatiality of counselling.
    Social and Cultural Geography 4:527–547
Bondi L, Fewell J and Kirkwood C (2003) Working for free: A fundamental value of
    counselling. *Counselling and Psychotherapy Research* 4:291–299
British Association for Counselling and Psychotherapy (2002) *Ethical Framework for
    Good Practice in Counselling and Psychotherapy*. Rugby: British Association for
    Counselling and Psychotherapy
Butler J (1997) *The Psychic Life of Power*. Stanford, CA: Stanford University Press
Eichenbaum L and Orbach S (1982) *Outside In ... Inside Out*. Harmondsworth:
    Penguin
Fournier V (1997) The appeal to "professionalism" as a disciplinary mechanism.
    Sociological Review 47:280–307
Freud S ([1926] 1959) The question of lay analysis. In J Strachey (ed) *The Standard
    Edition of the Complete Psychological Works of Sigmund Freud*, vol 20 (pp 179–258).
    London: Hogarth Press
Furedi F (2003) *Therapy Culture: Cultivating Vulnerability in an Age of Uncertainty*.
    London: Routledge
Kovel J (1988) *The Radical Spirit: Essays on Psychoanalysis and Society*. London: Free
    Association Books
Larner W (2000) Neoliberalism: Policy, ideology, governmentality. *Studies in Political
    Economy* 63:5–25
Lasch C (1980) *The Culture of Narcissism*. London: Abacus
Levitas R (ed) (1986) *The Ideology of the New Right*. Oxford: Polity Press
Lewis J, Clark D and Morgan D H (1992) *Whom God Hath Joined Together: The Work
    of Marriage Guidance*. London: Routledge
London Edinburgh Weekend Return Group (1979) *In and Against the State*. London:
    Pluto Press
Mackenzie C and Stoljar N (2000) Introduction: Autonomy refigured. In C Mackenzie
    and N Stoljar (eds) *Relational Autonomy* (pp 3–31). Oxford: Oxford University
    Press
Nolan J (1998) *The Therapeutic State*. New York: New York University Press
O'Neill O (2002) *Autonomy and Trust in Bioethics*. Cambridge: Cambridge University
    Press
Parker I (1997) *Psychoanalytic Culture*. London: Sage

Parker I (2003) Therapy from the left: The personal from the political. *European Journal of Psychotherapy, Counselling and Health* 6:1–5
Peck J and Tickell A (2002) Neoliberalizing space. *Antipode* 34:380–404
Phillips A (1995) *Terrors and Experts*. London: Faber and Faber
Rieff P (1966) *The Triumph of the Therapeutic*. London: Chatto and Windus
Rose N (1985) *The Psychological Complex*. London: Routledge and Kegan Paul
Rose N (1990) *Governing the Soul*. London: Routledge
Rose N (1999) *Powers of Freedom*. Cambridge: Cambridge University Press
Schön D (1983) *The Reflective Practitioner*. London: Temple Smith
Schwartz J (1999) *Cassandra's Daughters*. London: Allen Lane
Sennett R (1977) *The Fall of Public Man*. London: Faber
Turkle S (1979) *Psychoanalytic Politics*. London: Burnett Books
Wilensky H L (1964) The professionalization of everyone? *American Journal of Sociology* 70:137–158

Liz Bondi is Professor of Social Geography at the University of Edinburgh. Informed by her long-standing involvement in feminist geography, her current research focuses on counselling and psychotherapy as socio-spatial practices, and on emotional geographies. Founding editor of the journal *Gender, Place and Culture*, she has published in edited collections and journals such as *Antipode, Environment and Planning A, Progress in Human Geography, Social and Cultural Geography*, and *Society and Space*. She is co-author of *Subjectivities, Knowledges and Feminist Geographies* (Rowman and Littlefield, 2002) and co-editor of *Emotional Geographies* (Ashgate, 2005).

Chapter 6

Desiring Sameness? The Rise of a Neoliberal Politics of Normalisation

Diane Richardson

Introduction

In recent years there have been a number of interesting shifts in the political agendas of social movements concerned with the organisation of sexuality and gender. Rather than critiquing social institutions and practices that have historically excluded them, as did gay and lesbian/feminist activists in the 1960s and 1970s, over the last decade the politics of sexuality has increasingly been about seeking access into mainstream culture through demanding equal rights of citizenship (D'Emilio 2000). Feminist and queer critiques of this "sea change" in lesbian and gay politics (eg Richardson 2000a; Warner 2000) contest the rise of a "politics of normalisation" that is behind contemporary sexual citizenship agendas. Earlier normalising arguments are associated with the 1950s, a time of heightened discrimination and harassment of homosexuals. After World War II, in Europe and the USA a number of "homophile" organisations were formed in urban centres such as Los Angeles, San Francisco and London. These organisations, on the whole, adopted the political strategies of a minority group seeking tolerance from the heterosexual majority. They sought homosexual rights and aimed to reverse the medical model of homosexuality as pathology by claiming that homosexuals were normal people like heterosexuals (Richardson and Seidman 2002).

Fifty years later and a different politics of normalisation can be observed. This is a neoliberal politics of normalisation that, although it too deploys "sameness" with heterosexuals as a central aspect of its argument, differs in emphasising the rights of individuals rather than "gay rights" and in seeking "equality" with, rather than tolerance from, the mainstream. These "equal rights" approaches have become the dominant political discourse in the case of lesbian and gay movements in the USA, and are the favoured strategy of groups such as the

Human Rights Campaign and the National Gay and Lesbian Task Force. They have also increasingly become the dominant trend in Canada, Australia, New Zealand, and Europe (Richardson 2000a; Stychin 2003). In Britain, for instance, the cross-party campaigning and lobby group Stonewall can be seen, to greater or lesser extent, as following integrationist strategies to achieve social change.

I focus on the changing politics of sexuality in the context of new forms of social governance associated with neoliberalism, central to which is professionalisation and particular forms of knowledge construction. Before going on to map out my analysis of these trends, I want to first briefly clarify how I am using the term neoliberalism and why I consider it to be significant to my argument. Neoliberalism is commonly used to refer to monetary and trade policies that, although contested, are associated with a procorporate "free market economy" that has dominated Western politics and global markets since the early 1980s (Duggan 2002), as well as social policies concerned with personal, sexual and domestic life, including welfare reform, education, and recognition of domestic partnerships (Cooper 2004).

A primary goal of neoliberalism's policy agenda for both economic expansion and social governance is privatisation, in particular the "rolling back" of the state and the transfer of "public" services and functions to private (for profit) interests. Although strategies of governmentality in neoliberal states include direct intervention, the emphasis is on individual freedom and rights against the excessive intervention of the state. In this context, the role of government is to provide advice and assistance to enable self-governing subjects to become normal/responsible citizens, who voluntarily comply with the interests and needs of the state. However, it would appear that in the "policy arenas of cultural and personal life, neoliberalism is currently more pointedly conflicted" (Duggan 2002:178). For example, analysis of attempts to extend partnership rights to lesbian and gay couples through institutional recognition reveals that the policy environment often combines contradictory positions (Richardson 2004; Stychin 2003).

Neoliberalism can therefore be used to refer to the realms of both economic and cultural politics. Given the focus here, I will use the term primarily in the latter sense. That is, to aid my exploration of the changing politics of sexuality in the context of new forms of social governance associated with neoliberalism. However, this is not my only reason. As well as examining the question of how neoliberalism may inform new forms of sexual politics, I am also interested in how these new formations in sexual politics can be seen, at a more fundamental level, as influential in the development of neoliberal policies more generally. In this sense I am in agreement with Duggan when she states that "Neoliberalism in fact *has* a sexual politics" (2002:177).

The dominance of "equal rights" approaches and the question of the implications of extending various rights of citizenship to lesbians and gay men have received considerable attention in the literature (eg Bell and Binnie 2000; Kaplan 1997; Phelan 2001; Richardson 2000a; Seidman 2002; Weeks 1998). To date, however, there has been relatively little explicit discussion in the literature on the relationship between neoliberal governance and the politics of sexuality. (Notable exceptions to this include Bell and Binnie (2004) and Stychin (2003) in their discussion of contemporary transformations in sexual citizenship, and Duggan (2002) in her analysis of what she terms "the new homonormativity".) One possible explanation for this is that until relatively recently debates about sexuality, and homosexuality in particular, have been primarily configured through the epistemological authority of scientific, legal and religious discourses. A primary focus of lesbian and gay movements and political discourses, as a consequence, has been opposing "conservative" and moral right arguments, rather than contesting (neo)liberal understandings of (homo)sexuality. As I will go on to argue, this is further compounded by the fact that the "politics of citizenship" is the dominant discourse in sexual politics. In this respect, contemporary lesbian and gay movements rely implicitly on neoliberal language/concepts, which may also help to explain why neoliberalism tends to be ignored or is hidden from view.

As I indicated earlier, neoliberalism has been associated first and foremost with particular forms of economic policy, the "free market" economy, often considered separate to understandings of neoliberalism as social governance. Within this interpretative framework, the lack of critical discussion of neoliberalism in work on sexuality can be further explained by the fact that there has been relatively little written on how sexual politics, communities and identities are shaped by economic processes. A notable exception to this is D'Emilio's (1983) groundbreaking work in which he analysed the relationship between economic development and sexual identity in the USA, drawing out how industrial capitalism enabled the development of lesbian and gay identities and communities during the twentieth century. Other work has examined the relationship between urban economic change and sexual identity, in particular the role that gay men have played in the process of gentrification of certain neighbourhoods such as, in the 1970s, the Castro area in San Francisco (Castells 1983; Lauria and Knopp 1985). This facilitates, it is argued, the forging of identities through the economic colonisation of spaces within urban landscapes that, in turn, create gay identified places (Knopp 1992).

Although neoliberalism has not been a primary focus of analysis within the sexuality literature, a concern with the self-producing self-regulating subject is common to both. This is particularly apparent in Foucauldian-informed approaches to understanding sexuality, which draw on ideas of disciplinary power and the regulatory function of normalising techniques of control (Carabine 1996). Discussion of neoliberal modes of governance can also be found in a number of specific areas within the broader field of "sexuality studies". It is clearly evident, for example, in debates about health promotion in relation to sexuality. A good example is the AIDS education and prevention policy approach adopted by the UK and many other so-called "First World" nations (Lupton 1999). Such policies can be understood in terms of a "framework of governmentality", where the goal is for individuals to internalise new safer sexual norms in the interests of minimising HIV transmission. Following this argument, recent analyses of HIV antibody testing have argued that such testing can be understood as a technique of "surveillance medicine" closely aligned with neoliberal modes of governance (Adkins 2002; Lupton 1995; Waldby 1996).

Other areas, besides health, where ideas associated with neoliberalism have informed debates connected with sexuality include: theories of intimacy (Giddens 1992), the body (Lupton and Tulloch 1998), sexuality and the state (Cooper 2002), global sex (Altman 2001; Binnie 2004) and sexual citizenship (Bell and Binnie 2000; Weeks 1998). Of particular relevance here is the suggestion that (good) citizenship is increasingly constituted through the voluntary governance of the self (Richardson 2000a).

In the following section I will develop this argument through a consideration of the political claims of lesbian and gay movements for rights of citizenship (Ingebretsen 1999; Woods 1995). These changes in political organising, coupled with the growth in identity-based consumption and the greater visibility of lesbians and gay men as consumer citizens, have provided a variety of opportunities for new professional careers. I also discuss these developments and suggest that a key aspect of this increase in professionalisation is the construction of the gay and lesbian subject as part of a national and, in some instances, an international constituency. Finally, I consider how, in recent years, new forms of professionalisation of knowledge production about lesbians and gay men have emerged, not only in terms of political and market interests, but also in the academy.

Sexuality and Citizenship

Since the 1990s, a new form of sexual politics has emerged that has been highly influential in redefining the political goals and strategies associated with lesbian and gay activism. This is a politics that by invoking—and simultaneously constituting—a "gay movement" that seeks incorporation into the mainstream, rejects the earlier political language of women's, lesbian and gay liberation in favour of a "lesbian and gay equality" rhetoric. Before discussing this shift in more detail, it is important to clarify the frameworks of "equality" that these demands are based upon. One of the most common interpretations of equality in contemporary neoliberal societies such as the USA and Britain is equality of resources and recognition. Furthermore, what is implicit in such models is an emphasis on shared characteristics, the supposition that "equality" requires "sameness" (Cooper 2004). Although there are conflicts over the use of the term "equality", this is also the dominant model deployed by contemporary lesbian and gay rights movements. The case being made is for equality with the dominant group (heterosexuals) for a particular social membership (lesbians, bisexuals and gay men), where the subject of equality is interpreted as equal entitlement to recognition and to resources, centred upon demands for civil rights, access to welfare and rights as consumers (Vaid 1995; Warner 2000). More specifically, it is struggles over the civil recognition of domestic partnerships, including the right to marry, and the right to serve in the military that have emerged as primary concerns of lesbian and gay movements in Europe and the USA (Cooper 2004; Phelan 2001; Richardson 2000a).

A common justification of these and other demands for social inclusion—one that is made both by lesbian and gay movements themselves and neoliberal governments responsive to their rights claims—is that lesbians and gay men are "ordinary", "*normal*" citizens. This is exemplified in the arguments developed by neoconservative gay writers such as Bawer, who asserts that the "lifestyle" of mainstream gays is "indistinguishable from that of most heterosexual couples in similar professional and economic circumstances" (1993:33–34). Sullivan (1995) advances a similar argument, claiming that the majority of lesbian and gay individuals have the same values, aspirations and lifestyles as most heterosexuals and desire nothing more than to be fully integrated into society as it is.

These assumptions are problematic for a variety of reasons. First, the emphasis on sameness implies that lesbians and gay men, as well as heterosexuals, have shared interests and needs. In effect, sameness emerges from difference through two mechanisms: first through the appeal to a universal lesbian and gay citizen who deserves equal rights with heterosexuals; and second, through the dominant interpretation of equality as similitude, in this case between lesbians, gay men and heterosexuals. To the extent that lesbian and gay communities are socially heterogeneous, an obvious problem with this approach is that differences and the complex social locations within that group membership are obscured and inequalities such as those of gender, class, race and disability are not addressed. Given the difficulties associated with the construction of sameness, I have chosen to use lesbian/gay rather than "lesbian and gay" as a way of acknowledging the significance of gender differences.

Second, the emphasis on shared norms and inclusivity raises difficulties in relation to what constructions of lesbians and gay men are mobilised in order to establish the case for equality. Related to this is the question of what counts as "equal" recognition; what are the values and norms through which recognition of lesbians and gay men as the "same" as heterosexuals, as well as with each other, takes place. Critics have questioned the extent to which such a model of citizenship reinforces normative assumptions about sexuality and gender (Bell and Binnie 2000; Duggan 1995; Richardson 2000b; Warner 2000). The problem identified here is that a particular version of what it is to be lesbian or gay (as well as heterosexual) is privileged in demands for "equality", with the potential for creating "new social, economic and moral divisions between lesbians and gay men, between heterosexuals and across the heterosexual/homosexual divide" (Richardson 2004:405). As I go on to suggest below, the question of how the lesbian/gay "community" is represented by political organisations concerned with sexual politics is also connected to the increasing professionalisation of those organisations. In particular, we need to consider how the construction of a specific *normative* lesbian/gay citizenship may impact on the way political organisations are staffed and the styles of leadership they may favour.

A further reason to question the dominant tendency to interpret equality through similitude stems from the fact that, historically, homosexuality has been defined in ways that would seem to work against such a project. As Sedgwick (1900), Butler (1990) and others have argued in their discussion of the heterosexual/homosexual binary, central to the meanings of homo and heterosexuality is the notion of "difference". This takes the form of *sexualised difference*—the idea that heterosexuality and homosexuality are "different"—which is also connected to assumptions about *gender difference*, the idea that men's and women's sexualities are different though complementary. Thus, heterosexual desire is defined in terms of attraction to the so called "opposite" sex, and lesbians and gay men are constructed as "desiring sameness", that is sexual attraction to the "same" sex. (In claiming similitude with heterosexuals, lesbians and gay men are challenging this binary and, in an interesting twist, can be seen as "desiring sameness" on two different levels.) Such constructions of difference operate at a corporeal level, as evidenced by continuing attempts to identify a distinct "homosexual body" that is different to the heterosexual biological norm, at a cultural level, in terms of the different social meanings and values ascribed heterosexual and homosexual conduct, norms and lifestyles, as well as via sexualised constructions of space and the public/private divide. The following question therefore arises: how can sameness be intelligible—and the grounds for "equality" thereby established—against dominant constructions of "the homosexual" as "other"?

From being seen in the past as having little of positive value to contribute to society, lesbians and gay men are now constituted as citizens worthy of inclusion. Within traditional models of "normalisation", this is explained by reducing or eradicating forms of "difference" that are ascribed to people which render them devalued citizens. According to Warner (2000), this is achieved primarily through a process of "purification" or "gentrification", whereby lesbians but more especially gay men are reconfigured as desexualised normative citizens, and through a shift in the spatial differentiation of sexual identities and activities that relocates lesbians and gay men through the norms of proper place and responsibility within domestic settings. It is also the case that these discourses of sexual difference are also grounded in assumptions about gender differences, which produces contradictory tensions in the homo/heterosexual binary (Richardson 1992). Thus, heterosexual and gay men, and lesbians and heterosexual women, have been seen as "alike" in certain respects because of their common gender and the presumptions about values and conduct supposedly associated with this shared membership over and above their sexual "difference".

Other writers have pointed to economic participation of lesbians and gay men as consumer citizens, and support for and adherence to dominant cultural norms and values as key mechanisms of social inclusion (Bell and Binnie 2000; Cooper 2004; Evans 1993). As I have also argued elsewhere (Richardson 2004), the responsibility of lesbians and gay men is now to adopt disciplined sexual practices through the internalisation of new norms of identity and sexual practices associated with a certain (heteronormative) lifestyle, with various rights granted through demonstrating a specific form of "domestic" sexual coupledom. The forms of same-sex partnership registration schemes that have been introduced in many countries, including Canada, Australia, New Zealand, parts of the USA and Europe, giving same-sex couples access to civil rights such as next-of-kin, inheritance and pension rights, is supportive of this argument (Bell and Binnie 2002; Stychin 2003). Indeed, in the context of a neoliberalism's policy agenda for "rolling back" the state it is possible to see how governments are motivated to introduce civil recognition of lesbian and gay relationships insofar as these are seen as a form of private welfare, providing economic interdependency and support.

There are a number of important points to make here. First, in this model of citizenship the "risk" lesbians and gay men might pose to society is rendered governable through establishing the "ordinary" "normal" lesbian/gay as a category of persons who desire, and achieve, responsible citizenship primarily through civil registration. This is the self-regulating homosexual subject who chooses stable co-habiting relationships. This aspect of the contemporary sexual citizenship agenda has been subject to considerable critical discussion (see, for example, *Feminism and Psychology* 2003, 2004; Kaplan 1997; Richardson 2004). However, what is of relevance to this discussion is that there would appear to be a new partnership at work between activists and policymakers, in sharing common goals and political language. Having said this, we need to recognise that under the rubric of "normalisation" there are a range of approaches and viewpoints which may reflect different levels of engagement with neoliberal agendas. For some, a shared language may be strategic—a means to a political end; whereas, for others, there is a shared commitment to a politics of normalisation. This is an area where future empirical work could usefully develop theoretical frameworks. Second, in establishing their ordinariness and normality, good lesbian/gay citizens serve as a means for establishing new boundaries in relation to sexuality, ones which are constitutive of "other" sexualities that can be figured as problematic and in need of control (Seidman 2002). Third, what is especially significant in the adoption of such measures is the way in which they are presented by neoliberal governments as supportive of the choosing responsibilised lesbian/gay subject, who is demanding the right to make lifestyle choices that are approved of as "low risk" to society (Nussbaum 1999). Through such neoliberal techniques of governance, the promotion of lesbian and gay rights can appear to be necessary and benign, rather than ushering in a new politics of surveillance and control. In his analysis of the deployment of equality arguments in the specific case of age of consent legislation in the UK, Waites captures this nicely when he remarks:

> Conceived in this way, the achievement of an equal age of consent begins to appear less like straightforward liberalisation, and more as the consequences of a new balance of forces, embodying elements of both permissiveness and control. (2003:643)

However, in considering the consequences of "lesbian/gay normalisation" we should be careful of collapsing analysis into a dichotomy between the "old" homosexual (especially male) subject as in need of external regulation and control, and the newly emergent self-regulated neoliberal lesbian/gay subject who has internalised new norms of responsibilised sexual identity and practice. Arguably, it is a condition of their social oppression that lesbians and gay men have long been self-reflexive, self-regulating sexual subjects. The realities of living lives in "the closet", a "life shaping" social pattern that involves episodes of passing and coming out (Seidman 2002), both necessitates and shapes a self-monitoring self. However, what is significant is that there may be a shift from a "policing of the self" because of fears of violence and shame, to a desire for normativity and respectability. Lesbians and gay men were previously constrained by representations of themselves as mad, bad or sad; now they are being shaped through normative constructions of responsible and respectable sexual citizenship. Constructions that are structured through the processes of neoliberal self-regulatory governance, central to which is professionalisation and particular forms of knowledge construction.

Professionalisation of Sexual Politics

Having outlined contemporary developments in sexual politics, I will now go on to argue that these are associated with a movement towards professionalising acitivism. My aim is to examine what I have termed the "professionalisation of sexual politics" and how this is opening up new career paths for some activists as well as new funding regimes, which themselves shape the different modes of professionalisation that are emerging. The opening up of new career paths and professional roles can be observed in a number of other sites besides political campaigning and fund raising. As I argue in the following section on the professionalisation of knowledge production, the institutionalisation of lesbian/gay/queer studies within the academy is one such area of development. Another key site is the expansion of professional roles in businesses. Many investors, both mainstream and gay and lesbian entrepreneurs, have been keen to cash in on what they perceive as the niche market potential of the "pink economy" (Lukenbill and Klenert 1999). Such commercial growth relies on, and is productive of, both a lesbian/gay "consumer citizen" and the development of an expanding lesbian/predominantly gay "business community" that has become increasingly "professionalised". Although this is an important area of debate within the literature (see, for example, Chasin 2000; Gluckman and Reed 1997), discussion of the "pink economy" and how it relates to the changing conceptions of the lesbian/gay citizen within marketised neoliberalism is beyond the scope of this contribution. Here the focus is on how the politics of sexuality, and responses to lesbian/gay demands, are changing in a number of significant respects that afford opportunities for the construction of new lesbian and gay subjectivities, both as members of a political constituency and as professional activists.

The dominant political discourse of equal entitlement and "integration" or, as some describe it, "assimilation" that circulates throughout

North America, Europe, New Zealand and Australia would seem to call for a style of leadership that is acceptable to "mainstream society", to politicians and policymakers, and to sponsors. One that can represent both lesbians and gay men, *and lesbian and gay social movements*, as no longer "troubling" to mainstream society. One that can not only render intelligible and acceptable the idea of the "normal lesbian/gay", but also can "normalise" the lesbian and gay movement itself. This has led to claims that the "public face" of lesbian and gay movements is changing, and has prompted questions about what communities and which individuals are becoming *acceptably* visible, as others are being marginalised, through these mainstreaming effects. Given the lack of empirical studies of the significance of gender, racial and other differences within political organisations concerned with sexual politics, this is an interesting area for future research.

In the following section, I will go on to consider how the construction of the lesbian/gay subject as part of a national and, in some instances, an international constituency is connected to these processes of professionalisation.

National Communities

Commenting on the direction of sexual politics in the USA, Warner (2000) claims that increasing professionalisation is already evident in many lesbian and gay organisations. The conditions he identifies as significant in this process are the increasing role of the mass media as the "public voice" of the movement, a shift from local to national organising, and the growing importance of "big-money" in political campaigning.

> Over the past decade, movement politics on the national scale have been dramatically transformed. Its public face is now dominated by a small group of national organisations, an equally small group of media celebrities, connected to a network of big money politics that revolves around publicity consultants and campaign professionals and litigators. (Warner 2000:67)

The trajectory Warner describes mirrors, to some extent, the professionalisation of activism that occurred in relation to HIV/AIDS. The emergence of AIDS in the 1980s impacted on lesbian and gay lives, communities and politics in ways that have been as varied as they have been far reaching (Altman 2001). In the context of this discussion, however, what is significant is the importance of AIDS to both the nationalising and the professionalisation of lesbian and gay culture and politics. In the USA in particular, the 1980s witnessed an explosion of AIDS organisations and services (Watney 1994). Such developments were prompted both by the failure of governments and policymakers to anticipate and respond to the specific needs of gay men with HIV and AIDS, and by the introduction of neoliberal economic policies associated with the "rolling back" of the state, leaving the NGO sector to try to fill the gap. Located in major cities, these included health and social services programmes, advocacy, legal and other services for those with AIDS and HIV-related illness. The vast majority of these organisations were staffed by lesbians and gay men, and offered career paths for "activists". This move towards professionalisation in AIDS work led to the kind of ambiguities that are well rehearsed in debates about professionalisation, and that are echoed in the debates surrounding the mainstreaming of lesbian and gay politics since the 1990s. Thus, for example, while this move in AIDS activism provided vital social, health and educational services to many lesbian and gay communities, it was also regarded by some activists as overdetermining the form and direction of sexual/AIDS politics and activism. This, in turn, led to splits, for example, between Gay Men's Health Crisis, one of the first AIDS organisations in the USA, and the more radical confrontational politics of ACT-UP.

Alongside, and associated with, the scaling up of lesbian and gay groups and organisations over the last decade from local to national levels are a number of shifts in funding trends. In particular, there has been a significant growth in funding from corporate and donor funders who, as Chasin (2000) details in the USA, are more likely to allocate monies to mainstream, national organisations than to those that are local community-based and/or with more radical agendas (see also Cooper 1993). Chasin also highlights the growing tendency for mixed economy funding, involving "partnerships" between non-profit organisations and commercial interests. This represents a new relationship between activists and businesses, especially in the UK where, in the past, there has been a tendency within gay and lesbian/feminist movements to adopt an anti-commercial stance (Cooper 2004; Sinfield 1998). Financial support for lesbian and gay events and services was largely sought through public funding and through raising money within local communities. For many, being "self sufficient" was associated with greater autonomy and less risk of becoming co-opted and/or dependent on public funds that could be withdrawn at a later date. Over the last decade, however, the trend has been increasingly towards the pattern in the USA, with the financing of Gay Pride and similar events reliant on sponsorship deals with mainstream corporations such as Absolut Vodka and American Airlines (Woods 1995).

The increasing significance of "big-money" in political campaigning raises interesting questions about the possible effect this may have on both the structure and staffing of organisations, and for lesbian and gay movements more generally. Along with Warner (2000) and others, I would argue that it has resulted in an increasing profession-alisation of such organisations, or at least an appeal to the language of professionalisation, and the role of political activist/campaigner. The UK group Stonewall, for example, was founded in 1989 as a cross-party lobbying group to put the case for lesbian and gay equality on the mainstream political agenda. Since then it has become established as a national voice of lesbian and gay politics, and has expanded its activities to include work that involves promoting new research into lesbian and gay discrimination and "partnerships with organisations outside of Parliament". These "partners" include the police, local councils, health trusts and, through their "Diversity Champions" scheme, employers such as IBM and the major supermarket chain Sainsbury's. The organisation has also secured mainstream corporate sponsorship. Its principal sponsors include Barclays Bank and the investment bank JP Morgan, as well as sponsorship via the "pink economy" through Millivres Prowler Group, Europe's largest gay and lesbian company. These developments are described in ways that appeal to the "authority" of professionalisation. Thus, according to Stonewall, alongside this expansion, "the staff team has grown (to 20) and become highly professional" (http://www.stonewall.org.uk, accessed 13 August 2004). Others have drawn on the example of the changing nature of Gay Pride, held annually in many countries, to make a similar argument. Thus, for example, Chasin (2000) argues that as Gay Pride events in the USA have become more commercial-ised they have transformed themselves into professional organisa-tions, with paid positions for parade organisers and those whose job it is to obtain corporate sponsorship. This too would seem to call for a certain kind of "professional", someone who can project themselves in ways that will attract funding, who can manage large scale organisa-tions and budgets, and represent the normalising agenda through being seen as acceptable to the "mainstream".

In addition to the tendency of political organisations to scale up their activities from local to national levels, and draw on mainstream funding, during the last decade we have witnessed the globalisation of lesbian and gay politics and markets (Adam, Duyvendak and Krouwelm 1999; Altman 2001). Opportunities for lesbian and gay activism at a global level exist in organisations such as, for example, the International Lesbian and Gay Association (ILGA) and the International Gay and Lesbian Human Rights Commission (IGLHRC), which have been pri-marily concerned with promoting modern notions of human rights. The construction of an "international" gay community is also aided by the global visibility of lesbians and gay men in the market, through the international distribution of gay newspapers, magazines, books, films and other media, the expansion of international gay tourism to "gay- friendly holiday destinations" as well as travel associated with participation in international conferences, and access to the Internet (Cruz-Malavé and Manalansan 2002:1).

One of the most important aspects of the development of international lesbian and gay movements and markets is the complex question of how they are likely to impact on local sexual cultures and politics. A particular concern is that international human rights organisations such as IGLHRC use the terms "lesbian" and "gay" unproblematically in ways that produce the effect that these are universal terms, rather than terms that have particular local as well as global meanings (Puar 2002). In producing a new global lesbian/ gay citizen, whose rights claims go beyond single nation states, we need to be attentive to what circulates as the global definitions of lesbian and gay identities and politics. This requires a consideration of the power relations in intercultural exchanges in relation to knowledges about both sexuality, in particular the meanings attached to same sex desires and practices, and political organising (King 2002; see following section). The charge is that it is definitions of lesbian and gay produced over the last 30 years in the USA and Europe, where there is a key distinction made between sexual identity and sexual activity, that have colonised ideas of the "universal". Altman (2001) discusses this in terms of a tension between the global gay citizen and local (homo)sexualities, arguing that global definitions are inadequate to represent local sexual practices, activisms and identities. However, as he points out, in acknowledging the risk that local meanings and knowledge may be lost or undermined in this inter/nationalising process, we must be careful not to ignore the complexity of interactions between local sites and global contexts (see, for example, Cantú (2002) on the impact of queer tourism on Mexican male sexualities).

Finally, we might ask what are the implications of this "professionalisation" of sexual politics on the shape and direction of lesbian and gay movements themselves. As debates about professionalisation more generally have highlighted (see this volume), there is ambivalence in the responses to these processes. Some argue that the shift to larger, national organisations with scaled up budgets supported by corporate funding can benefit lesbian and gay movements through increased visibility and "authority", which is enabling to the prosecution of their causes (Bawer 1993). Others, even if they are in agreement with this, point to inherent tensions, in particular the ways in which such changes can constrain political activity in a number of important respects. Thus, Chasin, for example, claims that:

> ... among gay-related causes, the smaller, more local, more grass-roots organisations, and those working for radical social change, are

surely those the least favoured by funders. As a result, market-related funding mechanisms—while providing increased visibility for the larger national service-oriented organisations—can contribute to the invisibility and/or the de-resourcing of less mainstream organisations. (2000:202)

To put it in a slightly different way, there is a new level of *accountability* evident in lesbian and gay politics. It can be argued that the growing professionalisation and centralisation of gay politics by national organisations means that there is less direct accountability to those who organisations claim to represent. At the same time, such organisations are increasingly accountable not only to their political constituency, but to the corporate interests who fund them. Where these relationships of accountability are in conflict with one another, then organisations may feel constrained to act in ways that satisfy funders and further mainstreaming can occur.

In the final section, I will go on to consider the professionalisation of knowledge production where similar processes may be at work. There are, of course, a variety of sites of knowledge production that could be addressed. For example, McNair (2002) discusses the impact of the mainstreaming of gay music culture on "popular knowledge", whereas Carabine (2004) analyses social policy as a specific form of "professionalised" knowledge production about sexuality. While these raise interesting issues, the following discussion is limited to one particular area of knowledge production, that of "expert knowledge". Specifically, my focus is on the professionalisation of knowledge about lesbian and gay communities and individuals, and the shifts that have occurred through the institutionalisation of "lesbian and gay" and queer studies within the academy.

Professionalisation of Knowledge

In addition to the expansion of professional roles in businesses and political organisations, changes in the practices of knowledge production and dissemination over the last two to three decades have also provided opportunities for new professional careers. Efforts to understand the origins, meanings and treatment of "homosexuality" have been at the heart of many professions since the rise of sexology during the latter part of the nineteenth century. These new forms of knowledge about lesbians and gay men were produced by "experts" who deployed the power and authority of "scientific theory", primarily working in the fields of medicine and psychiatry. Furthermore, in so far as these "expert knowledges" defined homosexuality as pathological, they constituted a market for their own services: the homosexual as someone in need of treatment. There is, then, a long tradition of the professionalisation of homosexuality that has provided careers both in making sense of the subject and in offering services to "treat" the subject.

One of the primary goals and achievements of the gay and lesbian liberation movements that emerged at the end of the 1960s, beginning of the 1970s was to challenge such "expert" knowledge about "homosexuality", in particular the idea that homosexuality was abnormal and/or inferior (Terry 1999). In rejecting a professionalised model of homosexuality, such movements provided interpretations of same sex attraction that were productive of a new positive identity as lesbian and gay as distinct from that of homosexual, a negative identity associated with a medical category (Weeks 1990). This represented far more than new meanings for old realities. It also reflected a shift in the politics of knowledge as lesbians and gay men, in their struggles to redefine what it meant to be gay, became knowledge producers who claimed the authority "to speak for themselves". Interestingly, these attempts to institute lesbians and gay men as experts on their sexuality might be seen to resonate with later processes of neoliberal self-regulatory governance that require subjects to know themselves. As discussed earlier, Lupton (1995), for instance, has argued that discourses of health risk incite self-monitoring subjects who are obliged to deploy expert knowledge of their own body and lifestyle to make responsible decisions. However, here the obligation to deploy expert knowledge is personalised, at the level of individual agency, rather than politicised, at the level of collective agency.

The emergence of AIDS in the early 1980s, and the recognition that it may reach epidemic proportions, revitalised both religious and scientific–medical discourses on homosexuality (Watney 1994). Along with this, it brought a new impetus to the professionalisation of knowledge about sexuality, homosexuality in particular. The need for information in order to facilitate behavioural change that reduces the risk of HIV transmission, and for research into the treatment of those with HIV/AIDS, has provided an important focus for "work on homosexuality" within the medical profession, for social researchers and those working in public policy development. As Seidman points out, as a health crisis AIDS has forced "public officials to gather and publicise knowledge about homosexuality" as gaining "detailed empirical knowledge of homosexuality is deemed essential for public health reasons" (1997:183). This echoes the point made by Larner and Craig (2005) that there is a growing emphasis on the need for new professional knowledge *about* different communities that is connected to neoliberal attempts to better manage government services and resources.

In addition to lesbian/feminist and gay activism being productive of new ways of thinking about sexuality, academic research and scholarship over the past two or three decades has also helped to create an *affirmative* space for studying lesbian and gay issues within the academy. At first, this occurred principally within feminist, gender and women's studies courses. By the mid-1980s, however, new professional spaces and territories of knowledge opened up as lesbian and gay studies emerged as a field of study in its own right (Plummer 1992).

Over the last decade and a half, paralleling the development/mainstreaming of gender and women's studies, lesbian and gay studies has become institutionalised, especially in the USA, and is now an established position from which "to speak and work within the academy" (Spurlin 1998:74). This is evidenced in a variety of ways: by a growth in lesbian and gay studies courses on offer; the development of a number of lesbian and gay research centres and institutes at major universities with associated career opportunities and fellowships; the establishment of specialist groups within professional associations, for example, the Sexuality and Space Specialty Group within the American Association of Geographers, the Gay and/or Lesbian Study groups within the American Sociological Association and the British Sociological Association; the organisation of inter/national conferences; and, associated with these developments, the production of a rapidly expanding literature including new journals such as *GLQ: A Journal of Lesbian and Gay Studies*, first published in 1993, and textbooks in lesbian and gay studies (eg Abelove, Barale and Halperin 1993; Medhurst and Munt 1997; Nardi and Schneider 1997; Nast 2002; Richardson and Seidman 2002; Sandfort et al 2000; Wilton 1995).

The development and consolidation of the interdisciplinary field of lesbian and gay studies during the late 1980s and the 1990s was accompanied by the emergence of queer theory, which prompted claims to a further disciplinary formation: queer studies. The relationship between lesbian and gay studies, feminism and queer studies is the subject of much debate (see, for example, Merck, Segal and Wright 1998; Nast 2002; Richardson, McLaughlin and Casey forthcoming), in particular the extent to which it is appropriate to conceptualise queer as the "next stage" in disciplinary development, in keeping with dominant narratives of progressive change (Stacey 1997). What is of primary significance here, however, is the rapid expansion of queer studies in the academy, to the extent that some might want to claim that it has established "market dominance", although the dominance of queer agendas has been more apparent in the arts and humanities than the social sciences.

The institutionalisation of "sexuality studies" within the academy that I have briefly described is a further example of the tensions that are often associated with professionalisation. On the one hand, we can see such practices as associated with the greater visibility of

lesbians and gay men in mainstream culture, and as helping to establish rights of cultural citizenship. On the other hand, we might view
these developments more critically. Various writers, for instance, have
suggested that the greater cultural visibility, associated with new
forms of knowledge production, both in terms of "academic" knowledge and "popular" knowledge associated with the growth of commercial venues and services catering to lesbians and gay men and in
the media, can operate as new "spaces of control" (Cottingham 1996;
Jagose 1996; Torres 1993). Such developments have also given rise to
a number of concerns about accountability and legitimacy. More
specifically, that knowledge production within the academy, especially
within queer studies, is becoming more and more disconnected from
the political activities and the material lives of those living in communities that are the primary focus of analysis (Escoffier 1990; Stanley
and Wise 2000).

Summary

My aim has been to address a number of issues. The first concerns the
ways in which the politics of sexuality appears to be changing, as
exemplified by demands for "equal rights" for lesbians and gay men,
where a link is made between social norms and the achievement of
"equality". The second issue concerns the question of the inter-
relationship between neoliberalism and the emergence of new forms
of sexual politics. At the heart of neoliberal responses to homosexuality
there is frequently both a (continued) recognition and maintenance of
difference and, at the same time, an attempt to disrupt this through the
introduction of new policy measures that constitute lesbians and gay
men as "ordinary normal citizens". This is a significant change.
However, one question that needs to be addressed in future research
is whether the dominance of heteronormative values and practices is
consolidated as much by this reimagining of lesbians and gay men as
incorporated, as it was in the past through their location as excluded
"other"? The primary focus in the rise of a politics of normalisation is on
bringing about social changes so that lesbians and gay men may be
regarded as socially valued members of society, rather than
attempting to bring about changes in how societies operate in ways
that are productive of devalued categories of behaviour, identity and
persons. From this perspective, as I have suggested, it would seem that a
new "partnership" is in the process of being constructed between
neoliberal governments and organisations promoting lesbian and gay
rights and social inclusion. Unlike earlier social movements that sought
to transform key institutions, contemporary struggles for "equality" help
to reaffirm the regulatory power of the state by reinforcing the authority
of the institutions appealed to which confer rights and responsibilities

(in this case military, marriage, family), and through which sexualities are regulated.

The final section is concerned with how new forms of social governance associated with neoliberalism are linked to professionalisation and particular forms of knowledge production. In my analysis I have identified a number of areas for future empirical work. However, building on my discussion, I would argue that we need a theoretical framework that can allow us to critically engage with the challenges and insights provoked by these issues. The rise of a neoliberal sexual politics of normalisation is based on a whole set of assumptions that require critical analysis: the taken for granted meanings and value attached to "being normal", assumptions about what constitutes ordinary sexual and intimate relationships and "lifestyles", the continuing tradition of regarding sexuality as a key indicator of normality, and the idea that there is something we can call "normal".

References
Abelove H, Barale M A and Halperin D M (eds) (1993) *The Lesbian and Gay Studies Reader*. London: Routledge

Adam B D, Duyvendak J and Krouwelm A (eds) (1999) *The Global Emergence of Gay and Lesbian Politics*. Philadelphia, PA: Temple University Press

Adkins L (2002) *Revisions: Gender and Sexuality in Late Modernity*. Buckingham: Open University Press

Altman D (2001) *Global Sex*. Chicago, IL: University of Chicago Press

Bawer B (1993) *A Place at the Table: The Gay Individual in American Society*. New York: Poseidan Press

Bell D and Binnie J (2000) *The Sexual Citizen: Queer Politics and Beyond*. Oxford: Polity Press

Bell D and Binnie J (2002) Sexual citizenship: Marriage, the market and the military. In D Richardson and S Seidman (eds) *Handbook of Lesbian and Gay Studies* (pp 443–457). London: Sage

Bell D and Binnie J (2004) Authenticating queer space: Citizenship, urbanism and governance. *Urban Studies* 41(9):1807–1820

Binnie J (2004) *The Globalization of Sexuality*. London: Sage

Butler J (1990) *Gender Trouble*. New York: Routledge

Cantú L (2002) *De ambiente*. Queer tourism and the shifting boundaries of Mexican male sexualities. *GLQ: A Journal of Lesbian and Gay Studies* 8(1/2):139–166

Carabine J (1996) Heterosexuality and social policy. In D Richardson (ed) *Theorising Heterosexuality: Telling it Straight* (pp 55–74). Buckingham: Open University Press

Carabine J (ed) (2004) *Sexualities. Personal Lives and Social Policy*. Buckingham: Open University Press

Castells M (1983) *The City and the Grassroots*. Berkeley, CA: University of California Press

Chasin A (2000) *Selling Out: The Gay and Lesbian Movement Goes to Market*. New York: St Martin's Press

Cooper D (1993) An engaged state: Sexuality, governance and the potential for change. In J Bristow and A R Wilson (eds) *Activating Theory: Lesbian, Gay and Bisexual Politics* (pp 190–218). London: Lawrence and Wishart

Cooper D (2002) Imagining the place of the state: Where governance and social power meet. In D Richardson and S Seidman (eds) *Handbook of Lesbian and Gay Studies* (pp 231–252). London: Sage

Cooper D (2004) *Challenging Diversity: Rethinking Equality and the Value of Difference.* Cambridge: Cambridge University Press

Cottingham L (1996) *Lesbians Are so Chic ... that We Are not Really Lesbians at All.* London: Cassell

Cruz-Malavé A and Manalanasan IV M F (eds) (2002) *Queer Globalizations: Citizenship and the Afterlife of Colonialism.* New York and London: New York University Press

D'Emilio J (1983) Capitalism and gay identity. In A Snitow, C Stansell and S Thompson (eds) *Powers of Desire: The Politics of Sexuality* (pp 100–113). London: Virago

D'Emilio J (2000) Cycles of change, questions of strategy, the gay and lesbian movement after fifty years. In C A Rimmerman, K D Wald and C Wilcox (eds) *The Politics of Gay Rights* (pp 31–53). London: University of Chicago Press

Duggan L (1995) Queering the state. In L Duggan and N D Hunter (eds) *Sex Wars: Sexual Dissent and Political Culture* (pp 178–193). New York: Routledge

Duggan L (2002) The new homonormativity: The sexual politics of neoliberalism. In R Castronovo and D D Nelson (eds) *Materializing Democracy: Towards a Revitalized Cultural Politics* (pp 175–194). Duke: Duke University Press

Escoffier J (1990) Inside the ivory closet: The challenge facing lesbian and gay studies. *Out/Look* 10:40–48

Evans D (1993) *Sexual Citizenship: The Material Construction of Sexuatities.* London: Routledge

Feminism and Psychology (2003) Special Issue on Marriage (1) 13(4):411–543

Feminism and Psychology (2004) Special Issue on Marriage (2) 14(1):7–202

Giddens A (1992) *The Transformation of Intimacy: Sexuality, Love and Eroticism in Modern Societies.* Cambridge: Polity

Gluckman A and Reed B (eds) (1997) *Homo Economics: Capitalism, Community, and Lesbian and Gay Life.* New York: Routledge

Ingrebretsen E (1999) Gone shopping: The commercialization of same-sex desire. *Journal of Gay, Lesbian, and Bisexual Identity* 4:132

Jagose A (1996) *Queer Theory: An Introduction.* New York: New York University Press

Kaplan M B (1997) *Sexual Justice: Democratic Citizenship and the Politics of Desire.* New York: Routledge

King K (2002) "There are no lesbians here": Lesbianisms, feminisms, and global gay formations. In A Cruz-Malavé and M F Manalanasan IV (eds) *Queer Globalizations: Citizenship and the Afterlife of Colonialism* (pp 33–45). New York and London: New York University Press

Knopp L (1992) Sexuality and the spatial dynamics of capitalism. *Environment and Planning D: Society and Space* 10:651–669

Larner W and Craig D (2005) After neoliberalism? Community activism and local partnerships in Aotearoa New Zealand. *Antipode* 37(3):401–423

Lauria M and Knopp L (1985) Towards an analysis of the role of gay communities in the urban renaissance. *Urban Geography* 6:152–169

Lukenbill G and Klenert J (1999) *Untold Millions: Secret Truths about Marketing to Gay and Lesbian Consumers.* New York: Haworth

Lupton D (1995) *The Imperative of Health: Public Health and the Regulated Body.* London: Sage

Lupton D (1999) *Risk.* London: Routledge

Lupton D and Tulloch J (1998) The adolescent "unfinished body": reflexivity and HIV/AIDS risk. *Body and Society* 4(2):19–34

McNair B (2002) *Striptease Culture: Sex, Media and the Democratising of Desire.*
London: Routledge
Merck M, Segal N and Wright E (eds) (1998) *Coming Out of Feminism?* Oxford:
Blackwell
Medhurst A and Munt S (eds) (1997) *Lesbian and Gay Studies.* London: Cassell
Nardi P and Schneider B (eds) (1997) *Social Perspectives on Lesbian and Gay Studies.*
New York: Routledge
Nast H J (ed) (2002) Special issue: Queer patriarchies, queer racisms, international.
Antipode 34(5):874–909
Nussbaum M (1999) *Sex and Social Justice.* Oxford: Oxford University Press
Phelan S (2001) *Sexual Strangers. Gays, Lesbians and Dilemmas of Citizenship.*
Philadelphia: Temple University Press
Plummer K (1992) Speaking its name: Inventing a lesbian and gay studies. In
K Plummer (ed) *Modern Homosexualities* (pp 3–25). London: Routledge
Puar J K (2002) Circuits of queer mobility: Tourism, travel and globalization. *GLQ: A
Journal of Lesbian and Gay Studies* 8(1/2):101–138
Richardson D (1992) Constructing lesbian sexualities. In K Plummer (ed) *Modern
Homosexualities* (pp 187–200). London: Routledge
Richardson D (2000a) *Rethinking Sexuality.* London: Sage
Richardson D (2000b) Claiming Citizenship? *Sexualities* 3(2):271–288
Richardson D (2004) Locating sexualities: From here to normality. *Sexualities*
7(4):393–413
Richardson D and Seidman S (eds) (2002) *Handbook of Lesbian and Gay Studies.*
London: Sage
Richardson D, McLaughlin J and Casey M (eds) (forthcoming) *Intersections Between
Feminist and Queer Theory.* Basingstoke: Palgrave
Sandfort T, Schuyf J, Duyvendak J W and Weeks J (eds) (2000) *Lesbian and Gay
Studies: An Introductory, Interdisciplinary Approach.* London: Sage
Sedgwick E (1990) *Epistemology of the Closet.* Berkeley: University of California Press
Seidman S (1997) *Difference Troubles: Queering Social Theory and Sexual Politics.*
Cambridge: Cambridge University Press
Seidman S (2002) *Beyond the Closet: The Transformation of Gay and Lesbian Life.* New
York and London: Routledge
Sinfield A (1998) *Gay and After.* London: Serpent's Tail
Spurlin W J (1998) Sissies and sisters: Gender, sexuality and the possibilities of
coalition. In M Merck, N Segal and E Wright (eds) *Coming Out of Feminism?* (pp
74–101). Oxford: Blackwell
Stacey J (1997) Feminist theory: Capital F, capital T. In V Robinson and
D Richardson (eds) *Introducing Women's Studies: Feminist Theory and Practice*
(pp 54–76). 2nd ed. Basingstoke: Macmillan
Stanley L and Wise S (2000) But the empress has no clothes! *Feminist Theory* 2(1):
99–103
Stychin C F (2003) *Governing Sexuality. The Changing Politics of Citizenship and Law
Reform.* Oxford and Portland, Oregon: Hart Publishing
Sullivan A (1995) *Virtually Normal: An Argument About Homosexuality.* New York:
Alfred A Knopf
Terry J (1999) *An American Obsession. Science, Medicine and Homosexuality in
Modern Society.* Chicago, IL: University of Chicago Press
Torres S (1993) Prime time lesbianism. In H Abelove, M A Barale and D M Halperin
(eds) *The Lesbian and Gay Studies Reader* (pp 176–185). London: Routledge
Vaid U (1995) *Virtual Equality: The Mainstreaming of Gay and Lesbian Liberation.*
New York: Doubleday

Waites M (2003) Equality at last? Homosexuality, heterosexuality and the age of
   consent in the United Kingdom. *Sociology* 37(4):637–655
Waldby C (1996) *AIDS and the Body Politic: Biomedicine and Sexual Difference.* New
   York: Routledge
Warner M (2000) *The Trouble with Normal: Sex, Politics, and the Ethics of Queer Life.*
   Cambridge, MA: Harvard University Press
Watney S (1994) *Practices of Freedom: Selected Writings on HIV/AIDS.* London: Rivers
   Oram Press
Weeks J (1990) *Sex, Politics and Society.* 2nd ed. London: Longman
Weeks J (1998) The sexual citizen. *Theory, Culture and Society* 15(3–4):35–52
Wilton T (1995) *Lesbian Studies: Setting an Agenda.* London: Routledge
Woods C (1995) *State of the Queer Nation: A Critique of Gay and Lesbian Politics in
   1990s Britain.* London: Cassell

Diane Richardson is Professor of Sociology and Social Policy and
Director of the Centre for Gender and Women's Studies at the
University of Newcastle, UK. She has written extensively about feminism and sexuality, including articles published in, among other journals, *Sociology, Sociological Review, Sexualities, Journal of Gender
Studies, Critical Social Policy, Culture, Health and Sexuality.* She is
the author of *Theorising Heterosexuality* (Open University Press,
1996), *Rethinking Sexuality* (Sage, 2000) and, co-edited with Steven
Seidman, the *Handbook of Lesbian and Gay Studies* (Sage, 2002). Her
most recent book (with Mark Casey and Janice McLaughlin) is
entitled *Intersections Between Feminist and Queer Theory*, to be published in 2006 by Palgrave.

Chapter 7

Making Space for "Neo-communitarianism"? The Third Sector, State and Civil Society in the UK

Nicholas R Fyfe

Introduction

Recent years have seen a growing interest in the role of neo-liberalism in the remaking of urban space. Market-led economic and social restructuring, the hall-mark of the neo-liberal political project, has had a profound impact on cities in many parts of the globe, resulting in the intensification of uneven spatial development and prompting a "revival of the local" as a strategically important arena in which local and national political-economic elites are "aggressively attempting to promote economic regeneration from below" (Brenner and Theodore 2002a:342). Over time, however, there have been important shifts and changes in the nature of neo-liberal urban policy (Peck and Tickell 2002). During the 1990s, the urban became an important "institutional laboratory" for state-initiated policy experiments to address the social costs and political repercussions of economic polarization and social exclusion associated with neo-liberalism (Brenner and Theodore 2002b:374). These policy experiments have taken different forms in different places depending on institutional legacies and the balance of political forces. As Jessop (2002) outlines, such experiments have typically included neo-statism ("a market-conforming but state-sponsored approach to economic and social restructuring"), neo-corporatism ("a negotiated approach to restructuring by private, public and third sector actors") and, of specific interest here, neo-communitarianism, emphasising the contribution of the third sector "located between market and state" (463) to economic development and social cohesion.

Jessop's identification of the importance of the third sector within the context of neo-liberalisation clearly resonates with current policy developments in many advanced capitalist societies. The last ten years have witnessed a remarkable revival of interest in the role of the third sector as a possible "panacea" for the problems facing neo-liberalising states. Faced with fears about declining political participation, anxieties about meeting welfare needs, and worries about the nature of citizenship, the third sector has come to be regarded as "a place where politics can be democratised, active citizenship strengthened, the public sphere reinvigorated and welfare programmes suited to pluralist needs designed and delivered" (Brown et al 2000:57). Thus, as Jessop observes, "even where both the national and international levels are dominated by attempts to promote a neo-liberal regime shift", third sector organisations have become a central focus of neo-communitarian strategies for addressing problems of social exclusion at a local level (Jessop 2002:464). In the US, for example, the restructuring of a Fordist welfare state into a post-Fordist workfare state (Peck 2001) has involved the localisation of responsibility for welfare and an increasingly important role for voluntary, non-profit organisations. Similarly in Canada, Jiwani (2000) notes how "the combined forces of globalisation and neo-liberal ideology" have placed greater emphasis on the third sector in the delivery of public services. In the UK, which provides the immediate context for this paper, "New Labour's" programme of welfare reforms (Clarke, Gewirtz and McLaughlin 2000; Powell 1999) and Prime Minister Blair's "Third Way" political philosophy (Giddens 1998) have all contributed to the "mainstreaming" of the third sector into UK public policy (Kendall 2000).

In understanding the nature and implications of the role of the third sector in neo-communitarian strategies, it is vital to move beyond Jessop's overly simplistic characterisation of the third sector as lying "between market and state" (2002:463). The third sector is, of course, notoriously difficult to define. In general terms it is taken to include "self-governing associations of people who have joined together to take action for public benefit", that are independent, do not distribute profits and are governed by non-paid volunteers (Taylor 1992:171). But rather than lying "between" market and state, as Jessop suggests, the third sector is more accurately conceptualised as lying within a triangular "tension field", the cornerstones of which are the state, the market and the informal sector, with "the characteristics of the landscapes of organisations in the third sector ... simultaneously shaped by the respective influences coming from state institutions, the market economy and the 'informal sector' of family and community" (Evers 1992:162). From this perspective, assessing the nature and implications of contemporary neo-communitarian strategies requires close examination of the interplay between the third sector and the "cornerstones" of the "triangular tension" field that it occupies. As a first step in such an analysis, this paper examines the relationship between the third sector and the state and the wider implications of this relationship for civil society. Focusing on the UK, I first trace the *repositioning* of the third sector in contemporary political discourse. Under Prime Minister Blair's Labour government, the third sector has emerged as not only crucial to "New Labour's" programme of welfare reform but also to its wider ambitions of tackling social exclusion by reinvigorating civil society in terms of encouraging active citizenship and fostering social capital. According to Labour, government support has resulted in a "quiet revolution" with the "transformation of the third sector ready to rival market and state" (Brown 2004). In making space for neo-communitarianism, however, the government's strategy has also involved a fundamental *reconfiguring* of the governance of the third sector, evident in the voluntary sector compacts which are discussed in the following section. Then, case study evidence from the city of Glasgow is used to reflect critically on the wider assumptions within Labour's policy discourses that neo-communitarianism can create spaces for the development of social capital and active citizenship within civil society. In particular, this section shows that the *(re)structuring* of third sector organisations calls into question whether local voluntary activity is capable of rekindling a sense of active citizenship or reversing the decline of social capital as envisaged by national policy.

Repositioning the Third Sector: From "Shadowy Enclave" to "Centre Stage"

Within a few years of coming to power in 1997, the UK's Labour government had significantly repositioned the role of the third sector within national policy discourse. "From being a shadow enclave at the periphery of the mental map of policy makers and shapers" Wrigglesworth and Kendall observe, "the [third] sector has increasingly occupied centre stage in their minds" (2000:1). Addressing an audience of voluntary organisation representatives in 2004, Labour's Chancellor of the Exchequer, Gordon Brown, triumphantly declared that over the last decade there has been "a quiet revolution in how voluntary action and charitable work serves the community" (Brown 2004). However, this "quiet revolution" has its roots in the policies of the Conservative governments in the 1980s and 1990s. Articulating arguments advanced by many on the political right, the Conservatives championed the third sector as an antidote to an unresponsive, bureaucratic welfare state that stifles choice and community initiative. As a result, voluntary organisations came to play increasingly important roles in areas such as local community development, health, and social services, "often in contractual relationships [with government] through which they received substantial sums of money" (Plowden 2003:416). Indeed, by encouraging the devolution of service responsibilities to voluntary organisations, government funding for voluntary organisations, covering grants and contracts, rose from £1850 million in 1982/83 to £4198 million ten years later (Home Office 2001).

With the election of a Labour government in 1997 the momentum behind developing the role and responsibilities of the third sector in UK society has significantly increased as part of Labour's programme of welfare reforms (Clarke, Gewirtz and McLaughlin 2000; Powell 1999). The ideological and political foundations of this interest in the third sector lie with the interplay between neo-liberalism and neo-communitarianism which has characterised the development of Labour policy. Keen to distance itself from both "Old" Labour Left (pro-state, anti-market) and the Thatcherite Right (pro-market and anti-state), "new" Labour has embraced a new, Third Way political philosophy (Giddens 1998). While this contains a neo-liberal emphasis on the need to engage with the new "realities" of globalisation and embrace the market, choice and competition, it also adopts a neo-communitarian stance by stressing the strategic importance of civil society for social cohesion and economic vitality. Informed partly by the work of Amitai Etzioni (1995, 1997; see too Levitas 1998), this neo-communitarian emphasis on civil society has been crucial not only in providing Labour with the type of "post-Thatcherite edge it wants" (Driver and Martell 1997:36) but also in promoting the role of the third sector within Labour policy discourse. For Labour, the third sector represents the "organised vanguard" of civil society. "Civil society", Gordon Brown declares, "finds its greatest embodiment in the strength of voluntary organisations—a genuine third sector established not for self or for profit but for mutual aid and, most often, to provide help and support for those in need" (Brown 2004:4). For the third sector to flourish, however, Labour's third way philosophy draws on a further element of Etzioni's communitarianism: the importance of partnership between state and civil society. Etzioni maintains that "Though government should not seek to replace local communities, it may need to empower them by strategies of support" (1995:260), a view clearly echoed by Blair. "A key challenge of progressive politics", Blair argues, "is to use the state as an enabling force, protecting effective communities and voluntary organisations and encouraging their growth to tackle new needs in partnership" (quoted in Amin, Cameron and Hudson 2002:23).

An early indication of New Labour's commitment to the third sector was their pre-election publication *Building the Future Together: Labour's Policies for Partnership Between the Government and the Voluntary Sector* (Labour Party 1997). This explained that in rejecting the old and arid split between "public" and "private", Labour has recognised the richness and diversity of independent organisations and their potential (1997:3). Once in power, Prime Minister Blair underlined his own particular commitment for the third sector in his pamphlet *The Third Way: New Politics for the New Century*:

> We seek a diverse but inclusive society ... promoting civic activism as a complement to modern government ... The Third Way ... recognises the need for government to forge new partnerships with the voluntary sector. Whether in education, health, social work, crime prevention or the care of children, "enabling" government strengthens civil society rather than weakening it, and helps families and communities improve their own performance ... the state, voluntary sector and individuals working together. New Labour's task is to strengthen the range and quality of such partnerships (Blair 1998:14; quoted in Kendall 2000:16).

This commitment to the third sector has now been translated into a range of policy initiatives. At a strategic level, the Labour government has introduced voluntary sector "compacts", setting out commitments by the governments and the voluntary sector in each of the UK's four jurisdictions (England, Wales, Scotland and Northern Ireland) to improve the ways they work with each other. The government has also examined the potential for increasing the role voluntary organisations can play in public service delivery (HM Treasury 2002) and explored the scope for modernising the infrastructure for regulating the third sector (Cabinet Office 2002). More specific policy initiatives include the Active Communities Initiative, designed to increase the role of volunteering in community life, the New Deal for Communities focused on involving community organisations in the regeneration of deprived neighbourhoods, and "*future*builders", an investment fund to strengthen the service delivery role of voluntary organisations in the areas of health and social care, crime and social cohesion, in education and for children and young people (HM Treasury 2002:32).

In effectively "mainstreaming" the third sector into public policy, however, it is clear that the Labour government's repositioning of the third sector has two distinct but overlapping aims. First, at an instrumental level, the government wishes to make space for voluntary organisations to play a more prominent role in the delivery of public services. After years of privatisation under successive Conservative governments, voluntary organisations are recognised as having vital resources to tackle local problems of social exclusion that are now "outside the reach of state bureaucracy and beyond the interests of the private sector" (Morison 2000:105). As the government's review of *The Role of the Voluntary and Community Sector in Service Delivery* (HM Treasury 2002) makes clear, third sector organisations are seen as having a comparative advantage over agencies in other sectors which "enable them to operate in environments which the State and its agents have found difficult or impossible" (16). Public service workers, for example, "are often perceived as representatives of an authority which certain groups have learned to mistrust" whereas those in the third sector are "independent of government and therefore free to be unequivocally on the user's side" (16). But in making space for this expanded role for the third sector in public service delivery, it is also clear that the government wishes to rework the governance of the UK third sector via the voluntary sector compacts in ways which entail "seeking to mobilise a reserve army of support effectively and *on its own terms*" (Morison 2000:129, my emphasis). This reconfiguration of state–third sector relations is discussed in more detail in the next section.

The second aim of the government's repositioning of the third sector reflects Labour neo-communitarian inspired "philosophical enthusiasm for the third sector as an integral part of civil society" (Kendall 2000:542). As one government minister explained, "The Government is passionately committed to the work of the voluntary sector. We believe that voluntary and community sector organisations have a crucial role to play in the reform of public services *and reinvigoration of civic life*" (Boateng 2002:3, my emphasis). From this perspective, government policy clearly views third sector organisations as key local sites for promoting social cohesion via the development of citizenship and social capital. The localism of such organisations means that they are viewed as being better placed than state bureaucracies to develop "customised solutions to local problems of social exclusion" (Amin, Cameron and Hudson 2002:28). Furthermore, third sector organisations are seen as providing environments in which individuals can demonstrate their responsibilities as citizens as well as places that provide opportunities for empowerment by involving individuals in the delivery of services, providing "opportunities for social participation, for democratic involvement at the local level, and thus for active citizenship" (Turner 2001:200). The dependence of much of the third sector on voluntary effort thus neatly dovetails with the Labour government's doctrine that "individual rights must be earned through the acceptance of civic responsibilities" (Johnstone and Whitehead 2004:10). Labour has also embraced the arguments of Putnam and others that the third sector is a key site for the production and reproduction of social capital, those norms and networks that can improve economic efficiency and social cohesion (Putnam 1993). As Gordon Brown (2004) confidently declared, "We know from the theory and evidence on what is called social capital that societies with strong voluntary sectors and civic society institutions have lower crime, greater social cohesion and better performing economies than those without".

Against this background, it is clearly important to subject these twin elements of the government's neo-communitarian commitment to the third sector to further critical scrutiny. The next section focuses on the reconfiguring of state–third sector relations by examining the implications of the voluntary compacts for the governance of the sector. The following section draws on case study evidence from Glasgow to assess the contribution that voluntary organisations are making to the wider neo-communitarian agenda of fostering citizenship and social capital.

Reconfiguring the Third sector: The State, Governmentality and the UK "Compacts"

Representing "an unparalleled step change in the positioning of the voluntary sector in public policy" (Kendall 2003:46), the compacts between government and the voluntary sector launched in 1998 are the centrepiece of the Labour government's new found commitment to the third sector. The idea for a compact, however, was first suggested under the previous Conservative government but rejected on the grounds that it would "imply a more rigid relationship than is appropriate, given the diverse and dynamic nature of voluntary organisations" (quoted in Plowden 2003:419). Labour had no such doubts. After winning the 1997 general election, the Labour government initiated negotiations with the voluntary sector umbrella groups in England, Wales, Scotland and Northern Ireland, resulting in four national compacts (Home Office 1998; Northern Ireland Office 1998; Scottish Office 1998; Welsh Office 1998) and a commitment to develop local compacts between the statutory and voluntary sectors in each local authority area.

Comprising a series of agreed statements on the respective roles of government and voluntary organisations, the national compacts are essentially an "enabling mechanism" to enhance the relationship between government and the voluntary sector (Lewis 1999). The compacts spell out how central government will "recognise and support the sector's independence", including its right to: challenge policy; facilitate access to enable voluntary organisations to contribute to the policy development process; and "apply best practice in funding and in the administration of grants". For the voluntary sector, the compacts contain parallel undertakings. Voluntary sector groups agree: to "represent accurately and honestly the views of their sectoral constituencies"; to "promote the value of collaborative working with the public sector"; to "champion the importance of good management of financial resources"; and recognise that public funding is provided on the basis of its contribution to government "policy priorities".

While tempting to dismiss the compacts as "warm words, platitudes and generalities" (Morison 2000:113), many have argued these documents are central to a fundamental reworking of the relations between the state and the UK's third sector. Dahrendorf (2001), for example, has suggested that the compacts are a sign of nothing less than the incorporation of the third sector into the state, echoing concerns raised by Wolch (1989:201) of the dangers posed by the development of a "shadow state" apparatus, comprising voluntary organisations "with collective service responsibilities previously shouldered by the public ... but controlled in both formal and informal ways by the state". Although Dahrendorf's conclusion has been dismissed as overly simplistic (Craig et al 2002), the changes in the governance of the UK's third sector initiated by the compacts exemplify Foucauldian ideas of governmentality (Morison 2000). For Foucault, a key question concerning the exercise of state power was how is it possible for governments to shape and control increasingly disparate and numerous subjects in ways that facilitate effective governance to take place? (Raco 2003:76). The answer lay, Foucault contended, in the "emergence of new and distinctive mentalities of government and governmental rationalities which involve a calculating pre-occupation with activities directed at shaping and channelling and guiding the conduct of others" (Hunt and Wickham 1994:26). The compacts, along with their associated codes of practice (covering areas such as funding, consultation and volunteering), represent just such an attempt by government in the cultivation of subjectivity and are a way of mobilising the voluntary sector in its own governance. As Morison has noted:

> Through the compacts process, the sector is being encouraged to exercise a "responsibilised autonomy" and pursue its interests through a framework where the "systems of thought" and "systems of action" emphasise and reinforce an economic rationality alongside the more traditional welfare ethos ... Standards, guidelines and reporting mechanisms together will transform the ways in which at least some of the voluntary sector think about themselves and exercise choices within a newly constructed framework that reinforces economic forms of reasoning. What may be presented as increasing autonomy, a chance to govern oneself, is in fact a reconfiguration of rationalities so that the self-interest of (part of) the sector aligns with the interests of a state seeking to mobilise a reserve army of support effectively and on its own terms. (Morison 2000:119, 129–130)

In addition to their role in constructing new subjectivities, however, the development of the compacts also illustrates the crucial interplay between governance, space and state power. As Raco has noted, "one of the defining features of advanced liberal governance is the shift towards new scales of action with 'local' or more 'in touch' scales being promoted as the basis for new forms of social action and conduct" (2003:78). The compact process reflects this at two levels. First, at a UK scale, individual compacts have been negotiated separately for England, Wales, Scotland and Northern Ireland. Thus, although each compact contains an identical "message from the Prime Minister", there are specific forewords from the chairs of the national bodies representing voluntary sector organisations in each part of the UK and there are subtle variations in the specific details of each compact. The "shape" of the English compact, for example, is symmetrical, containing obligations and commitments for both government and the voluntary sector. The compacts for Wales, Scotland and Northern Ireland, however, are asymmetrical, emphasising the obligations of government and with less emphasis on the commitments of the voluntary sector (Hayton 2003:22). Second, at a local authority level, central government has encouraged the adoption of local compacts based on similar principles and undertakings that characterise the national compacts. A mapping exercise examining the development of local compacts revealed that the process has been highly uneven. In some areas, changes in local government policy resulting in cuts in funding to voluntary organisations had undermined the trust needed to negotiate a successful compact. There is concern, too, that the compact process is not reaching beyond the main umbrella organisations. As Bridge and Taylor (2001) observe, "For voluntary and community organisations, the 'abstract' principles of a compact may not feel like a priority when there are many more immediate pressures". Despite a government target for 100% coverage of England by March 2004, there were still 270 local authorities that by March 2003 had not established local compacts, leading to concern that "momentum will be lost and confidence that the rhetoric of partnership can work in practice will ebb away" (Carrington 2002:12–13). Indeed, this uneven spatial development of local compacts illustrates "there is no such thing as complete or total control of an object or set of objects—governance is necessarily incomplete" (Malpas and Wickham 1995:40).

The (Re)Structuring of the Third Sector and the Differential Development of Social Capital and Citizenship

Although it is still too early to establish precisely what impact the compacts are having on individual third sector organisations in the UK, several commentators have drawn attention to the ways in which the compacts contribute to a restructuring of the third sector into two broad elements: "one genuinely voluntary, happily remote from government ... and the other linked to government ... subject to all sorts of controls and rules, and voluntary in name only" (Dahrendorf 2003:xiv). "[I]t is hard to overlook the fact", Dahrendorf (2001) suggests, "that there is a Compact sector which benefits from organised relations with government and a non-Compact sector which does not need such relations". Similarly, as Morison observes, the compacts provide a mechanism whereby the more "managerially minded" parts of the voluntary sector are being encouraged by the state to pursue their interests through a framework of "good practice" which emphasises and reinforces an economic rationality rather than a traditional volunteering ethos. Such speculation over the bifurcation of the third sector is not new. Over ten years ago, Knight (1993) reflected on the "divorce" that was occurring between "grassroots" voluntary organisations and much larger, "corporatist" organisations. Far from being a source of anxiety, Knight believed this divorce to be "highly desirable" (1993:297). It would leave "grassroots" organisations free to pursue an agenda of change and reform, while large corporatist organisations would focus on service delivery. Against the background of Labour's neo-communitarian agenda, however, the bifurcation of the sector has important implications in relation to the wider contribution of voluntary organisations to the development of civil society. In particular, the assumption within policy discourses that voluntary organisations are key sites for the production of social capital and active citizenship is increasingly being questioned as evidence of the differential development of social capital and citizenship emerges linked to both the structural characteristics and contextual conditions of third sector organisations. In order to illustrate this, this section draws on case study evidence from Glasgow to show how the structure and political context of the city's third sector has had important implications for the differential development of social capital and citizenship. It will be useful to begin, however, by providing a brief sketch of the wider context and character of Glasgow's third sector.

An Overview of the Development and Structure of Glasgow's Third Sector

With its glittering array of new cultural institutions, high-class shopping malls and gentrified enclaves, Glasgow perhaps more than any other UK city has increasingly come to be represented in academic discourses in terms of a transition from the urban managerialism of the "welfare city" to the urban entrepreneurialism of the "neo-liberal city" (Brenner and Theodore 2002b). As Macleod (2002:615) notes, the city is now "regularly distinguished as a successful model of place-marketing and urban entrepreneurialism" while "the city's elite appears to be suspending any remaining managerialist commitment to extend social citizenship and spatial justice". Yet such a conclusion seems premature. With some of the highest concentrations of unemployment, poverty and ill-health of any major city in the UK (over half its wards are among the most deprived 10% of wards in Scotland; Fyfe and Milligan 2003), the city faces huge challenges in addressing the economic and social problems associated with neo-liberal urbanism and part of the response to these challenges has involved a neo-communitarian emphasis on the role of the third sector.

The roots of this higher profile for the third sector in Glasgow can be traced back to the1980s and 1990s when successive Conservative central governments used legislation to enable a process of substituting collective public service provision by private and voluntary sector provision at a local level. Although this contributed to a period of voluntary sector expansion in the city, weakening municipal dominance of service delivery, this process came to an abrupt halt in the mid-1990s with the shift from regionalism to localism in the governance of the city. The abolition of Strathclyde Regional Council and the tightening of the boundaries of the new Glasgow City Council precipitated a fiscal crisis as the city lost some of its more affluent suburbs and saw its total population decline. The resulting drop in revenues led the City Council to introduce a £68 million package of spending cuts, partly though cutting grants to third sector bodies (Carmichael and Midwinter 1999). Although data on the precise impact of these cuts are unavailable, the fact that local authority funding is one of the main sources of income for many of the third sector organisations in the city meant that those working in voluntary organisations in this period observed significant reductions in the size of some organisations while other organisations disappeared altogether. In relation to the city's social economy, for example, it has meant that this now tends to be dominated by much larger organisations than might otherwise have been the case because they have had the resources to "ride out" some of the changes in funding regimes that have occurred (Amin, Cameron and Hudson 2002:65–66).

Following devolution and the establishment of a Labour-controlled Scottish Parliament in 1999, the third sector has, as elsewhere in the UK, clearly enjoyed a political renaissance. As Burt and Taylor (2002:93) observe, "there seems to be a genuine commitment on the part of the Scottish administration to engage voluntary organisations in the governance of Scotland" and that underpinning this commitment is a neo-communitarian concern that the voluntary sector can "prove effective in resolving major social 'problems' that fall between the interstices of public and private provision". Evidence of this repositioning of the third sector at a Scottish level include new institutional arrangements within the Scottish Executive, involving the expansion of the Voluntary Issues Unit, the re-launching of the Scottish Compact in 2003 (Scottish Executive 2003) and the recommendations of the Scottish Charity Law Commission for a more politically active third sector. This national level support for the third sector to play a more influential role has had important implications at the local level. Evidence of this within Glasgow is provided by the formation of the Glasgow Alliance in 1998. The Glasgow Alliance comprises representatives of central government (the Scottish Executive), local government (Glasgow City Council), the business community and the third sector, and is charged with developing and implementing a strategy for the social and economic regeneration of the city. Exemplifying the shift from government to governance within cities, the Glasgow Alliance oversees the city's five Social Inclusion Partnership (SIP) areas that cover those districts of the city with particularly acute problems of multiple deprivation and which have been allocated over £100 million of government funding between 1999 and 2004. As the most recent of a series of area-based state funding programmes to support the role of the third sector in deprived areas of the city, the SIPs are of crucial significance to understanding the uneven spatial development of the sector within the city. With most of the city's voluntary organisations heavily reliant on public funds for their survival (Fyfe and Milligan 2003; Maloney, Smith and Stoker 1999), the SIPs have become the focus of what one voluntary sector representative graphically described as a "feeding frenzy" among voluntary organisations from across the city, contributing to a geography of third sector activity which is strongly skewed towards localised areas of high social deprivation in the northeast, northwest and south of the city.

In terms of the organisational characteristics of the city's third sector, evidence from two recent surveys of voluntary organisations in the city indicate a high level of structural diversity. Maloney, Smith and Stoker's (1999) survey of 300 organisations revealed that they range in size and income from quite small (4% had less than 10 members and 8% had an annul income below £1000) to very large, well-resourced groups (3% had over 10,000 members and 10% had an annual income of over £1 million). This survey also indicated that over a third of the city's voluntary organisations rely on the state for their main income, a finding underlined in Fyfe and Milligan's (2003) more narrowly focused survey of 147 organisations within the city's voluntary welfare sector. This showed that for 52% of organisations their single largest source of funding came from the state. Fyfe and Milligan's survey also highlighted the structural diversity of the city's third sector: 46% of welfare voluntary organisations were local independent groups, 23% were independent groups but affiliated to regional and national organisations, and 31% were branches of larger regional and national organisations operating across the city and elsewhere in Scotland. Most organisations, however, were relatively small. Of all the organisations that responded to the survey, 44% had no full-time paid staff and of those that did have full-time staff, a third only employed one or two people.

The Differential Development of Social Capital

These structural characteristics of Glasgow's third sector and the local political context have important implications in relation to the development of social capital and citizenship. In terms of social capital, Maloney, Smith and Stoker (1999) studied the relationships of trust and information flows among the city's voluntary organisations and between local voluntary organisations and Glasgow City Council. Using a questionnaire survey of voluntary organisations (n = 307), this study revealed some of the contours of this uneven distribution of social capital. Although there were high levels of trust among voluntary organisations in the city (72% of organisations agreed with the statement that they trusted other voluntary groups in the city), only 37% of organisations agreed that there were high levels of trust between their organisation and Glasgow City Council, and even fewer organisations (14%) believed there were high levels of trust between the city's voluntary sector as a whole and Glasgow City Council. The structural characteristics of voluntary organisations appear to have an important impact on these perceptions of trust. In terms of relationships with the Glasgow City Council, levels of trust were consistently higher for organisations regularly involved in City Council consultation forums such as SIPs, those that had regular contact with councillors and council officers, those that had an annual income of over £50,000 and those for whom a City Council grant was a very important source of income. In terms of relationships within the voluntary sector, voluntary organisations regularly involved in the City Council's consultation forums have higher levels of trust in other voluntary organisations as do those that are members of voluntary organisation umbrella groups in the city. In terms of perception of information flows, those organisations that believed there were good information flows with the city council also tended to be those with regular contact with the councillors and council officers, who had an annual income of over £50,000 and for whom a council grant was an important source of income.

These findings are important because they indicate that the connections between the third sector and social capital are more complex than either the assumptions of the national policy discourses or the "Putnam school" of social capital allow for. Social capital in Glasgow is clearly differentially distributed between different types of voluntary organisation. "[T]here is", Maloney, Smith and Stoker (1999) conclude, "a distributional quality to social capital—certain groups may be excluded from accessing inter-organisational social capital. The important finding here is that trust and information flows are related to levels and quality of contact". Thus, it is not simply the number of voluntary organisations in an area that is important in terms of the development of social capital; the characteristics of those organisations are also significant. Moreover, this Glasgow case study also exposes an important weakness in national policy discourses. Echoing Putnam's formulation of social capital, national policy discourse offers a "bottom up" or "society-centred" perspective (see also Mohan and Mohan 2002) with social capital viewed as flowing from civil society to the state. Yet this ignores the crucial role played by political structures and institutions in shaping the context of voluntary activity and hence the creation of social capital. The findings of this Glasgow case study clearly point to the way in which social capital can be actively generated and promoted by the city council though the establishment of consultative forums, outreach work and the funding regime. However, given that local authorities "do not have the resources or even the will to engage with all [voluntary] groups in the city ... it becomes clear that in urban areas, inter-organisational social capital is neither brokered equitably nor distributed evenly" (Maloney, Smith and Stoker 1999).

The Differential Development of Citizenship
In addition to these findings concerning the differential development of social capital, there is also evidence of the differential development of citizenship among third sector organisations in Glasgow. Drawing on interviews ($n = 32$) with voluntary organisation staff from three areas of social welfare in the city (health, crime and criminal justice, and black and ethnic minority issues), Fyfe and Milligan (2003) revealed important contrasts between, on the one hand, grassroots groups committed to non-hierarchical structures and maximising the decision-making inputs of service users and, on the other hand, more "corporatist" groups characterised by processes of bureaucratisation and professionalisation. These "corporatist" voluntary organisations have very different implications for the development of citizenship

than more traditional "grassroots" or "activist" organisations (see Brown et al 2000). The latter are typically characterised by organisational structures which attempt to maximise participant input, routinely draw on the rhetorics of empowerment and participation and are thus closely associated with the development of active citizenship. Exemplifying these features was a local mental health organisation:

> The objectives of the organisations were to develop a community-led initiative, empower service users and put in place services where they [the users] want to see them ... it was constantly going into local communities saying, "OK, how is it you want us to deliver services? Where is it you want us to deliver services? What services is it that you want us to deliver?" (Co-ordinator of local mental health organisation)

By contrast, "corporatist" voluntary organisations are characterised by hierarchical, bureaucratic structures with an internal division of labour between managers, welfare professionals and volunteers. Such organisations are more oriented towards the development of passive forms of citizenship, where service users are consumers of welfare delivered by a professionalised workforce of paid staff and highly trained volunteers. The emergence of these more corporatist characteristics often reflected a process of organisational growth and restructuring in an attempt to deliver services to greater numbers of people. As a respondent from the Glasgow branch of a national mental health organisation explained:

> As an organisation gets bigger, and puts in more and more systems, and there are more and more people to manage, you lose that tremendous flexibility you had when you were very small. But it's a catch 22 situation: if you want to grow big enough to provide the levels of service needed, so some extent, those layers of management and administration are absolutely essential or it would be *chaos*! (Co-ordinator of national mental health organisation)

The existence of such "differential citizenship" within the third sector cannot be understood simply in terms of internal characteristics of the organisations themselves. As Lake and Newman (2003:117) argue, "[I]nternal organisational characteristics ... are a symptom rather than a cause, ... and are themselves a function of the larger social, political and institutional context situating the non-profit sector, allocating its resources, and delimiting its programmatic capability". There was clear evidence in support of this argument in Glasgow, where the pressure on third sector organisations to become more bureaucratic and professional often came directly from government. One example was a criminal justice organisation which was restructured from seventeen local, independent groups scattered across the city to become one centrally managed organisation with "branches" providing comprehensive coverage of the city. As the organisation's director explained:

> we were the subject of a management review by the Scottish Office [which became the Scottish Executive after devolution] ... and they were essentially saying that, "Well what you've done up to now is absolutely great, but frankly in the current climate you need to be able to deliver services on a more consistent basis across the city. It's not kind of politically acceptable [to have ad hoc organisations]. (Director of national criminal justice organisation)

While such processes of bureaucratic restructuring can bring important benefits in terms of service delivery, the hierarchical and asymmetrical power relations that can result from this process may be profoundly disempowering to those that work within an organisation at a local level. As a member of staff working in the local branch of a national voluntary organisation explained, "we don't get as much support as we used to ... The decision making structures are becoming more bureaucratic and distant".

In parallel with the bureaucratic restructuring of third sector organisations, there have been attempts to professionalise services. In some cases this is through the use of "professional social entrepreneurs" rather than local people to lead regeneration partnerships, while in other fields it involves providing greater training to volunteers or, in some cases, abandoning the use of volunteers all together because of a concern at the lack of "professionalism" displayed by some volunteers in the delivery of complex services. However, although increasing the professionalisation of welfare voluntary services allows organisations to provide more complex services, it clearly circumscribes the opportunities for volunteering and thus for fostering active citizenship. As one health organisation explained:

> In terms of [being a voluntary organisation] we are 400 people, and the only people who regularly volunteer are the board of management. It's very much a staff organisation, and we're looking at how to make use of the volunteering bit ... we don't have the scale to make it worthwhile in terms of the time and trouble in investing in managing volunteers to run a service. (Co-ordinator of regional health organisation).

Moreover, professionalisation, like bureaucratisation, can disempower citizens by reproducing the distinction between client and bureaucrat and lead to service users becoming passive recipients of standardised welfare programmes.

These tensions arising as a result of the bureaucratic restructuring and professionalisation of voluntary welfare organisations highlight some of the unresolved ambiguities that surround the Labour government's neo-communitarian commitment to the third sector as a space for fostering active citizenship. As the earlier discussion of the UK compacts indicates, by emphasising the importance of "professionalism" and "economic rationality" rather than a traditional volunteering ethos, Labour's approach to the third sector is contributing to an increasing division between grassroots voluntary groups and "a new breed of professionalised, well-funded and well-organised voluntary organisations" (Morison 2000:103). As the evidence from Glasgow indicates, this has important implications for the connections between voluntarism and citizenship.

Concluding Comments

The structure and dynamics of Glasgow's third sector clearly disclose some of the tensions that underlie the UK government's neo-communitarian strategy of using the third sector organisations to provide "professional" and cost-effective welfare services *and* expecting such organisations to contribute to the reinvigoration of civil society by fostering the development of social capital and citizenship. Indeed, current policy developments in the UK appear to exemplify what Brown has termed "the paradox of the shadow state" (1997:116). If third sector organisations are to conform to the localised vision in national policy discourse by being essentially neighbourhood-based, grassroots groups, they are unlikely to be able to contribute to service delivery in the way that the government hopes. Yet it is clear that organisations that do professionalise and restructure their services run the risk of disempowering citizens both within organisations as a result of developing a hierarchical structure with clear divisions between volunteers and paid staff, and outside organisations by reproducing the bureaucrat–client relationship characteristic of government organisations. Such a scenario means that third sector organisations often fail to contribute to the government's wider neo-communitarian agenda of fostering active citizenship and "the reinvigoration of civic life" (Boateng 2002:3).

Faced with this dilemma, some have argued that it is vital for third sector organisations to distance themselves from the state. Amin, Cameron and Hudson (2002:125), for example, insist that for third sector organisations to realise their potential means resisting pressures to conform to "the image of the mainstream" and instead acting as a space of "alterity" based around "advocacy for another way of life; … social commitment, ethical/environmental citizenship, and work as a vehicle for self and social enhancement". Similarly, in the

United States where there have been calls for the third sector to embrace the "modern reality of … working collaboratively with government" (Salamon,1999:20–21), Wolch (1999) has articulated a counter-argument, advocating that the third sector should act more as a "space of resistance" and less as a shadow state (26). Wolch's concern is that the partnership approach, exemplified in the UK by the compacts, is deeply problematic for third sector organisations. Such organisations are, she contends, typically "junior partners" so that "when government defunds social programs delivered by voluntary organisation partners, crises ensue, revealing the sector's vulnerability as contract or shadow-state partner" (26). Moreover, Wolch argues that the notion of citizenship envisaged in partnership arrangements (and underpinning the UK government's neo-communitarian agenda) is one narrowly defined in terms of "a political identity of rights and responsibilities" (Brown 1997:5) and does not allow for a "radical openness to alternative standpoints, and active incorporation of different, marginalised voices from the periphery into a [third] sector traditionally dominated by society's mainstream groups" (Wolch 1999:29).

The scope for third sector organisations to act as spaces of "alterity" or "resistance" clearly remains within the UK given that many organisations will choose not to subscribe to the government's neo-communitarian strategy with the result that "[c]ivil society will invariably remain incompletely domesticated" (Morison 2000:131). Nevertheless, there is also evidence that in some contexts the ability of communities to resist the government's attempts to drive forward its neo-communitarian agenda may be limited. Returning to Glasgow, the city recently witnessed the transfer of 85,000 local authority homes to the not-for-profit Glasgow Housing Agency (GHA). The rationale for this housing stock transfer from the public to the third sector, articulated by members of the Labour administrations in London and Edinburgh and endorsed by Glasgow City Council, is that it will permit community ownership and "bring benefits in empowerment, management and financing" (Mooney and Poole 2004:11). The government's hope is that "the stereotypical welfare dependent council tenant" will be transformed into "someone who will play a greater role in the management of their community" (2004:11). However, the transfer proposals were fiercely opposed by many grassroots groups. There were concerns that the transfer of the housing stock was a form of privatisation given the role that banks and other financial institutions will play in the management of transferred housing, and that stock transfer involves the removal of publicly owned assets from local democratic control. Moreover, there are already concerns that the operation of the GHA is proving profoundly disempowering because tenants are heavily outnumbered on the GHA management committee by professional GHA officials. While supporters of the housing stock transfer claim it is giving tenants in the non-market sector the benefits of choice in how their homes are owned, managed and financed, for critics such developments exemplify the perception that "New Labour's Third Way exhibits a ... neo-liberal economic sensibility camouflaged in the legitimating rhetoric of neo-communitarianism" (Hay and Watson 1999:172).

Acknowledgements

The very helpful comments of the three referees are acknowledged. I am also grateful to Christine Milligan for allowing me to draw upon our joint research on voluntary organisations in Glasgow funded by the Economic and Social Research Council (award reference number R000223093).

References

Amin A, Cameron A and Hudson R (2002) *Placing the Social Economy*. London: Routledge

Blair T (1998) *The Third Way: New Politics for the New Century*. London: The Fabian Society

Boateng P (2002) Foreword. In HM Treasury *The Role of the Voluntary and Community Sector in Service Delivery: A Cross-Cutting Review* (p 3). London: HM Treasury

Brenner N and Theodore N (2002a) Preface: From the "New localism" to the spaces of neoliberalism. *Antipode* 34(3):341–347

Brenner N and Theodore N (2002b) Cities and the geographies of "actually existing neoliberalism". *Antipode* 34(3):349–379

Bridge G and Taylor M (2001) Evaluating the significance of local compacts. Joseph Rowntree Foundation, *Findings* February

Brown G (2004) Speech to the National Council for Voluntary Organisations Annual Conference. http://www.ncvo-vol.org.uk accessed 25 September 2004

Brown K, Kenny S, Turner B and Prince J (2000) *Rhetorics of Welfare: Uncertainty, Choice and Voluntary Associations*. London: Macmillan

Brown M (1997) *Replacing Citizenship: AIDS Activism and Radical Democracy*. London: Guilford Press

Burt E and Taylor J (2002) Scotland's voluntary sector. In G Hassan and C Warhurst (eds) *Anatomy of the New Scotland: Power, Influence and Change* (pp 85–93). Edinburgh: Mainstream Publishing

Cabinet Office (2002) *Private Action, Public Benefit: The Organisational and Institutional Landscape of the UK Wider Nonprofit sector*. London: Cabinet Office

Carmichael P and Midwinter A (1999) Glasgow: Anatomy of a fiscal crisis. *Local Government Studies* 25(1):84–98

Carrington D (2002) *The Compact: The Challenge of Implementation*. London: Home Office

Clarke E, Gewirtz S and McLaughlin E (eds) (2000) *New Managerialism, New Welfare?* London: Sage

Craig G, Taylor M, Wilkinson, Bloor K, Monro S and Syed A (2002) *Contract or Trust? The Role of the Compact in Local Governance*. Bristol: Policy Press

Dahrendorf R (2001) *Challenges to the Voluntary Sector*. Arnold Goodman Lecture, 17 July 2001. Tonbridge: Charities Aid Foundation

Dahrendorf R (2003) Foreword. In J Kendall (ed) *The Voluntary Sector* (pp xiii–xiv). London: Routledge

Driver S and Martell L (1997) New Labour's communitarianisms. *Critical Social Policy* 52:27–46

Etzioni A (1995) *The Spirit of Community: Rights, Responsibilities and the Communitarian Agenda*. London: Fontana

Etzioni A (1997) *The New Golden Rule: Community and Morality in a Democratic Society*. London: Profile

Evers A (1992) Part of the welfare mix: The third sector as an intermediate area. *Voluntas* 6:159–182

Fyfe N R and Milligan C (2003) Space, citizenship and voluntarism: Critical reflections on the voluntary sector in Glasgow. *Environment and Planning A* 35:2069–2086

Giddens A (1998) *The Third Way: The Renewal of Social Democracy*. London: Polity Press

Hay C and Watson M (1999) Neither here nor there? New Labour's Third Way "Adventism". In L Funk (ed) *The Economics and Politics of the Third Way* (pp 171–180). Hamburg: LIT

Hayton K (2003) *Scottish Compact Baseline Review*. Edinburgh: Scottish Executive

HM Treasury (2002) *The Role of the Voluntary and Community Sector in Service Delivery: A Cross-cutting Review*. London: HM Treasury

Home Office (1998) *Getting it Right Together: Compact on Relations Between Government and the Voluntary and Community Sector in England*. London: Home Office, Cm 4100

Home Office (2001) *Central Government Funding of Voluntary and Community Organisations, 1982/83 to 1999/2000*. London: Home Office

Hunt A and Wickham G (1994) *Foucault and Law: Towards a Sociology of Law as Governance*. London: Pluto Press

Jessop B (2002) Liberalism, neoliberalism, and urban governance: A state-theoretical perspective. *Antipode* 34(3):452–472

Jiwani I (2000) Globalization at the level of the nation-state: The case of Canada's third sector. *Innovations: A Journal of Politics* 3:27–46

Johnston C and Whitehead M (2004) Horizons and barriers in British urban policy. In C Johnstone and M Whitehead (eds) *New Horizons in British Urban Policy* (pp 3–21). London: Ashgate

Kendall J (2000) The mainstreaming of the third sector into public policy in England in the late 1990s: Whys and wherefores. *Policy and Politics* 28(4):541–562

Kendall J (2003) *The Voluntary Sector*. London: Routledge

Knight B (1993) *Voluntary Action*. London: Centris

Labour Party (1997) *Building the Future Together: Labour's Policies for Partnership Between Government and Voluntary Sector*. London: Labour Party

Lake R W and Newman K (2003) Differential Citizenship in the Shadow State. *Geojournal* 58:109–120

Levitas R (1998) *The Inclusive Society? Social Exclusion and New Labour*. London: Macmillan

Lewis J (1999) Reviewing the relationship between the voluntary sector and the state in Britain in the 1990s. *Voluntas* 10(3):255–270

MacLeod G (2002) From urban entrepreneurialism to a Revanchist city? On the spatial injustices of Glasgow's renaissance. *Antipode* 34(3):602–624

Maloney W, Smith G and Stoker G (1999) "Social capital and urban governance: Civic engagement in Birmingham and Glasgow." Paper presented at the Annual Meeting of the American Political Science Association, Atlanta, GA

Malpas J and Wickham G (1995) Governance and failure: On the limits of sociology. *Australian and New Zealand Journal of Sociology* 31:37–50

Mohan G and Mohan J (2002) Placing social capital. *Progress in Human Geography* 26: 191–210

Mooney G and Poole L (2004) "'The only game in town?' Debating housing stock transfer in Glasgow." Unpublished manuscript

Morison J (2000) The government–voluntary sector compacts: Governance, governmentality and civil society. *Journal of Law and Society* 27(1):98–132

Northern Ireland Office (1998) *Building Real Partnership: Compact Between Government and the Voluntary and Community Sector in Northern Ireland.* Belfast: Northern Ireland Office, Cm 4167

Peck J (2001) *Workfare States.* New York: Guilford Press

Peck J and Tickell A (2002) Neoliberalizing space. *Antipode* 34(3):380–404

Plowden W (2003) The compact: Attempts to regulate relationships between government and the voluntary sector in England. *Nonprofit and Voluntary Sector Quarterly* 32(3):415–431

Powell M (ed) (1999) *New Labour New Welfare State? The Third Way in British Social Policy.* Bristol: Policy Press

Putnam R (1993) *Making Democracy Work: Civil Traditions in Modern Italy.* Princeton, NJ: Princeton University Press

Raco M (2003) Governmentality, subject-building, and the discourses and practices of devolution in the UK. *Transactions of the Institute of British Geographers* 28(1):75–95

Salamon L (1999) The non-profit sector at the cross roads: The case of America. *Voluntas* 10:5–23

Scottish Executive (2003) *The Scottish Compact.* Edinburgh: Scottish Executive

Scottish Office (1998) *The Scottish Compact: The Principles Underpinning the Relationship Between Government and Voluntary Sector in Scotland.* Edinburgh: Scottish Office, Cm 4083

Taylor M (1992) The changing role of the non-profit sector in Britain: Moving toward the market. In B Gidron (ed) *Government and Third Sector* (pp 147–175). San Francisco: Jossey Bass

Turner B S (2001) The erosion of citizenship. *British Journal of Sociology* 52:189–210

Welsh Office (1998) *A Shared Vision: Compact Between the Government and Voluntary Sector in Wales.* Cardiff: Welsh Office, Cm 4107

Wolch J R (1989) The shadow state: Transformations in the voluntary sector. In Wolch J R and Dear M (eds) *The Power of Geography: How Territory Shapes Social Life* (pp 197–221). Boston, MA: Unwin Hyman

Wolch J R (1999) Decentring America's nonprofit sector: Reflections on Salamon's crises analysis. *Voluntas* 10:25–35

Wrigglesworth R and Kendall J (2001) The impact of the third sector in the UK: The case of social housing. Centre for Civil Society Working Paper 10. London School of Economics

Nicholas Fyfe is Reader in Human Geography at the University of Dundee. His main areas of research are contemporary geographies of voluntarism and the geographies of crime and criminal justice. He is the author of *Protecting Intimidated Witnesses* (London: Ashgate, 2001), editor of *Images of the Street: Planning, Identity and Control in Public Space* (London: Routledge, 1998) and co-editor with Judith Kenny of *The Urban Geography Reader* (London: Routledge, 2005).

Chapter 8

Caught in the Middle: The State, NGOs, and the Limits to Grassroots Organizing Along the US–Mexico Border

Rebecca Dolhinow

Introduction

Rebecca: What do you want for your colonia?

Alicia: Very specifically, I want us to have a sewage system. I want us to have the water system. I want us to have the gas [natural]. I mean I want us to have all the things that people need. It's just the basic things we need, and I want us to have them all. Do I think we are going to get them? Do I see any hope? Not really. I mean right now, just looking at what people say, people that have been here longer than us, it would be a miracle. It would be, I don't know, the new President coming in and looking at the colonia and just feeling embarrassed about the conditions. I don't know what it would take, but it's bleak.[1]

Alicia is not the average colonia resident. She speaks English fluently, has a college degree, and was born in the US. Yet she lives in a colonia and experiences on a daily basis the resource deprivation that characterizes these primarily immigrant communities. Alicia's quote demonstrates the frustration and hope that simultaneously exist in the lives of most colonia leaders. This contradictory situation is an important element of activism in the colonias. Both women leaders, like Alicia, and the NGOs that serve these communities are full of hope for a more just future in the colonias, a future in which colonias no longer lack the basic necessities of a healthy community. But they are also filled with frustration at the many obstacles that stand between them and their goals. Together, women leaders and NGOs create physical improvements that include the provision of potable water and the creation of community parks and childcare centers. Yet it is harder for them to produce more politicized communities that challenge their marginalized position as Mexican immigrants. As a mediator between state-based or state-financed donors and grassroots activists, NGOs in the colonias often present neoliberal solutions, such as self-help,[2] to address the colonias' resource deprivation. In this way, NGOs can obscure and limit the discussion of alternative discourses of development and social change, such as those that acknowledge the economic, political, and social marginalization of Mexican immigrants and make demands on the state to improve their situation. I critically examine women's leadership and NGO interventions in the colonias in order to focus on the role of NGOs in neoliberal governance. I point to the complex, contradictory, and ambiguous position of colonia leaders in this the latest iteration of the American ideal of self-help and self-sufficiency.

In this contribution, I look at the role of NGOs[3] in women's activism and argue that in many interventions, NGO attempts to empower women actually employ practices that produce de-politicizing effects by isolating colonia communities. These striking contradictions are explained through ethnographic data that demonstrate how the multiple scales at which NGOs work, from federal agencies to grassroots communities, often put conflicting demands on NGOs. Two interrelated arguments are made here. The first addresses the growing demands of professionalism many funders are putting on NGOs. Demands that make NGOs justify and account for projects in increasingly burdensome manners, demands that drive a wedge, made up of endless meetings, paperwork and accounting, between communities and NGO workers. The second argument also focuses on the distance donor demands can create between NGOs and their client communities, but in a slightly different manner. As NGO funding becomes more competitive, NGOs often find they must follow donor agendas in order to keep their funding. As NGOs push the more fundable projects they move away from community needs and closer to the neoliberal interventions preferred by many donors (Edwards and Hulme 1996b). The resulting disabling of activism relates directly to the multiple and simultaneous processes of professionalization that are growing in importance in civil society as a whole (Mawdsley et al 2002).

I argue that both of these pitfalls are avoidable, but only when NGOs and communities are aware of them and seek to avoid them. I agree with Miraftab who writes, "it is discernable that the increased attention and financial support received by NGOs have affected drastically their original character and the nature of their activities" (1997:362). I saw these changes in the discrepancies between the discourses and practices of the NGOs in the colonias; employees spoke of empowerment and politicization while they planned projects that helped to enhance neoliberal forms of governance. Increasing trends toward professionalizing NGOs mean organizations that used to operate in opposition to the state, maintaining their distance in part through their less professional and more grassroots approaches, are now being encompassed in greater and greater numbers by the neoliberal state.

The following section sets the stage for the arguments to follow by introducing colonias as a form of affordable housing and describing the colonias in which this research took place. Next, I examine how the growing focus on civil society in the US plays out in the colonias. The role of NGOs in the processes of neoliberal governance is a central focus of this section. Then I explore the sometimes disabling role of NGOs in the colonias through a story that demonstrates the complex relationships that exist between the state, NGOs, and grass-roots communities. Last, I examine the politics of NGOs and, in particular, their growing stress on professionalism, in order to better understand how the relationships between NGOs, their funders, and the state play out at the scale of daily life in the colonias.

Context: Colonias in the US

Although colonias exist on the Mexican side of the international boundary, the colonias that are the focus of this research are located in the US. According to the federal government a colonia is any identifiable community in the US–Mexico border regions of Arizona, California, New Mexico, and Texas that is determined to be a colonia on the basis of objective criteria, including lack of a potable water supply, inadequate sewage systems, and a shortage of decent, safe, and sanitary housing. As detailed as this definition is it leaves out more than it says. The federal definition rests solely on the absence of services and infrastructure, and in highlighting these negative characteristics of the colonias, validates the discriminatory treatment many colonia residents experience at the hands of the state. The colonias of southern New Mexico are Mexican immigrant communities with strong transnational ties to Mexico. Like their Mexican counterparts, colonias in the US are a direct result of large-scale processes such as global economic restructuring, immigration, and neoliberal social policy. But, unlike their Mexican counterparts, US colonias are not as widely accepted as an alternative form of affordable housing.

Colonias exist to house the constantly increasing population of Mexican immigrants on which the border economy relies. Global economic restructuring on the border can be seen as far back as 1942's Bracero Program, which brought Mexican labor to the US to support the wartime economies of the southwest. Several of the women in my sample had their first experience with the US when their fathers left Mexico as Braceros. Estella, a leader from the colonia named Recuerdos, remembers the Bracero program as an important part of her childhood:

My papa was a Bracero. Always, since we knew we were growing up, we always saw that he was never in the house. Because he came with the Braceros, he always worked in the United States. He would cross the bridge [from Ciudad Juárez to El Paso] and there were buses that took people to different places to work ... He was in Chicago; he was in Wisconsin, Colorado, in various places.[4]

More recently, NAFTA is an example of economic integration on the border. As NAFTA breaks down Mexico's traditional agricultural economy, it forces great numbers of formerly agricultural workers from the country's interior to the border region's manufacturing sector, and from there many move into the US (Massey, Durand and Malone 2002; Nevins 2002; Staudt 1998).

In New Mexico a great deal of colonia development took place after the Immigration and Reform Control Act (IRCA) of 1986. For many Mexican men working without documentation in the agricultural fields of southern New Mexico, IRCA meant the opportunity to reunite their families in the US. Once these families were documented and united in the US, a whole new set of obstacles were encountered, not least of which was a tremendous lack of affordable housing. The search for affordable housing forced many Mexican immigrants to turn to colonia communities for land to buy (Dolhinow 2003). Once settled in the colonias, Mexican immigrant families began the struggle to get necessary infrastructure. It was usually women who led this struggle.

Much like the "super madres", which have become the symbol of women's activism in social movements across Latin America, colonia leaders are motivated by the needs of their individual families (Chaney and Bunster 1989). The debilitating effects of neoliberal social policy are felt widely in the global South where the differing effects of global economic restructuring on women and men have been noted in many contexts, particularly in reference to structural adjustment programs (Bakker 1994; Brodie 1994; Moser 1993; Runyan 1999; Tanski 1994). The colonias are no exception. As the primary caretakers in their homes, colonia women experience the lack of basic services in more daily and intimate ways than do the men in their communities. The women in my sample described these daily deprivations as a great motivation for their activism.

Sylvia: Women have to drive the streets day in and day out, take the kids to school. They're more involved as far as water goes because they're the ones that use it more than anything, they're the ones that wash, they're the ones that cook with it, they're involved with the gas more because they're the ones that are cooking and knowing if they're running out of gas or not. Well one [women] needs the services more, right? The man, not really. The man, he finishes

work, comes home from work, eats and baths and that's it. We need
to do more, to take care of the kids. We meet and get the services.[5]

When colonia developers fail to deliver necessary infrastructure,
colonia residents and women leaders, like many working poor groups,
find that the state offers them little help, and they must turn to NGOs
(Desai and Imrie 1998; Hammack 2002; Larner and Craig 2005:1;
Wolch 1989).

In response to declining services and shrinking economic opportunities due to neoliberal policies, Latina heads of households in the US
and across Latin America are forming important relationships with
NGOs that tie them in subtle ways to the institutions of neoliberalism
(Chant 1997; Laurie et al 1999; Varley 1996). In addressing these
relationships I want to stress, as Desai and Imrie (1998) do, that all
examples of global economic restructuring and its attending neoliberal policy are very localized, highly uneven, and complex. For this
reason, it is necessary to have grounded and concrete data, such as
ethnography, when examining these processes and relationships
(Molyneux 2001).

Activism in the colonias primarily results in the creation of physical
infrastructure in the form of roads, water and waste water systems, and
community parks. Through the process of creating these improvements
to their communities, leaders learn new "people skills", including how to
better communicate with their communities and county officials. A few
women expressed their increased awareness of their marginalized
position as immigrants, but not all leaders expressed themselves in
these more politicized ways. What activism does not produce as clearly
in the colonias is a community-wide awareness of their marginalization
or greater politicization. Why is politicization so limited in the colonias?
The answer revolves around the role of NGOs.

NGOs often play a central part in the complex processes that
produce colonia leaders and activists as political subjects who unintentionally serve the interests of the neoliberal state. To employ the
parlance of development studies, NGO-supported projects in the
colonias address "practical" needs while often obscuring more "strategic" needs (Moser 1993). By "practical" needs I mean indispensable
resources, such as potable water, that most US citizens take for
granted. "Strategic" needs are resources and relationships that have
more outwardly political ramifications and less tangible results, such
as picketing the county commissioner's meeting for better
representation.

For example, the colonia of Recuerdos needed a majority decision
in order to create a mutual water association that would allow them to
buy and sell water at wholesale prices. In order to get residents to the
meeting the colonia leaders and NGO staff went door-to-door to tell

the community about the project and the organization meeting. During this canvassing the project was primarily described in terms of needs and not rights. Canvassers asked residents if they needed better and more affordable access to potable water and encouraged residents to attend the meetings to show support for a much needed project. The meeting was not billed as a place to discuss why colonia residents were currently being charged almost twice what nearby town residents paid for water. Many projects in the colonias are introduced and described like this, in terms of improvements to the conditions of daily life. Organizers often tend to appeal to the resource deprivation colonia women experience every day and stress how improvements will help women to meet their currently unmet needs. An alternative approach would address the project in terms of basic human rights, rights such as a healthy environment in which to live free from discrimination. Such a rights-based approach could highlight the unequal power relations that led to and reinforce the substandard living conditions in the colonias.

Methodology

This contribution is based on research that took place over 11 months in 2000. During my year-long study and subsequent follow-up visits to the colonias between 2000 and 2003, I witnessed a series of projects initiated and several completed. I address a number of these projects, including a housing project, a water project, and several waste water projects. The majority of my work with local NGOs was with the Community Organizing Group (COG). I attended the COG's weekly staff meetings and helped with project research and planning. My relationship with the COG began when I approached them with my research and requested their help with introductions to the communities. As a well-known NGO working in the colonias, the COG was the obvious place for me to begin my research.

Once the project was under way I was a daily visitor to the colonias and attended all colonia meetings. I spent time with the women leaders, who I identified based on COG records and community perceptions. I visited with leaders in their homes—cleaning kitchens and ironing clothes, at the homes of their relatives—cooking endless pots of menudo (tripe stew) and chile, and in local community centers—joining them for training on topics such as sex education for children and diabetes awareness. In the company of colonia leaders I went to baptisms in local Catholic parishes, dances at night-clubs and bars, and long early morning walks.

The three colonias in which this research took place are Los Montes with a population of approximately 30 households, Recuerdos with 35 households, and Valle de Vacas with over 200 households. On several occasions I heard non-colonia residents describe colonias as "the Third World in our backyard". Colonia residents, on the other hand, see past the obvious poverty. Juana's description of Recuerdos is a good example of how colonia residents feel about their communities: "I like the peacefulness, that there is not so much moving around, not so much running around—zoom, zoom, all the time. I like it for my kids that there is so much free space … It's a peaceful thing, that's what I like about it."[6]

Los Montes is a small colonia built around two parallel dirt roads that are poorly graded and full of potholes. At least once every summer during the rainy season the colonia floods and the roads become impassable and many residents must walk in from the highway. With its striking poverty Los Montes became the poster child of colonias in the area and most tours for federal visitors or possible funders go through Los Montes. Flora and Esperanza are the leaders I followed in Montes, both are single mothers who speak very little English. Nearly 20 years ago, Flora came by herself to the US. She worked as an undocumented maid for a few years until she met and married her husband who was a US citizen. Unlike many of the other leaders, Flora works most of the time. She prefers manual labor because she "likes to feel like she is really working". Flora's outgoing and always cheerful personality helped her deal with the pressures of life as a single mother and colonia leader. She also received help from her mother who spent part of the year living with Flora and her family. While I was in the colonias, Esperanza was dealing with a difficult divorce and her ex-husband's serious psychological problems. She saw her activism as a way to stay busy during her hard times and a way to create a new life for herself.

Valle de Vacas was the most mixed community in which families in stick built homes with central air conditioning lived next to families living in 1950s travel trailers with holes in the floors and ceilings. Even though it was the largest colonia in my research, Valle had the least consistent leadership. Marie had been a leader in the colonia for nearly a decade and she single-handedly kept Valle involved with the local NGOs, even when there were no projects under way. Marie had a deep devotion to activism and often cited her father, a Mexican labor organizer, as her role model. She kept her father's papers in a drawer in the kitchen and on several occasions she brought them out to show me. While I was there, Alicia, a school teacher, and Rosa, a mother and homemaker, also became active in the colonia's leadership. The size of Valle both helped and hindered activism. For large-scale projects, such as building a waste water system there were more than enough people to help out. But it was also very difficult to get the colonia together to discuss possible projects.

Recuerdos was a quiet and rural community in a small and out of the way valley in a busy agricultural area. Residents of Recuerdos often commented on the isolation of their community and felt it offered their families a life more like that they left behind in rural Mexico. Yet their hidden and tranquil colonia was also the site of numerous border patrol raids and a green and white "migra" truck was a constant presence on the hill above their little valley. Estella and Juana had been best friends and co-leaders in Recuerdos for several years. Together they had organized their colonia to build a road for the school bus, and a waste water system. Estella came to leadership in part through the influence of her brother Mario, the only COG employee who lived in a colonia. Juana became involved through her friendship with Estella.

Working in the colonias for more than ten years, the COG, like other NGOs, experienced community participation as a cyclical process. The COG's director, Elena, described working in the colonias as unpredictable: "gusts of activity can be followed by periods of total disinterest". While I was in the colonias, interest was beginning to grow again after a period of little involvement. Recent publicity during the 2000 presidential elections created a greater awareness of colonias in the US as George W. Bush was questioned about his work in Texas colonias while he was governor. Yet even during an upswing in interest, only a handful of residents were committed to colonia leadership.

The COG facilitates the community organizing process by searching out activists and providing them with leadership training. Based on the COG's mission statement, "empowerment" is a central goal of their work. They define empowerment in terms of responses to marginalization and need. From my observations of the COG at work, it is clear that the goals of the COG and their actual results did not always overlap. The COG often found themselves in contradictory and difficult positions. On the one hand, they strove to politicize colonia residents, encourage them to question their position as immigrants and working poor, and challenge the state to provide them with the basic resources that were available to other groups. On the other hand, in order to procure funding, the COG often found it necessary to sign onto projects that were based in much less progressive policy agendas, projects that pushed colonia residents towards neoliberal ideals of self-reliance and self-sufficiency. While I was working with the COG they were constantly negotiating this complex terrain between possible empowerment and further marginalization at the hands of neoliberal social policy.

The COG also acts as an intermediary between other NGOs, such as Affordable Housing Inc (AHI) and the Border Water Group (BWG), which want to work in the colonias but do not have contacts in the communities. AHI primarily builds low-cost housing in urban settings by procuring state and private funds to underwrite construction costs. AHI is much less concerned with empowerment and hands on politicization than the COG. Run by a politically well-connected local woman, AHI is primarily committed to procuring funds and building houses, leaving the community organizing to the COG. BWG designs and builds low-cost waste water treatment systems and helps colonia communities to manage their own water systems. BWG is committed to community activism as a means to politicization but, like AHI, leave the political work to the COG.

NGOs, Civil Society, and Colonias: Theory and Practice

Before I go on to discuss the particulars of my examples, I want to speak more generally about the central roles carried out by the NGOs serving in the colonias and other working poor communities. There are currently a large variety of NGOs doing work in impoverished communities. These NGOs vary in size from small groups with a handful of personnel to large and well-established organizations that employ dozens of people. Some have endowments that make them virtually self-sustaining and others, like those described here, are constantly battling for the funding necessary to keep them afloat. The format in which NGO interventions take place is, in my experience, another important distinction between NGOs. Some NGOs choose to offer specific services, while others help more generally with community organizing, trying to teach communities how to access the services they need on their own. Both types are common in the colonias. For the arguments presented here, the most important distinction between NGOs is that of consistency between goals and results. There are NGOs that are outwardly committed to empowerment and a rights-based approach to community activism; these groups often only accept funds from equally progressive institutions. Then there are those that work well within neoliberal institutions and policy agendas, with little interest in social justice or revolutionary change. Finally, there are those committed to progressive social change and justice, but who in their search for funding must turn to less progressive institutions for money. All the NGOs discussed here fall into this third category. In the colonias, the focus on basic needs and infrastructure makes it very easy for individually centered neoliberal solutions to take over and NGOs must work hard to maintain their social justice agendas.

Leaders expect to see COG organizers at least once a week, and residents do not look twice when COG organizers drive by with potential donors or county officials. During one of many door-to-door campaigns to interest a colonia's residents in a new project, I was struck by how uninterested residents were in Los Montes. Residents are so acclimatized to the workings of NGOs that the presence of a young gringa walking through their all-Mexican community barely provoked interest. Most colonia residents simply accept NGOs as part of their life, and it is often through the workings of NGOs that colonia residents experience neoliberal policy measures.

To understand how NGOs became so commonplace in the colonias it is necessary to examine the role civil society plays in the current neoliberal or "advanced liberal" order (Barry et al 1996; Dean 1999; Rose 1999). Two of the most powerful theoretical approaches to the state and civil society are those offered by Gramsci and Foucault. Although these two theorists address the powers and processes of the state from very different points of view, they can be used productively together to conceive of civil society as simultaneously "both object and end of government" (Burchell 1996:25). Hansen and Stepputat (2001) call for these two theories to be held in "a productive tension" and, in so doing, introduce a healthy element of ambiguity into theories of the state.

Together Gramsci and Foucault's theories of the state and governmentality work well to theorize the often-contradictory role of NGOs in colonias. According to Gramsci, "the State is the entire complex of practical and theoretical activities with which the ruling class not only justifies and maintains its dominance, but manages to win the active consent of those over whom it rules ... " (Gramsci 1989:244). In this definition, the state, a class-based entity, encompasses the domain of civil society. In the close relationship Gramsci formulates between the state and civil society, the space NGOs inhabit becomes very important. In Gramsci's theory it is the state's localized and everyday forms that are of the greatest importance. The state in Gramsci's view is a bundle of sites and scales of governance and authority that shift, grow, and continuously change. In the modern state's advanced liberal form, NGOs can play a key role in the state's continuous construction and reconstruction.

Foucault, rather than focusing on what constitutes the state, creates a theory of governmentality to examine what the state does and how. In Foucault's theory of governmentality, the state is more than just the strictly political institutions and powers commonly associated with the state. It also encompasses the institutions that govern more broadly by controlling and shaping everyday behavior. Foucault describes governing as delineating "the conduct of conduct" (Gordon 1991:2). Governmentality encompasses the rationalities of rule as well as the forms of knowledge and expertise necessary to produce governable subjects. As Hart (2004) notes, Foucault decenters the state and brings to light the multiplicity of other sites that factor in important ways into the production of political subjects.

NGOs occupy one such site. In the colonias, NGOs play a significant role in what Hansen and Stepputat (2001) term a key "language of governance", producing resources and ensuring the population's well-being. NGOs in the colonias help with resource acquisition and in so doing can become "transmitters" of neoliberal governance.

Together, Gramsci and Foucault allow us to acknowledge both the essential political instability and partiality of the state (Gramsci) as well as its constantly reworked processes of governmentality (Foucault). Within liberalism as currently experienced, "civil society is brought into being as both distinct from political intervention", and as such a site for possible resistance to neoliberal politics, "and yet potentially alignable with political aspirations" (Barry et al 1996:9). Together, Foucault and Gramsci can be used to theorize civil society as a dynamic space that is not inherently liberating or oppressive, but has the potential for both. The decentered advanced liberal state produces political subjects from many sites and although many NGOs in the colonias attempt to use their position within civil society to work for social justice, they often become a site of neoliberal governance and end up reinforcing the very production of neoliberal political subjects they seek to deconstruct. I argue here that one central way NGOs are brought into neoliberal governance is through techniques of professionalization. The accountability, professionalism, and development of expertise that currently occupy much of the time and energy of NGOs (including those discussed here) are part and parcel of the neoliberal project. These "technical" concerns of governmentality can be just as important as ideology.

While the increasing presence of neoliberalism in the realm of civil society in the colonias was obvious, there was also a more libratory conception of civil society present. The potential for civil society as a revolutionary space was an underlying theme in the work of many NGOs. Although this libratory space rarely materialized, it is important to acknowledge its presence, especially in relation to the current plurality of thinking on civil society. Howell and Pearce (2001) distinguish between two primary theories of civil society, the mainstream and alternative approaches. I focus on the spread of mainstream thinking about civil society that views civil society as primarily relevant to solving the state's dilemmas and providing for the state's agendas. Yet, alternative ideas about the role of civil society are also present in the colonias as activists "embrace the concept of 'civil society' as expressing a role for NGOs beyond that of implementing the donor agenda" (Howell and Pearce 2001:16).

Following Habermas' theorization of the failure of seventeenth and eighteenth century bourgeois public sphere, activists and others seek to "decolonize the life world" of "personal relationships and communicative action" in order to create a more receptive space for alternative models of civil society (Howell and Pearce 2001:57). Similarly, Keane (1998) points to the "unharnessed potential" that the alternative perspective holds to "develop new images of civil society that alter the ways in which we think about such matters as power, property ... and violence" (1998:190). It is firmly in the alternative perspective that, I believe, the NGOs in the colonias would position themselves. But, as I demonstrate, the demands of mainstream civil society appear to be too strong to resist.

In the colonias, NGOs encourage leaders to organize their communities around self-help projects that neatly fit into the neoliberal state's focus on individual self-reliance. NGOs often facilitate the state's divestment from the colonias by providing private services and at the same time act as a transmitter of dominant forms of governance from the neoliberal state to the colonias. Martin argues, "governance theories highlight an increasingly blurred relationship between private and public actors in public policy and service provision" (2004:395). This blurring was an important characteristic of NGO work in the colonias.

Colonias were developed in relative isolation as a response to the lack of state-sponsored affordable housing during the late 1980s and early 1990s in the "roll back" stage of neoliberalism—a period characterized by "the active *destruction and discreditation* of Keynesian-welfarist and social-collectivist institutions (broadly defined)" (Peck and Tickell 2002:384, emphasis in original). More recently colonias have been the site of the "roll out" of neoliberalism as colonias have been brought into the fold by both state agencies and NGOs. In turn, NGOs and the state add to the production of colonia leaders and residents as political subjects who consistently chose neoliberal solutions to their problems rather than make demands on the state. Civil society in the colonias thus "flourish[es] precisely as a consequence of state action" (Hyatt 2001:227).

A great deal of work has been done on the changing role of civil society in developing countries and the key position of NGOs in this change (Bebbington 2000; Hintjens 1999; Mohan 2002; Morris-Suzuki 2000). In the colonias, as in many other immigrant communities across the US, "local neoliberalisms" (Peck and Tickell 2002) developed alongside similar global-scale neoliberal processes and structures. A focus on the specific and local manifestations of neoliberalism in the colonias allows me to situate Mexican working poor communities in the US alongside other marginalized communities within the global scale processes and structures of neoliberalism. My work thus has implications for how we understand marginalized communities within an overarching neoliberal context. The story to follow exemplifies the many pitfalls NGOs must avoid and the pivotal role they play in shaping activism in the colonias.

NGOs and Change in the Colonias
Who Profits from Non-Profits?

Many of the problems I observed while in the field revealed the large-scale difficulties that exist between NGOs and their clients. I found, just as Edwards and Hulme (1996a) did nearly a decade ago, that problems could arise from the differences between funder goals and those of the grassroots communities that NGOs serve (Bebbington 1997). In the worst of situations, the NGOs insert their own priorities into the process, which obscures the desires of the communities. When funding priorities do not match community priorities, the former, which determine the viability of NGOs, often win out (Townsend, Porter and Mawdsley 2002). Because much of the time the clients of the NGOs have little or no contact with the funders, as is the case in the colonias, it can be difficult or impossible for them to realize that community goals are not being accurately transmitted to the donors.

For two years starting in November 2000, the colonia of Montes was the site of a new housing project designed to build dozens of new homes. But in the end, only two households, both headed by single mothers, expressed interest. The apparent failure of this much-needed project reveals the problems created by the growing emphasis on professionalism and competition in NGO circles. My first experience with this project came at a COG meeting in which Elena, the NGO's director, announced that she had been contacted by the director of another local NGO, AHI, which wanted to start a housing project in the colonias in which the COG worked. In this relationship the COG would provide entrance into the colonias and organize support for the project that would be funded by AHI. AHI had put together a funding scheme, based on state and private money, that would allow colonia residents to build new homes using self-help and sweat equity methods and to finance the projects at very low interest rates. All the COG had to do was administer a survey to demonstrate the need for such housing, elicit interest in the colonias, and help residents complete the rather long and complex application forms. Because the project required intensive labor from the COG, AHI had budgeted monies to pay for the part-time services of one of the COG's organizers. Like most NGOs, the COG constantly searches for more funding. The opportunity to secure money for its payroll provided more incentive to join this seemingly beneficial project.

The housing project in Los Montes is an example of the many ties between NGOs, such as the COG and AHI, and the state that funded the project. In her discussion of NGOs, Jennifer Wolch (1989) describes the cutbacks of state-sponsored public services as "public sector retrenchment" and points to the simultaneous privatization of public services, such as affordable housing. The growth of voluntary sector organizations, such as NGOs that fill the needs left open by the state's move away from service provision, leads to the "formation of a 'shadow state' apparatus" (Wolch 1989:198). Wolch's "shadow state" takes the "form of voluntary organizations with the collective responsibilities, which operate outside traditional democratic controls, yet are strongly affected by state resources and constraints" (198). The sources of funding they solicit and the ways in which the federal government often controls this funding determine, in part, the activities of the NGOs. In Los Montes the availability of donor money made housing a priority, even though it had not been on the colonia's list of projects. The list included such things as paved roads and a working waste water system. For the leaders and community members who, with the COG's help, developed this priority list, communitywide projects were of primary importance. The housing project did not fit this criterion.

A meeting early on in the planning process showed signs that this project lay in the hands of the "professionals", in this case NGO personnel and county planners, and not in those of the colonia leaders. At this meeting, representatives from the COG and AHI discussed the proposed project with the county planning office. No colonia residents were in attendance, even though the project would build homes in their community. Attitudes at the meeting ranged from condescending and dismissive county planners, who thought the colonias were a waste of time and money because people should know better than to buy unimproved land, to genuinely concerned and motivated county officials and NGO employees. After much debate and a few concessions, the project was approved. Next it was time for the project to move into the colonias. The COG staff and I administered the survey. Because the survey was in both English and Spanish none of the colonia leaders were asked to help. At this point, colonia residents had no real role in the project. On several occasions, Flora asked me for information about the housing project. I answered as best as I could and then asked the COG organizer in her community to provide the information, which he did do. However, Flora and the other leaders remained on the outside of this project, and, in the long run, their absence spelled failure for the project.

While I split my time between the three colonias, I needed help keeping up with all the events in each community and I often asked the women to fill me in on the events I missed. It struck me that these summaries were full of details regarding colonia politics and more than a little *chisme* (gossip). But what the NGOs did once they left the colonias, for example, how they were going to deal with a colonia request for a meeting with a county commissioner, these details were

never part of the summaries. When I asked for details on these
matters the women expressed their interest, but always said they did
not know much about "those things". The women had little or no
knowledge of how the NGOs did business once they left the communities. This lack of transparency is, I believe, yet another symptom of
the distance a stress on professionalism can create between NGOs
and their clients. When I mentioned this apparent lack of communication at NGO meetings, both COG and AHI personnel said they
would like to explain more, but there was no time; with more experience the women would pick some of it up on their own. To this end
the COG regularly invited the women to attend the county commis-
sioners' meetings. But when the women did attend these meetings
they always expressed frustration because they couldn't follow the fast
moving meetings that were held in English and even with translation
they did not know enough of the, often technical, terminology to
really understand what was going on.

Flora and Esperanza were the only two residents to take part in the
housing project. It is no coincidence that they were both the heads of
single mother households. Families headed by married couples all
declined to apply for the project for the same reason. The women all
supported the project, but their husbands did not want to go further
into debt, especially when they believed they could build the houses
themselves and for less money. Many men in the colonias have built
rooms onto their trailers and a few have built new homes from the
ground up. With owner-built housing a common occurrence, many
men expressed skepticism about the need for architectural plans and
building permits, two aspects of the housing project that created what
they considered to be extra costs.

By the fall of 2003, three years after the housing project began, only
two new houses stood in Montes and the importance of community
support for a project was clear. If it had succeeded, the project would
have produced very obvious results. But, the project failed to produce
many new houses. What this story shows most dramatically is that
NGOs play multiple roles in their own daily operations. They must be
organizers and activists alongside publicists, accountants, and finan-
ciers. The toll these roles take on NGOs can lead to problematic
situations such as the housing project. Though not a community
priority, better housing was clearly needed, and the COG easily
justified its role in the project. In her work with Nicaraguan NGOs
that serve women's heath needs, Ewig found "a grant with a man-
dated focus detracts from the mission of the movement as a
whole ... Thus financial dependence on donations can quickly
become a problem in diverting attention from the mission of the
movement and ultimately threatening its base if NGOs are unable
to obtain sufficient funding" (Ewig 1999:80). In the case of Los

Montes, the money that moved housing to the top of the priority list was not enough to make the project successful.

When funding for house construction is all that is available, many NGOs, such as the COG, will divert their activities to accommodate funding trends. In the case of the housing project in Montes, this new focus not only overshadowed community priorities, it also led the COG into a very complex situation. The COG was caught up in a cycle of professionalism. Eagerness to complete a really big project meant that the realities of colonia life were not taken into account. These realities included the fact that projects that involve little or no financial burden are most popular with men and without the support of the colonia's men, more costly projects become impossible. By taking the initiative without fully consulting the whole colonia, the COG put itself and the project in jeopardy. Yet when NGO employees did discuss the project with leaders, the lack of male support was not apparent. NGOs are forced to work within a system that puts so many demands on their time and resources that it becomes very easy to lose sight of the client goals and the daily politics of community organizing. Misunderstandings and misinterpretations of community dynamics are a constant problem for NGOs. This problem is often intensified, as it was here, by the increasing pressures outside organizations, such as donors, put on NGO operations. Part of the professionalization process is the development of continuing sources of funding, and this increased focus on funding can be detrimental to the fulfilment of client needs.

The two houses that were built represent a vast improvement in the lives of two families. But the relationships that NGOs develop with communities produce more than material improvements. These relationships can also justify and reinforce the unequal power relations that led to these poorly planned communities in the first place. Townsend, Porter and Mawdsley (2002) found the international aid system to be a "chain of dependency inducing relationships" and that those "partnerships do not emerge in a vacuum. They emerge from an existing institutional architecture" (Ling 2000 in Townsend, Porter and Mawdsley 2002:834). In colonias, NGOs often focus on short-term, immediate projects as opposed to long-term structural changes that potentially politicized colonia leaders who understand the processes of their own marginalization can enact. It is the crucial processes and relationships of marginalization that many NGOs strive, yet ultimately fail, to illuminate. Hammack (2002) points to the historical role of NGOs in moving social conflict out of the open and into more controlled outlets such as community organizing.

Petras and Veltmeyer (2001) describe NGOs' role in the processes of global economic restructuring as: "local micro-projects, apolitical 'grassroots' self-exploitation and 'popular education' that avoids class

analysis of imperialism and capitalist profit-making" (128). NGOs in
the colonias fit into this model when they become tools of the state
that address and provide necessary social services. By focusing on the
immediate needs and daily desires of colonia residents, NGOs, often
lose sight of the more political questions of rights and resources that
lie at the heart of the social service cutbacks these communities
experience.

The Politics of NGOs

Many NGO projects fail to produce the desired effects, at both the
material and theoretical levels. In Montes, the NGO project produced
neither houses nor politicization. Why was this the case? To start
with, empowerment and politicization are processes. For self-help
projects to encourage the development of these processes, continuity
between projects and interventions of local NGOs needs to exist.
Here lies one of the crucial impediments in the empowerment and
politicization processes: competition between NGOs. For NGOs,
such as the COG, nurturing politicization at the same time as organizing projects to pave roads is an enormous challenge. Even though
politicization and empowerment are part of the COG's mission statement the challenge sometimes appears to be too big. In order to get
funding and be considered a serious and professional organization,
NGOs must be highly competitive and have proven in the past that
they can get the job done. The COG worked hard to create and
maintain its reputation but some of this work also contributed to
the growing distance between the NGO and the colonias that, in
turn, disabled activism.

Not only are NGOs now expected to be experts and professionals,
but they are also expected to compete like full-blooded capitalists—
even though they are usually not supposed to make a profit. The stress
on quantifiable concrete and practical changes in individual communities that fuels this competitive system can limit the development of
political awareness and empowerment in colonias by obscuring the ties
between colonias and other marginalized communities (Desai and
Imrie 1998; Mawdsley, Townsend and Porter 2005). Some see "frag-
mented politics" as the result of this stress on individual projects
(Mohan 2002), others see "de-politicization" (Manji 1998).

More and more commonly, NGOs must transform themselves into
market competitive organizations in order to acquire funding
(Feldman 1997). To compete they must present themselves as
experts, create a unique niche, and defend their territory. As NGOs
become more entrenched in this system, they are less likely to serve
the desires and needs of their clients, and the networks NGOs have

worked so hard to create less likely to bring marginal communities together to examine the processes of their own marginalization.

Conclusion

Global economic restructuring and neoliberal policies lead women to take a greater responsibility in the processes of social reproduction, and NGOs play an important part in this repositioning of responsibility by providing technical and organizational support. In the colonias Mexican immigrant women organize and work to provide their communities with the most basic of resources. Most NGO interventions in the colonias try to alleviate practical problems. But that is not all NGOs do. They have another, even more important and less obvious job. They tie colonia residents to the neoliberal state through their position in civil society, often propagate dominant neoliberal discourses of leadership and activism, and at times reinforce dominant and marginalizing forms of social governance (Duffield 2001). By influencing projects and community organizing, NGOs engage in a form of governmentality. It is in these daily and disabling relations that NGOs can play an important role in "the conduct of conduct", shaping an acceptance of, and even preference for, neoliberal policy in the form of self-help techniques. Unfortunately, popular representations of NGOs often overlook these limiting relationships (Feldman 1997).

This research suggests the failure of NGOs to foster lasting social change rests, in part, on the landscape in which they work. NGOs lie at the mercy of the capitalist system, a constraint that affects their work in the colonias and other populations most affected by capitalism. Through their position in the "shadow state", NGOs, such as the COG, must comply with both their funder's priorities (often based on state trends in funding) and the state's regulations and agencies (local housing codes and Housing and Urban Development [HUD]). In this playing field, designed and managed by others, it is no wonder that some NGOs have trouble meeting their stated goals of empowerment and positive and lasting social change.

Based on the examples used here, it is possible to lay out a rough model of the impediments to social change in the colonias. At the base of this model rests the scale of daily life which encompasses "the fleshy, messy, and indeterminate stuff of everyday life" (Katz 2002:711) played out in the actions of women leaders and their families in the colonias. Next lies the scale of civil society and NGOs, whose interventions constitute part of daily practice, yet are also circumscribed by their relationship with the state. At the top lies the state, which functions at multiple levels as it constrains NGOs and uses various forms of governance to reproduce the dominant mode of production. The relationships among these three scales are contentious, limiting, impeding, and supportive all at once. Although the state deals most closely with civil society and NGOs, it still affects the daily lives of colonia leaders. It is critical to examine the links between the state and daily life and movement between the two, because in these spaces exist the vast potential for social change. It is in the microgeographies of daily life that we can find the "tools with which to imagine alternative models of globalization [and economic restructuring] that might spring from more egalitarian relationships, from social and economic justice ideals ... " (Cravey 2003:604).

The women leaders whose activism NGOs often disable represent a powerful resource that must be nurtured and developed. NGOs that seek social justice need to produce discourses and practices that challenge their own production as tools of neoliberal governmentality. This research points to the need for politically progressive NGOs to challenge the dominant state structure, as seen in funding priorities and self-help technologies, in order to support grassroots activists and create politicization, empowerment, and social change. It is important for NGOs to understand their role in the processes of neoliberalism and to look for opportunities to diverge from the desires of the neoliberal state. In order to use their influential role to work on an alternative form of civil society and to facilitate change, NGOs must be fully aware that they can also bridge the gap between the current neoliberal order and possible alternatives.

Acknowledgements

This contribution is based on research generously funded by the National Science Foundation, UCMexus, and the Institute for Labor and Employment at the University of California. I am also grateful to the Rockefeller foundation for funding my postdoctoral fellowship at the University of Texas at Austin where I carried out this work. Many readers made indispensable contributions, including Allan Pred, Gillian Hart, Caren Kaplan, Nitasha Sharma, Aaron Bobrow-Strain, David Kamper, and Jessica Teisch. Finally, I would like to thank the reviewers who made valuable comments and helped me to clarify my arguments in important ways.

Endnotes

[1] Alicia interview, 5 September 2000. To supplement my daily observations and notes, I administered a set of four in-depth interviews with the women leaders. I chose to do four interviews spaced out during the year in order to create a set of focused conversations on similar themes, such as household gender relations and personal long-term goals. I did similar interviews with a handful of non-leaders. I also interviewed many NGOs working in the colonias, including all Community Organizing Group (COG) employees and the directors of two other local NGOs: Affordable Housing Inc (AHI) and Border Water Group (BWG). The final set of interviews I did

was with the local district attorney assigned to the colonias, a state lawyer who worked on the laws concerning colonia development, and several local politicians who were involved in the legislation as well. In all, 40 plus formal interviews were done. The names of all colonia residents, NGO employees, NGOs, and colonias are pseudonyms. I chose not to use real names to protect the anonymity of leaders who are already taking risks by speaking out in public about the conditions in their colonias.
[2] In the colonias self-help solutions range from community built waste-water systems to "sweat equity" projects that employ resident labor alongside contractors in the construction of new homes or paved roads. The long history of self-help in both Mexico and the US is well documented by Ward (1999). Self-help is a very controversial concept among colonia scholars. The debate is primarily between those who see self-help as an empowering and suitable solution in itself to resource deprivation in the colonias and those, myself included, who have more skeptical views on the merits of self-help and point to the strong and dangerous ties between self-help rhetoric and neoliberal ideology (see Lemos et al 2002).
[3] The primary NGOs that work in these colonias are COG, AHI, BWG.
[4] Estella interview, 25 August 2000.
[5] Sylvia interview by correspondence, December 2000.
[6] Juana interview, 14 September 2000.

References

Bakker I (1994) Introduction: Engendering macro-economic policy reform in the era of global restructuring and adjustment. In I Bakker (ed) *The Strategic Silence* (pp 1–29). London: Zed Books
Barry A, Osborne T and Rose N (1996) *Foucault and Political Reason: Liberalism, Neoliberalism, and the Arts of Government*. Chicago, IL: University of Chicago Press
Bebbington A (1997) Reinventing NGOs and rethinking alternatives in the Andes. *The Annals of the American Academy of Political and Social Science* 554:117–136
Bebbington A (2000) Reencountering development: Livelihood transitions and place transformations in the Andes. *Annals of the Association of American Geographers* 90:495–520
Brodie J (1994) Shifting boundaries: Gender and the politics of restructuring. In I Bakker (ed) *The Strategic Silence* (pp 46–60). London: Zed Books
Burchell G (1996) Liberal government and techniques of the self. In A Barry, T Osborne and N Rose (eds) *Foucault and Political Reason: Liberalism, Neoliberalism, and the Arts of Government* (pp 19–36). Chicago, IL: University of Chicago Press
Chaney E and Bunster X (1989) *Sellers and Servants Working Women in Lima, Peru*. Massachusetts: Bergin and Garvey Publishers Inc
Chant S (1997) *Women-headed Households: Diversity and Dynamics in the Developing World*. Basingstoke: Macmillan
Cravey A (2003) Toque una Ranchera, Por Favor. *Antipode* 35(3):603–621
Dean M (1999) *Governmentality*. London: Sage
Desai V and Imrie R (1998) The new managerialism in local governance: North–south dimensions. *Third World Quarterly* 19(4):635–650
Dolhinow R (2003) "Borderlands Justice: Women's community activism in the Colonias of Doña Ana County, New Mexico." Unpublished PhD dissertation, University of California, Berkeley
Duffield M (2001) Governing the Borderlands: Decoding the power of aid. *Disasters* 25(4):308–320
Edwards M and Hulme D (1996a) Introduction: NGO performance and accountability. In M Edwards and D Hulme (eds) *Beyond the Magic Bullet: NGO*

Performance and Accountability in the Post Cold War World (pp 1–20). West Hartford: Kumarian Press

Edwards M and Hulme D (1996b) Too close for comfort? The impact of official aid on nongovernmental organizations. *World Development* 24(6):961–973

Ewig C (1999) The strengths and limits of the NGO women's movement model: Shaping Nicaragua's democratic institutions. *Latin American Research Review* 34(3):75–102

Feldman S (1997) NGOs and civil society: (Un)stated contradictions. *The Annals of the American Academy of Political and Social Science* 554:46–66

Gordon C (1991) Introduction. In G Burchell, C Gordon and P Miller (eds) *The Foucault Effect: Studies in Governmentality* (pp 1–52). London: Harvester Wheatsheaf

Gramsci A (1989) *Selections from the Prison Notebooks.* New York: International Publishers

Hammack D (2002) Nonprofit organizations in American history. *American Behavioral Scientist* 45:11

Hansen T B and Stepputat F (2001) Introduction: States of imagination. In T B Hansen (ed) *States of Imagination: Ethnographic Explorations of the Postcolonial State* (pp 1–38). Durham, NC: Duke University Press

Hart G (2004) Critical ethnographies of development in the era of globalization. *Progress in Human Geography* 28:1

Hintjens H (1999) The emperor's new clothes: A moral tale for development experts? *Development in Practice* 9:382–395

Howell J and Pearce J (2001) *Civil Society and Development.* London: Lynne Rienner Publishers

Hyatt S (2001) From citizen to volunteer: Neoliberal governance and the erasure of poverty. In J Goode and J Maskovsky (eds) *The New Poverty Studies: The Ethnography of Power, Politics, and Impoverished People in the United States* (pp 201–235). New York: New York University Press

Katz C (2002) Stuck in place: Children and the globalization of social reproduction. In R J Johnston, P J Taylor and M J Watts (eds) *Geographies of Global Change: Remapping the World* (pp 248–260). 2nd ed. Malden, MA: Blackwell

Keane J (1998) *Civil Society: Old Images, New Visions.* Stanford: Stanford University Press

Larner W and Craig D (2005) After neoliberalism? Community activism and local partnerships in Aotearoa New Zealand. *Antipode* 37(3–4):this issue

Laurie N, Dwyer C, Holloway S and Smith F (1999) *Geographies of "New" Femininities.* London: Longman

Lemos M C, Austin D, Merideth R and Varady R (2002) Public–private partnerships as catalysts for community-based water infrastructure development: The Border WaterWorks program in Texas and New Mexico colonias. *Environment and Planning C* 20:281–295

Ling T (2000) Unpacking partnership: The case of health care. In J Clarke, S Gertwitz and E McLaughlin et al (eds) *New Managerialism, New Welfare?* (pp 82–101). London: Sage

Manji F (1998) The depoliticization of poverty. In D Eade (ed) *Development and Rights* (pp 12–33). Oxford: Oxfam

Martin D (2004) Nonprofit foundations and grassroots organizing: Reshaping urban governance. *The Professional Geographer* 56(3):394–405

Massey D S, Durand J and Malone N J (2002) *Beyond Smoke and Mirrors: Mexican Immigration in an Era of Economic Integration.* New York: Russell Sage Foundation

Mawdsley E, Townsend J and Porter G (2005) Trust, accountability and face-to-face interaction in North–South NGO relations. *Development in Practice* 15(1) 77–82.

Mawdsley E, Townsend J, Porter G and Oakley P (2002) *Knowledge, Power and Development Agendas: NGOs North and South*. Oxford: INTRAC.

Miraftab F (1997) Flirting with the enemy: Challenges faced by NGOs in development and empowerment. *Habitat International* 21(4):361–375

Mohan G (2002) The disappointments of civil society: The politics of NGO intervention in northern Ghana. *Political Geography* 21:125–154

Molyneux M (2001) Ethnography and global processes. *Ethnography* 2(2):273–282

Morris-Suzuki T (2000) For and against NGOs: The politics of the lived world. *New Left Review* 2:63–84

Moser C (1993) Adjustment from below: Low-income women, time and the triple role in Guayaquil, Ecuador. In S Radcliffe and S Westwood (eds) *"Viva" Women and Popular Protest in Latin America* (pp 173–196). London: Routledge

Nevins J (2002) *Operation Gatekeeper: The Rise of the "Illegal Alien" and the Making of the U.S.–Mexico Boundary*. New York: Routledge

Peck J and Tickell A (2002) Neoliberalizing space. *Antipode* 34(2):380–404

Petras J and Veltmeyer H (2001) *Globalization Unmasked: Imperialism in the 21st Century*. London: Zed Books

Rose N (1999) *Powers of Freedom: Reframing Political Thought*. Cambridge: Cambridge University Press

Runyan A (1999) Women in the neoliberal frame. In M K Meyer and E Prugle (eds) *Gender Politics in Global Governance* (pp 210–220). New York: Rowan and Littlefield

Staudt K (1998) *Free Trade? Informal Economies at the US–Mexico Border*. Philadelphia, PA: Temple University Press

Tanski J (1994) The impact crisis, stabilization and structural adjustment on women in Lima, Peru. *World Development* 22(11):1627–1642

Townsend J, Porter G and Mawdsley E (2002) The role of the transnational community of non-governmental organizations: Governance or poverty reduction? *Journal of International Development* 14:829–839

Varley A (1996) Women heading households: Some more equal then others? *World Development* 24(3):505–520

Ward P (1999) *Colonias and Public Policy in Texas and Mexico: Urbanization by Stealth*. Austin: University of Texas Press

Wolch J (1989) The shadow state: Transformations in the voluntary sector. In J Wolch and M Dear (eds) *The Power of Geography* (pp 197–221). Boston: Hyman

Rebecca Dolhinow is an assistant professor in the Women's Studies Program at the California State University, Fullerton. Her ongoing research focuses on the intersections of community activism and governmentality in immigrant communities. She is also beginning a project on the political activism of young women in southern California. Her work on colonias in the US is part of the edited volume *Border Women in Movement*.

Chapter 9

"The Experts Taught Us All We Know": Professionalisation and Knowledge in Nepalese Community Forestry

Andrea J Nightingale

Introduction

Neoliberalism is an elusive concept and, as its usage has become more prevalent in policy and academic circles, it has come to stand for an increasingly wide range of market–society relations. Here I place the daily practices of development and negotiations over power and knowledge into an analysis of neoliberalism. Using the example of community forestry in Nepal, I seek to illustrate how neoliberalism is constituted and contested in localities and thus takes specific forms in particular places (Rankin 2001; Scott 1998; Sivaramakrishnan and Agrawal 2003; Watts 2003).

My purpose here is to contribute to work done more explicitly on the economic aspects of neoliberalism in Nepal by investigating how its ideological features are increasingly prevalent within environment–development programmes (Laurie, Andolina and Radcliffe 2003; Peck and Tickell 2002; Rankin 2001; Watts 2003). In Nepal, one key change has been a move from promoting technology transfer to the promotion of particular kinds of knowledges. Many programmes aim to facilitate the "diffusion of knowledge" or encourage new "knowledge regimes", which are assumed to culminate in development (Adams 1990; Crush 1995; Escobar 1995; Sivaramakrishnan and Agrawal 2003). As a result, many development practitioners seek to teach new skills to what are perceived to be backward populations and localities. Community forestry in Nepal is no exception and the programme is rife with mechanisms to promote learning in relation to forest conservation and scientific forestry.

Wendy Larner (2000) has distinguished three types of scholarship on neoliberalism. First, work which explores neoliberalism as a policy framework; second, research which focuses on the ideological aspects; and third, that which examines it as a form of governmentality. All of these approaches assume neoliberalism is characterised by the scaling back of the welfare state in Post-Fordist capitalism and a privileging of market forces to organise social–political–economic life (Jessop 2002; Larner 2000). The economy of Nepal cannot be characterised as "Post-Fordist" as it has not gone through a Fordist stage, but rather, like many developing countries, has features of both feudal and capitalist relations of production characteristic of so-called "transition" economies (de Janvry 1981; Jessop 2002; Rankin 2004). While systematic studies of the impact of neoliberalism on the development process in Nepal have not been done, through structural adjustment and other economic programmes, aspects of neoliberal orthodoxy can be identified in the current political economy of Nepal (Rankin 2001, 2004).

Here I want to distinguish between neoliberalism as an economic programme and neoliberalism as a set of ideas about the appropriate mechanisms for social and economic progress (Peck and Tickell 2002). While neoliberalism is difficult to separate neatly from processes of modernisation or post-colonialism (Hart 2002), I am interested in exploring aspects of the modernisation process that have been shaped by neoliberalism. The need to examine the daily practices of development and neoliberalism and how these are linked to knowledge has been discussed by a number of authors (Agrawal and Sivaramakrishnan 2000; Escobar 1995; Gupta 1998; Peck and Tickell 2002; Sivaramakrishnan and Agrawal 2003; Watts 2003). This work explores the embedding of professionalism, the promotion of individuals as agents of development, and market relations as they are constituted through processes of globalisation and economic change (Peck and Tickell 2002; Watts 2003). In particular, I emphasise two key strands that are often seen to define neoliberalism as a mechanism of change: one, the promotion and embedding of professional and expert knowledges within a range of services and activities; and two, the valorisation of market and quasi-market relations across a range of social and political arenas. Community forestry in Nepal is in many respects in direct opposition to these processes of neoliberalism because of its emphasis on collective practices; nevertheless, it has become an arena within which these ideologies are appropriated, contested and entrenched.

Economic processes of globalisation have only somewhat tangential effects on remote areas of Nepal, but the impact of neoliberalism is experienced in at least three ways. First, in the assumption that there is a distinction between local and professional knowledge (see also Gururani 2000; Sivaramakrishnan and Agrawal 2003). This is often manifest in the emphasis on teaching villagers proper, *scientific* forest management. Second, there is an emphasis on implementing programmes that decentralise state control by turning over forests and local development to villagers. Third, development programmes such as community forestry are important arenas within which key social relations, particularly around caste and gender, are (re)inscribed. Community forestry thus also needs to be recognised as constitutive of neoliberalism as the programme itself is embedded within overall development ideologies and, through its enactment, what "neoliberalism" means within specific localities is specified.

Before elaborating on how neoliberalism is manifest within development–environment programmes in Nepal, a bit of background on community forestry will help to contextualise the following discussion. Forests in Nepal provide crucial inputs to agro-forestry systems in the form of leaf litter, fodder for animals and firewood for cooking. Their apparent degradation has been the focus of international attention since the early 1970s and a number of programmes have been instituted to reverse degradation in what are perceived to be dangerously fragile mountain ecosystems (Gilmour and Fisher 1991; Graner 1997). The most visible of these programmes is community forestry, a government and foreign donor-sponsored programme that turns the management of forests over to village user groups. Legally villagers are given responsibility for the daily management and oversight of their forests and are allowed to set restrictions on the harvesting and sale of forest products. The statutory authority, the District Forest Office (DFO), however, denies the groups collective choice rights (cf Arnold 1998; Ostrom 1992); in other words, the villagers are not able to change their management strategies without the approval of the DFO staff. In order to take over the management of a community forest, a user group must first map the forest and develop an operational plan (Shrestha et al 1995). The DFO staff and, where relevant, foreign-donor project staff, provide substantial assistance to user groups during this phase. Once the forest has been surveyed, mapped and the operational plan approved, the amount of assistance villagers are given for the daily functioning of their management committees is highly variable. Foreign donor-sponsored groups tend to receive substantial assistance, whereas others, like the groups I worked with in Mugu District of northwestern Nepal, receive very little.

To understand the contradictory embedding of neoliberalism in rural Nepal (cf Jessop 2002; Larner 2000), I explore the ways that the professionalisation of forestry in Nepal authorises particular kinds of knowledges, discourses and practices related to forest management. Issues of who has knowledge, who needs to be taught and what they are taught are central to contestations over who can be legitimate managers of natural resources and what information they need to be effective. Knowledge intersects with the promotion of quasi-market relations and idealised visions of "community" (closely linked to key political changes) to re-figure caste and gender relations, although here I focus primarily on caste relations. Which users embrace the discourses and practices of professionalism and for what purposes lends insight into the workings of neoliberalism and how it is implicated in the reconfiguring of social and power relations within localities and, in this case, the consequences of this for ecological change.

I argue that the promotion of scientific forestry practices potentially undermines three of community forestry's key objectives: to include the poorest of the poor, to promote democratic institutions to manage forests, and to promote forest ecosystem health. While in some sense these objectives are counter to the goals of neoliberalism, especially those that seek to foster competitive market relations to stabilise social and economic inequalities, the programme can also be seen to be embedded within a neoliberal logic of property relations that seeks to privatise common resources through the promotion of collective management (Mansfield 2004). As Mansfield has argued, the promotion of common resources as "property" is firmly situated within a neoliberal logic that assumes rational, profit-seeking economic subjectivities and thus the need to regulate use of resources through property arrangements. Key to these ideas within community forestry is the vision of a recognisable and uncontested "community" to which management of forests can be given. In the case that follows, the disputes I recount show the complex appropriations and resistances to these neoliberal subjectivities and reveal the contested nature of "the community". Similar complexities are evident in the ways in which the re-figuring of caste and gender are the outcome of these resistances, appropriations and acquiescence of neoliberal forms of knowledge and quasi-market relations. This analysis of a programme designed to empower local people helps to illustrate some of the internal contradictions of neoliberalism. The programme offers possibilities to contest neoliberal social and power relations and take control over crucial resources, but these opportunities also serve to further entrench discourses of development and professionalisation into the daily practices of forest use. As such, the programme undermines immediate state control over natural resources, yet simultaneously promotes neoliberal notions of property and "professional" subjectivities that strengthen state control from afar, ultimately serving to entrench particular neoliberal ideologies into the most remote places of Nepal.

The establishment of DFOs was one of the first steps in the process of professionalisation in the forestry sector of Nepal (Bhattarai, Conway and Shrestha 2002). The offices brought professional foresters into all areas of Nepal, but beyond attempts at enforcing national forest rules,[1] they had little contact with villagers. Community forestry, in contrast, is a programme that gives villagers control over the management of their forests, with input from the District Forest

Officer and the staff of rangers. Through this input, community forestry can be seen as a vehicle for expanding neoliberal notions of "professional", community and scientific forestry into villages all across Nepal and yet also as a key mechanism through which villagers are able to resist aspects of scientific logic and state control.

To explore how neoliberalism shapes subjectivities within community forestry, I draw from feminist theory and discourse analysis to look at how people's subjectivities are linked to the mobilisation of particular discourses. Feminist theories of subjectivity have examined the ways in which people internalise different identities such as gender, caste, class, but also more subtle forms of social hierarchy and oppression (Butler 1997; Nightingale 2006; Mahoney and Yngvesson 1992; Mehta and Bondi 1999). In this kind of conceptualisation, identities are not assumed to be linked to pre-given characteristics, but rather are the result of social interactions. Thus the meanings and significance of gender and caste are not static or stable but rather are performed, (re)defined and (re)negotiated in daily interactions (Bondi and Davidson 2004; Butler 1990, 1992). A key insight from this work is that many forms of resistance require people to first internalise their oppressed status (Mahoney and Yngvesson 1992). In other words, people are able to draw on dominant discourses of social difference in order to contest their status within them or to draw into question the discourse itself. Yet by doing so, they must first acknowledge and internalise that discourse as dominant and thus (re)produce it. In the context of community forestry, I examine how people draw on scientific knowledge in order to assert authority, but in a more complex dynamic, I also explore how people use a lack of scientific knowledge to exert power and the importance of their own knowledge. How and when social hierarchies become salient in natural resource management lends insight into how neoliberal processes of professionalisation, knowledge and legitimate rights to manage the forest are embedded within power relations and the daily practices of forest use. In short, we see aspects of neoliberalism and the contestation of it in action.

Community Forestry in Mugu

I worked with a user group that was formed in 1991 and had their operational plan approved in 1993, allowing the forest (named Pipledi) to be officially handed over to them. They have been responsible for managing it with some oversight from the DFO ever since.[2] The mixed-caste group consists of four different castes: highest-caste Brahmins and Thakuris, middle-caste Chhetris and lowest-caste (or so-called "untouchable") Kamis. In this part of Nepal, caste and gender continue to be very significant social relations that shape the division of labour as well as a variety of spatial and bodily practices associated with ritual pollution. The relationships between work, caste, gender, labour relations and class are very complex, but I provide a brief outline here. Some of these relationships will become clearer below.

Work is a key domain within which social differences are defined and maintained and thus is a symbolic as well as material enactment of social power. Due to bodily practices associated with caste and class, high-caste men (Brahmins and Thakuris) are reluctant to do manual labour and when they are wealthy enough, hire low-caste men and women to work their fields. Most of the resources needed on a daily basis, including water, firewood, animal fodder and leaf litter, are thus gathered by women of all castes. Lower-caste men (Chhetri and Kami) also participate in these activities, but if they have access to a cash income or any kind of "office work" they avoid these chores. Working in offices—in Mugu generally government agencies such as the DFO or the handful of foreign-aid sponsored offices[3]—requires literacy skills and confers significant social and economic power. Kami men and the vast majority of women are essentially excluded from such opportunities because of their social status and because they are illiterate. A Kami man who had obtained his School Leaving Certificate complained bitterly of the lack of appropriate opportunities for him because of his caste status. Office jobs thus confer status because of the literacy skills and high-caste status of the men who hold them, and are only available to those who fit that profile. This is one of the important ways in which neoliberal processes are evident in rural Nepal. Development has become equated with cash incomes and education, among other attributes (Pigg 1996), and significant social and political power can be gained from being developed.

In many respects these processes are not new. Literacy skills have conferred social status and power within Mugu at least since the early twentieth century and perhaps longer. Oral histories indicate that the ancestors of many of the current leaders within the village were educated men who were well aware of and strategically utilised the legal system. The *mukiya*, or village tax collector and headman, and his brother, a clerk responsible for a variety of legal tasks, were instrumental in obtaining control of Pipledi forest in 1919. Both men were given these positions by the Rana government that ruled Nepal from 1846 to 1951 and their eldest sons were expected to continue in those roles after them. The *mukiya* has very little power now since he no longer collects taxes, but he is nevertheless given respect and continues to safeguard and interpret old documents that show title to land and, importantly for this user group, forests. Many of the high-caste men in the village are descended from the *mukiya*, although only direct descendants try to claim political and social power based on their heritage. All of them have been educated at home, therefore only a few adult high-caste men cannot read proficiently. Now, however, with the increasing professionalisation of knowledge, having a degree is more important than literacy skills and some people have implied that powerful high-caste families have actually paid for their sons' degrees when they were unable to pass the exams.

In addition, neoliberal processes have led to substantial changes in labour relations. According to oral histories, historically the Chhetris and lower castes worked for the highest castes in feudal and bonded labour arrangements until sometime in the second half of the twentieth century. Now the lowest castes have lands of their own that have very recently been brought under cultivation and they have a variety of wage labour opportunities available to them through state and foreign donor-sponsored building projects in Mugu. As a consequence, the high-caste people complain that the low castes do not "mind" anymore and are slow to come and work their fields for the food and small cash payment that is offered. This has led to significant reconfigurations of work expectations and has served to firmly establish a cash-based economy in Mugu. Until the institution of government offices and various work opportunities for both high and low caste men, the economy in Mugu was largely based on barter and primary production. Now primary production continues to be the main source of subsistence for most people, but cash-based exchanges have replaced many barter and feudal labour relations. In addition, the People's War which brought in multi-party democracy in 1990 (Hoftun, Raeper and Whelpton 1999), has intersected with these economic changes to reconfigure caste relations in significant ways. Both the high and low-caste people explained that because (high-caste) politicians need the votes of the lowest castes, they can no longer dominate them to the same extent. Many of my respondents concluded that not much had changed, yet there was an overall sense that at least legally and politically, they were all equal. Thus both the low castes and high castes are actively involved in appropriating new forms of authority within political and social arenas and community forestry is no exception. Below I detail the ways in which caste hierarchies are mobilised, contested and re-entrenched as an example of the appropriation of and opposition to neoliberalism (see also Gupta 1998).[4]

In this context it is perhaps not surprising that high-caste men have claimed positions of authority within the community forestry user group based on caste status and literacy skills. What is more interesting, however, is how literacy, and the knowledge to which it gives certain people access, is contested and mobilised within the user group. It is important to highlight here that while literate, high-caste

men claim the right to control the user group and develop management priorities, it is the low-caste, illiterate men and illiterate women
of all castes who do the vast majority of the harvesting and other work
in the forest.

The relationships between literacy, knowledge and power were well
illustrated in a dispute over two houses that had been built within the
community forest boundaries by two lowest-caste brothers. The clear-
ing of forest land for agriculture or for building purposes is strictly
forbidden by both national forest and community forest rules. The
two houses in question were well within the community forest boundaries but, perhaps more significantly, their presence had been
reported to the DFO leaving the user group the task of punishing
the violators. If the issue had not been reported to the DFO the user
group might have had more flexibility in how they dealt with the issue.
As it was, the extent to which they believed they had to follow the
operational plan to the letter was central to the conflict and thus the
operational plan became a highly contested arena. The operational
plan is a legal, binding document and if the DFO or the group so
choose, they could bring legal proceedings against someone for vio-
lating the rules. In practice, however, this is highly unlikely, but the
document and the threat of legal action is used to force compliance
with the rules. In the incident over the houses, people appealed to it
in different ways to suit their interests. For example, at one meeting
the following discussion took place:

Kami man [angry]: Who has to pay a fine? We will move the
house ... After everyone thinks about it, what could happen (*ke
lagyo*)? (ie "what's the big deal"). The committee can decide to
take a lot of money or a small amount of money, if the committee
decides one can put up a house, whatever the committee decides,
that can be done. For this we have the committee, otherwise what
[kind of] committee is this?

A Thakuri man looks at the management plan and reads the rules
slowly to the Kami men.

Kami man: The government has made these rules, you made [this
plan] by looking at the forest regulations, this is something that is in
the committee's hands. (Community forestry meeting, 19 June 1999)

The Kami man in the above exchange insists that because the rules
have been written by the user group they also have the power to
change them. He refuses to take the operational plan as the final
authority and rather appeals to the committee as the final authority—
a committee of which he considers himself a member. Technically, he
is not a committee member but only a user-group member; thus he

does not have formal decision-making authority but he does have a voice in the process. From his perspective, the operational plan is almost meaningless; it is the negotiations in the user group that count. The operational plan is in many ways representative of the state and the authority of the legal system, a system which in the eyes of the Kamis has rarely served the interests of the lower castes. Perhaps more importantly, it is a system they feel unable to negotiate to their advantage in most circumstances.

The high-caste men, in contrast to the Kami man, view the operational plan as a semi-sacred authority. They have a very high regard for official documents and they are well familiar with their legal power. When the community forest was formed, the 1919 document that conferred legal control over the forest to the *mukiya* was critical to establish and legitimate the group's claim to that particular piece of land. Thus the high-caste men approach the operational plan from a very different perspective than the low-caste men; for them, it is often an authority to legitimate their decisions. It is representative of the state, the legal system and other national powers that they in some ways fear, but also seek to keep on their side. It has served them in the past and thus they deliberately cultivate good relationships with the DFO staff and other key government officials in the locality.

The issue was not resolved quickly and at many of the meetings the management plan was brought out and read; sometimes people read it out loud to themselves and at other times out loud to the Kamis, slowly and deliberately at high volume as if reading to a non-native speaker. When reading to the Kami men, the high-caste men often said they needed to teach the Kami men or make them "aware". Awareness in Mugu is used as an indicator of being developed and literate (see also Pigg 1996). The Kamis were thus considered to lack knowledge and needed to be taught much like children. Community forestry, then, becomes a context in which neoliberal notions of appropriate knowledge and the authority that is conferred on those who are most "professional" is entrenched into even very remote places of Nepal like Mugu. The high-caste men have appropriated new forms of authority based on written documents and the ability to read them, undermining and devaluing the verbal processes of building consensus that are equally central to the idealised implementation of community forestry.

The structure of community forestry and indeed development discourses in Nepal encourage this kind of dynamic. According to a local, literate informant, when training sessions are given by the DFO they ask for literate members to be sent by the user group. Some of these training sessions include foreign donor-sponsored all expenses paid tours to other parts of Nepal, a much coveted and rare opportunity for people from Mugu.[5] The sessions do not involve reading or writing but literate people are considered more progressive ("aware"), smart and able to learn. While ostensibly sessions to train "rural villagers", the professionalisation of forestry encourages DFO staff and even the participants themselves to prefer those with a set of recognisable skills and knowledges as evidenced by degrees and levels of literacy. Literacy thus is promoted as a necessary requirement for understanding professional forestry practices and gives privileged access to scientific forestry knowledge, DFO staff and associated opportunities. User-group members then mobilise this discourse of understanding and literacy within decision-making forums to exert and resist power.

Another example illustrates this well. In addition to the operational plan, the map of the forest is similarly considered to be an authoritative, immutable document and the Kamis' lack of literacy used to argue that they are not capable of understanding it. It is upheld as a very important document conferring legal and de facto rights to that land and in many ways symbolises the user group and its ability to control their land. Thus one Thakuri man said, when trying to understand why two influential men had not shown up for a meeting:

> We have a map, we have surveyed our forest, Chhatyalbara [nearby village] hasn't. We have a record of the permits we've given. Who else has such a record? ... We have a good management plan. Who else has a good plan?"

And he went on to ask why the people who needed to be at the meeting had not come. For him, the map and the plan are symbolic and material representations of the group and because they are good documents, the group should function well. The high-caste people thus appeal to these symbols to try to bring unity in the group and use their ability to read and interpret them to maintain control over the group. This was reflected in the following exchange:

> Kami man: Did we build a house in the forest? Others have built houses in the forest.

> Thakuri man: If the DFO thinks we have mis-used the forest, he will take it back. We need to do things that won't affect either the little people (*sanno manche*) or the people with big posts (*thulo manche*).

> Thakuri man #2: If there's a map, they can't ignore it. Since there is a map of Pipledi [the forest], they can't change it to allow someone to encroach on community forest land.

> Chairman says to the Kamis sitting outside: Don't make a joke, this is a law.

Kamis outside: We haven't cut down the forest. We just built a house. We didn't take timber from the forest.

Later a Thakuri man said: In the minds' of these *Dums* (untouchables) this map of the forest is only a map, these numbers don't correspond to [real] land (*jugga*). They think, "where are the numbers on this land (*jugga*)?" But they have to follow the rules; they need to move the house. (Community forestry meeting, 19 June 1999)

For the high-caste men the map is an extension of the forest. They recognise it as representative of the forest on the ground and in fact almost more "real" than what's on the ground. The forest can be taken away—and was when the forests were nationalised—but the map can be used for legal challenges now and in the future. It offers some protection from the changing fashions of development and state control. For the Kami men, however, it represents none of these things. They feel under the control of the high castes and do not see the state as a reliable ally in combating that oppression, especially since the vast majority of all state employees and officials are from the high castes.

The map and the operational plan are direct outcomes of the professionalisation of community forestry. The programme requires that these legal documents are produced and approved by the DFO before the user group is considered legitimate. The high-caste, literate men seek to maintain good relations with the DFO to further their political power and readily adopt and use these symbols of professionalisation and development. Within the user group they have privileged access to them because of their abilities to read and they use this privilege strategically to maintain control over the user-group process when in fact they do very little forest harvesting. As the "developed ones", they place themselves in the role of educating the illiterate members, (re)producing the assumption implicit in community forestry as a national programme that local users lack the appropriate knowledge to effectively manage and conserve their forests.

The high-caste men must first accept and internalise a neoliberal discourse that equates illiteracy with backwardness and lack of knowledge to manipulate these discourses in this manner (see also Gupta 1998; Mahoney and Yngvesson 1992). While this is not surprising as it serves their interests and articulates with their own understandings of themselves as superior and having rights to dominate the lower castes, the lower-caste men themselves internalised and manipulated their subjectivity in somewhat different and conflicting ways.

In the dispute over the houses, the Kami men evidently did not believe they needed to be taught and rather used their illiteracy as a counter weapon. On more than one occasion after the rules had been read out loud, the Kami man said, essentially: "how do I know what's written there? You could just be pretending to read and say whatever you want". They firmly believed that the user group could make whatever decision they wanted and it was simply a question of using the right kind of influence within the user group, influence that did not necessarily depend on literacy. In order to use this kind of counter weapon, the lower-caste men must first accept the authority of the operational plan to undermine the Thakuris' reading of it. Thus while it appears that they are resisting the authority of the operational plan and the map—and processes of professionalisation—this resistance is only partial. By highlighting their illiteracy, they serve to further legitimate the neoliberal conflation of knowledge with development (Bondi and Davidson 2004; Larner 2000; Mahoney and Yngvesson 1992).

Their belief that the committee is the real authority was not far off the mark, however, or so it seemed from the treatment of other conflicts including one related to the forest houses. As part of a counter strategy, the Kamis accused middle-caste Chhetri families of encroaching on the community forestry boundaries to create more agricultural land (which they had done). The stipulated fine of Rs 1000 is the same as that for building the houses, but the Chhetris who have substantially more social power within the group were able to negotiate for a far lower fine of only Rs 250. In their case the committee argued that the crime was not as severe because it had occurred on the boundaries of the forest instead of in the middle, and agricultural land was cast as less permanent than a house. More importantly, however, their encroachment had not been reported to the DFO and therefore the committee felt they did not need to impose the Rs 1000 fine stipulated by the operational plan. It was also clear from various discussions at the community forestry meet-ings and more informal conversations that the leadership of the committee did not believe they would be able to collect more than Rs 250 from the Chhetris, whereas they believed they could force the substantially poorer Kamis to pay the entire fine.

People of different castes had different opinions about this issue and whether or not it was fair to the Kamis. Many people made reference to the underlying power dynamics and the way that various groups were trying to exert power by either ignoring the rules or enforcing them to the letter. In reference to the large fine given to the Kamis and the much smaller fine given to the Chhetris, one Brahmin man said:

> The law needs to be the same for all … if you dig up a little bit of land or a lot, you have dug it up. The Chhetris are influential (*thulo*

manche), they do not do any harm to themselves, and they try to dominate the small and the poor. (Interview, 25 July 1999)

This same man had suggested during the community forestry meeting that since the complaint about the houses had been written on one piece of paper that the fine could be applied to them as if it was one case. If so the two men could share the Rs 1000 fine. The Chhetris and other Brahmin and Thakuri men, however, argued strongly that the full fine needed to be applied to both of them. It is important to note that not all the high-caste men (women had very little involvement in this issue) were in favour of the way that influence was used in the user group, but they also felt powerless to stop it.

A Kami man who I asked about the issue initially responded by saying that the higher castes dominate the lower castes and thus the two men were treated unfairly. But when we told him the Chhetris also had to pay a fine, albeit quite a bit less, he said: "Oh, [they] also need to pay? Oh, then it is good. We need to use our own arena, that is good" (interview, 13 July 1999). His main concern it seemed, was that the community forestry committee was an arena within which all violators should be punished. He went on to say that the two Kami men knew exactly what they were doing and should not have encroached on the forest to build their houses: "what the committee decided was OK". Here the low-caste man was most concerned about oppression of the Kamis through the user group and not whether the two men had committed a crime. By protesting on these grounds, it is necessary for him to (re)assert that caste defines social hierarchies. He sees this issue as symbolic of the treatment of all lowest-caste people and thus the fine is unjust when only applied to the Kamis. In his mind, provided the Chhetris are also fined, then community forestry is not being used as a mechanism for oppressing the lowest castes, but rather as an arena for management of the forest. When analysed through this kind of framework, his lack of concern over the amount of the fines is perfectly consistent with his positionality, as what is at stake here for him is whether or not all violators of community rules are punished. It is important to point out, however, that the amount of the fine was significantly linked to caste hierarchies, thus I can only conclude that this informant agreed with the assessment by the rest of the user group that the houses were a more severe crime than the agricultural land.

The most interesting aspect of this episode is the way that people unsettle caste hierarchies through these oppositions to and mobilisations of neoliberal processes. The higher castes appropriate the symbols of professionalisation and use their literacy skills to assert their understanding of the community forest rules and the potential legal consequences. The Kami men, in contrast, use their lack of literacy skills in exactly the same way but to resist the domination of the higher castes. They insist that reading out loud from the operational plan is not sufficient evidence for them because they cannot verify what is written. It is only by accepting their inferior status and lack of understanding, however, that the Kamis are able to mobilise a discourse of ignorance. This kind of strategy requires them to manipulate power relations and the cultural practices of caste with somewhat conflicting results. By making it clear that they cannot read the operational plan, they accept and publicly reinforce their status as illiterate members. Yet, because they use their lack of literacy as a way to resist the authority of the higher-caste men, they are both contesting the right of the literate to control the group and challenging the idea that the operational plan is the final authority. In these somewhat contradictory ways, they both reinforce and redefine power relations based on caste.

In addition, by making literacy so central to this conflict, literacy is defined as another way in which caste distinctions are maintained, somewhat shifting yet also reinforcing social hierarchies based on caste. It is only those who are ignorant and unaware who are poor, low-caste and thus liable to break community forestry rules and need to be taught proper appreciation for the forest rules. It is not surprising, therefore, that the same labels are not applied to the Chhetris, rather it is their educated and powerful status that makes them likely to break community forestry rules and claim impunity. Each caste group draws on these discourses of knowing, awareness, literacy and power to contest the actions of the other members. It is through these processes that the contradictions of neoliberalism are evident. The strategies of both the high castes and low castes serve to further embed ideologies of professionalisation, yet there is a simultaneous unsettling and opposition to that.

To Market? Relations of Poverty, Knowledge and Power

Caste relations are deeply entwined with labour relations and it is in this domain that important contradictions of neoliberalism are also constituted. While markets in Western Nepal are hybrid processes with barter, patron–client and feudal relations continuing to be very important alongside more recognisably capitalist relations, there is nevertheless an embedding of a quasi-market logic into these relations. This embedding, however, is not straightforward or consistent, and hegemonic discourses about poverty, knowledge and power are not always used to exert power. In other cases they are invoked to allow for flexibility and tolerance of rule breaking in community forestry, indicating a level of cohesiveness in the group that contradicts neoliberal processes. For example, in 1994 a high-caste friend and I observed some Kami men selling firewood in the market town. At that time, it was prohibited to sell firewood to people outside the user group. I asked my friend why she did not stop them and she replied, "They are poor, what can they do? If they don't sell firewood they can't eat. It is destroying our forest, but what to do?" In this case then, flagrant breaking of community forestry rules is tolerated *because* of poverty. Just as in the earlier example, however, mobilising discourses in this way reinforces the caste and wealth distinctions upon which social power and cultural understandings of poverty are based. This kind of mobilisation of discourses of poverty does not serve to destabilise the processes that entrench quasi-market relations into rural societies, but there is not a direct attempt to exert power either. Rather a discourse of poverty is used to allow the Kamis to mitigate their poverty somewhat by selling firewood in opposition to ideologies of competitiveness and individualism.

In fact, the selling of firewood has been very important in changing labour relations based on caste, and in this sense has had profound effects on destabilising caste and power relations. As I mentioned above, there has been an increase in wage labour opportunities and these have served to undermine historical relations between the castes. Yet neoliberal processes do not subsume historical relations completely or generically. Rather, antecedents shape the kinds of appropriations and oppositions that occur, leading to highly uneven and unpredictable outcomes. So while in this instance poverty discourses are not used to exert power, in an indirect way, they serve to afford the Kamis more power. Very poor high-caste people do not and socially could not sell firewood to mitigate their poverty because it would reduce their social status (see also Gidwani 2000). High-caste men in particular, but also women, are very reluctant to engage in activities that are considered the domain of the low castes and therefore leave the quite significant economic opportunity to sell firewood to the lowest castes. This kind of rejection of lucrative opportunities defies a strict market logic. Through such material practices, both the low-caste and high-caste people (re)produce the symbolic meaning of work associated with caste. Yet by perpetuating these discourses about work, the Kamis are afforded the opportunity to change their economic impoverishment even if symbolically they are "poor" because they are low caste and sell firewood. Poverty and caste continue to be reproduced as important social distinctions, albeit to destabilise somewhat the economic but not symbolic foundations upon which social power is exerted.

Similarly, members of the user group assert their knowledge of forest management in different ways that do not necessarily follow the kind of pattern expected from the account I've given so far; although when understood as enacting subjectivities and embedded within new, partial appropriations and oppositions to neoliberal processes, it is consistent. The high-caste men who control the user-group committee describe how community forestry has taught them everything they know about managing the forest. One Thakuri man said:

> At the beginning we didn't know anything … One day [the DFO] asked all us *janne manche* (literate, knowledgeable people—literally "going somewhere people") if we wanted to take our forest. We didn't understand, but he spoke to our older brother (a village leader) and he said, "OK, we do not understand, but we are ready to try it."

In another informal discussion, a Brahmin man told me that community forestry had taught them all they know about managing the forest. Here literate, powerful men are portraying themselves in much the same light as they portray the Kamis.

Women mainly of the higher castes, however, are insistent that they had important knowledge about managing the forest. Women do most of the harvesting of firewood, fodder and leaf litter, thus they have extensive knowledge of these resources and the logistics of managing their collection (Nightingale 2005). A Thakuri woman said it this way:

> Long before, when our forest had become degraded, we had the idea [to protect it]. Then we heard on the radio about other places … three rangers and [high-caste Thakuri men—village leaders] got together and decided to form the community forest. (Interview, 20 February 1999)

A Chhetri woman, after saying that she had been afraid and did not really understand what community forestry would be, asserted, "The men gave their wives a lot of trouble. The men didn't know how to manage the firewood, they wanted to have permits for that too. The first time that they wanted to do this, the women [of all three villages] … scolded their husbands" (interview 14 June 1999). Other women also talked about how they had prevented the men from trying to regulate firewood and leaf litter with permits—resources that are collected almost daily—arguing that it was unrealistic to try to insist on permits for such things. Here, the women, in contrast to the men, assert that their knowledge is important, yet at the same time they also talk about how they did not understand community forestry and if it had not been for the vision of a few high-caste men who are village leaders, they would not have tried it. One Brahmin woman said:

> [In the beginning] when we were in community forestry meetings, the men would applaud the things the women said. They thought

our ideas were good. The men were educated (*parde-lekeko*) and we were not, so we needed both men and women for the community forest. (Interview, 20 February 1999)

In this example, the women are quite clear about the importance of their contributions, but they contrast these contributions with the educated knowledge of the men. Similarly, the men contrast their knowledge—or lack of it—in relation to the professional knowledge of the DFO staff.

As in the example of selling firewood, the use of these contrasting discourses does not map easily onto social and power relations, unless one understands that the mobilisation of these discourses is possible only by accepting the subjectivities of caste, gender and literacy and the power they confer on one. The high-caste men accept the dominance and knowledge of the experts and they utilise a discourse of ignorance to demonstrate to me how developed they are because they have followed the way shown to them by professionals. This helps illustrate the extent to which ideologies of neoliberalism have been internalised within remote parts of rural Nepal. The professionalisation of forestry and its origins outside of Nepal are especially evident in the following quote. When asked how community forestry was started, a Brahmin man replied:

Until 2034 (1977) all the forests were national forests. Then scientists, specialists, and scholars came from different countries and thought that the forest was for the people, and it is better to give the right to the people to conserve their own forest. (Interview, 12 June 1999)

In fact, he is basically right as community forestry was initiated by the World Bank, FAO and the Worldwide Fund for Nature, although there were important inputs from Nepalis as well, most of whom had been educated abroad. There is quite a lot at stake here for these men in Mugu beyond their desire to manage the forest effectively. They need to convey to the outside world (through me and my writing) that they have learned how to manage their forests "properly" and properly is defined as scientific forestry as taught by the DFO staff. In addition, by giving deference to the DFO staff, they hope to gain political favour that can benefit them in a variety of ways locally and even nationally. Furthermore, they are keen to demonstrate that they follow the prescriptions of community forestry to legitimate their control over the committee. Finally, because these men are known to be educated and "aware", at a fundamental level they do not need to prove that to me. In many ways, being "aware" means that they are able to learn from experts and therefore it is not necessary to assert their knowledge.

The women, however, have entirely different positionalities and this opens up the possibility for them to insist on the importance of their knowledge. The women generally don't have much interaction with the DFO staff and therefore are not as keen to position themselves favourably in relation to them. More importantly, because they know they are uneducated, they do not need to negate their own skills and knowledge to assert that they are "aware". While both men and women saw me and my work as potentially legitimating their claims, the women were keen to insist that they do have knowledge even if they do not have literacy. This insistence does not disrupt the hierarchies produced by literacy—they say that because they are illiterate the men are needed in community forestry—but it does disrupt the idea that literate knowledge is sufficient for forest management. This assertion contests but does not undermine the professionalisation of community forestry and the literate knowledge upon which such claims are based.

The Professionalisation of Forest Care

Professionalisation in community forestry does not only occur symbolically and in relation to control over the management process, it also occurs in relation to active management. By active management I mean activities like thinning, pruning and seedling rearing. It is a critical part of both the transmission of knowledge from the DFO to the user group and the user group's sense of conserving their forest. Thinning and pruning was taught by the DFO at a training session I attended in 1994 and five others have been conducted district-wide since that time. The training was required for at least one member of each household and had participation from a broad cross section of the user group, people of all castes and both men and women. It was done in the forest controlled by the user group described here, although people were present from other user groups as well. The District Forest Officer worked alongside the villagers and made it clear to me and the others that he had expert knowledge. He scolded the women for focusing too much on collecting firewood[6] instead of trimming off the young, green branches of the saplings and explained carefully to everyone how it was to be done.

The user group now has a small demonstration plot (less than 1 ha) that they have thinned and pruned. Interestingly, the stand is just outside the boundary of the community forest proper. It is shown off during district-wide training sessions as an example of what a forest can look like. The trees are relatively even-aged blue pines, regularly spaced with virtually no understory growth. This example is emblematic of the western, professional forestry bias in community forestry that promotes the growth of monoculture stands of timber species over other forest products (Häusler 1993). The objectives of thinning and pruning are to allow the remaining trees to grow faster in the absence of competition for light and nutrients, which will maximise eventual yield of timber (Wenger 1984). Raymond Borgen, a forester who worked with me during the fieldwork, believes that the work they are doing is inadequate and therefore not necessary. The pruning of lower branches is the focus of their work, but these branches would self-prune as the forest develops. They do not appear to be thinning (removing whole saplings), but even if they have cut some, they are not removing nearly enough. In Borgen's opinion, the demonstration stand is still far too thick to accomplish these objectives. As a consequence, the stand will not grow great timber nor does it provide for any other kinds of forest products except some firewood from pruned branches.

The user group has incorporated these "scientific" ideas of good forest management and show off the demonstration stand as evidence of their care for and knowledge of forestry. Yet, these activities cannot produce the kind of forest the user group really wants and needs. Already there are conflicts brewing within the user group over the amount of grazing land available and the fire suppression policy that reduces understory foliage good for grazing. Scientific forestry was developed in Germany and the United States to produce timber for industry and while in many places this kind of forestry is being re-thought, the forestry practices advocated in Nepal are still rooted in older models of forest dynamics (Alverson, Kuhlmann and Waller 1994; Scott 1998; Wenger 1984). The management techniques promoted by the DFO are thus intended for the production of timber, not multi-species, multiple resource "subsistence" harvesting such as that done in Nepal. Perhaps fortunately, the thinning and pruning activities are done on such a small scale that they will have little impact on the forest as a whole unless the effort intensifies. Nevertheless, professionalisation of forestry in Nepal and the ways in which such practices and knowledges are transmitted and incorporated into community forestry user groups all across Nepal potentially have serious ramifications for producing the kinds of forest ecosystems necessary for survival.

Conclusion

Community forestry is a highly complex arena for the entrenchment of neoliberalism. The programme itself is oriented around collective values which in many ways are in direct opposition to neoliberal values. Collectively owned and managed forests belie the individualistic and private property ideologies that are considered emblematic of neoliberalism. Yet, despite this opposition, the programme is quickly becoming enrolled in various neoliberal processes. I have explored how the professionalisation of forestry knowledge and practice has intersected with antecedent social relations and forestry practices to provide new avenues for resisting and appropriating power. The case study demonstrates how people exploit the artificial distinction between professional and local knowledges to claim authority and exert power and resistance. These processes are not clean and universal as neoliberalism is often portrayed, rather they are shaped by the contexts through which they are invoked and the contestations of them that occur within the daily functioning of user groups. This case emphasises the incomplete and unpredictable outcomes of neoliberal processes and the ways in which they are increasingly becoming embedded within development practices that in many ways were designed to counter such trends.

To return to the three key objectives of community forestry that are undermined, the overall devaluing of so-called local knowledge potentially has serious ramifications for forest ecosystems and community forestry. Scientific forestry cannot produce the kind of forests and resources people need for daily survival in Nepal because the kind of scientific forestry taught in Nepal is not designed to produce multi-use forests. Already the effects of this are becoming evident in Mugu and how the user group will respond to this change in their forest is unclear. More dialogue is needed between user groups and their (sometimes conflicting) needs and the DFO to tailor management priorities to the needs of each group, drawing from the rich locally embedded ecological knowledge of forest users.

Secondly, the symbolic way in which only literate people are considered legitimate forest managers serves to effectively exclude the poorest of the poor from the community forestry management process. But, more significantly, it defines forest management as separate from forest harvesting and the daily practices of resource use. It is only by making that symbolic shift that the knowledge of those who use the forest most often—illiterate, low-caste men and women of all castes—can be dismissed as inadequate for understanding community forestry. Thus it was considered inappropriate for the women to be gathering firewood during the pruning and thinning exercise, rather than seeing the potential for firewood collection as a means of thinning the forest. Through these processes and from the examples I have given, it is clear that the focus on scientific knowledges and development within community forestry undermines the ability of the programme to promote democratic access to forest management processes because of the way that some users are marginalised. Fundamentally, all villagers need to be seen to already have important knowledge about forest management that can be supported by community forestry, rather than community forestry teaching them to care for their resource.

Acknowledgements

I wish to thank Liz Bondi and Nina Laurie for organising the session "Between grassroots activism and incorporation? Processes and politics of professionalisation in the (neo)liberal world" at the AAG conference, New Orleans, 4–8 March 2003, where the original draft of this contribution was presented. Nick Blomley, Pamela Richardson, Maggie Chapman, Liz Bondi, three anonymous reviewers, Noel Castree and the participants in the session all contributed very helpful comments on earlier drafts. I would especially like to thank one of the anonymous reviewers and Noel Castree for pushing me to theorise neoliberalism more carefully and Pamela Richardson for her insights. Any errors that remain are my own. The fieldwork was supported by the National Science Foundation under Grant No 9900788, a Fulbright-Hays Doctoral Dissertation Award and a University of Minnesota Graduate School Special Grant. I am deeply grateful for the support they have provided. Thank you to HMG Government of Nepal for allowing me to conduct research on several different occasions and a very special thanks to the people of Mugu for their participation in my research.

Endnotes

[1] In 1957, all the forests in Nepal were brought under the control of the Ministry of Forests and, with the exception of a few private forests, all forested land was considered property of the state. This served to undermine some local systems of forest management, but in other places led to the evolution of new local systems (Messerschmidt 1987).

[2] Since I left the field in late 1999, Maoist groups operating in western Nepal have periodically disrupted affairs in Mugu. The latest reports I have are that the Maoists do not have a permanent presence (they do in Jumla, two days walk to the south) but do demand food and support when they come through. In Jumla, the Maoists have undermined community forestry user groups and intimidated foreign-aid sponsored staff trying to promote community forestry. I do not know what the situation is in Mugu, but have good reason to suspect that even if officially the group has been disrupted, it continues to operate informally.

[3] I believe the foreign donor-sponsored offices that were established in Mugu in the late 1990s, including the Karnali Local Development Project (KLDP), have closed their offices due to Maoist disruptions.

[4] Gender relations are also being re-configured and contested in ways that are embedded within and similar to caste relations. I focus on caste largely because the particular ethnographic events I describe were mainly contestations of caste. See Nightingale (2006) for an analysis of the intersections of gender and caste.

[5] These training sessions are the only direct support given to villagers in this region for community forestry. The donors also sponsor training for DFO staff. In other parts of the country, foreign donors provide more intensive direct support to user groups. Staff

members attend user-group meetings, help resolve disputes and utilise various "community mobilization" strategies.
[6] One woman said to the others that she was not going home without firewood after walking that far into the forest. She considered it a wasted trip otherwise.

References

Adams W M (1990) *Green Development*. New York: Routledge
Agrawal A and Sivaramakrishnan K (2000) Introduction: Agrarian environments. In A Agrawal and K Sivaramakrishnan (eds) *Agrarian Environments: Resources, Representation and Rule in India* (pp 1–22). Durham: Duke University Press
Alverson W S, Kuhlmann W and Waller D M (1994) *Wild Forests: Conservation Biology and Public Policy*. Washington, DC: Island Press
Arnold J E M (1998) *Managing Forests as Common Property*. Rome: Food and Agriculture Organization of the United Nations
Bhattarai K, Conway D and Shrestha N (2002) The vacillating evolution of forestry policy in Nepal. *International Development Planning Review* 24:315–338
Bondi L and Davidson J (2004) Troubling the place of gender. In K Anderson, M Domosh, S Pile and N Thrift (eds) *Handbook of Cultural Geography* (pp 325–344). London: Sage
Butler J (1990) *Gender Play: Feminism and the Subversion of Identity*. New York: Routledge
Butler J (1992) Contingent foundations: Feminism and the question of "postmodernism". In J Butler and J Scott (eds) *Feminist Theorize the Political* (pp 3–21). London: Routledge
Butler J (1997) *The Psychic Life of Power*. Stanford: Stanford University Press
Crush J (1995) Introduction: Imagining development. In J Crush (ed) *Power of Development* (pp 1–26). New York: Routledge
de Janvry A (1981) *The Agrarian Question and Reformism in Latin America*. Baltimore, MD: Johns Hopkins University Press
Escobar A (1995) *Encountering Development: The Making and Unmaking of the Third World*. Princeton, NJ: Princeton University Press
Gidwani V (2000) Labored landscapes: Agroecological change in central Gujarat, India. In A Agrawal and K Sivaramakrishnan (eds) *Agrarian Environments: Rule, Resources and Representations in India* (pp 216–250). Durham: Duke University Press
Gilmour D A and Fisher R J (1991) *Villagers, Forests and Foresters: The Philosophy, Processes and Practice of Community Forestry in Nepal*. Kathmandu: Sahayogi Press
Graner E (1997) *The Political Ecology of Community Forestry in Nepal*. Saarbrücken: Verl für Entwicklungspolitik
Gupta A (1998) *Postcolonial Developments: Agriculture in the Making of Modern India*. Durham and London: Duke University Press
Gururani S (2000) Regimes of control, strategies of access: Politics of forest use in the Uttarakhand Himalaya, India. In A Agrawal and K Sivaramakrishnan (eds) *Agrarian Environments: Resources, Representation and Rule in India* (pp 170–190). Durham and London: Duke University Press
Hart G (2002) Geography and development: Development/s beyond neoliberalism? Power, culture and political economy. *Progress in Human Geography* 26:812–822
Häusler S (1993) Community forestry: A critical assessment. The case of Nepal. *The Ecologist* 23:84–90
Hoftun M, Raeper W and Whelpton J (1999) *People, Politics and Ideology: Democracy and Social Change in Nepal*. Kathmandu: Mandala Book Point

Jessop B (2002) Liberalism, neoliberalism, and urban governance: A state-theoretical perspective. *Antipode* 34:452–472

Larner W (2000) Neo-liberalism: Policy, ideology, governmentality. *Studies in Political Economy* 63:5–25

Laurie N, Andolina R and Radcliffe S (2003) Indigenous professionalization: Transnational social reproduction in the Andes. *Antipode* 35:463–491

Mahoney M A and Yngvesson B (1992) The construction of subjectivity and the paradox of resistance: Reintegrating feminist anthropology and psychology. *Signs* 18:44–73

Mansfield B (2004) Neoliberalism in the oceans: "Rationalization", property rights, and the commons question. *Geoforum* 35:313–326

Mehta A and Bondi L (1999) Embodied discourse: On gender and fear of violence. *Gender, Place and Culture* 6:67–84

Messerschmidt D A (1987) Conservation and society in Nepal: Traditional forest management and innovative development. In P D Little, M M Horowitz and A E Nyerges (eds) *Lands at Risk in the Third World: Local-Level Perspectives* (pp 373–397). Boulder, CO: Westview Press

Nightingale A (2006) The nature of gender: Work, gender and environment. *Environment and Planning D: Society and Space* (forthcoming)

Ostrom E (1992) The rudiments of a theory of the origins: Survival, and performance of common-property institutions. In D Bromley (ed) *Making the Commons Work: Theory, Practice, and Policy* (pp 293–318). San Francisco: ICS Press

Peck J and Tickell A (2002) Neoliberalizing space. *Antipode* 34:380–404

Pigg S L (1996) The credible and the credulous: The question of "villagers' beliefs" in Nepal. *Cultural Anthropology* 11:160–201

Rankin K N (2001) Governing development: Neoliberalism, microcredit, and rational economic woman. *Economy and Society* 30:18–37

Rankin K N (2004) *The Cultural Politics of Markets: Economic Liberalization and Social Change in Nepal*. London: Pluto Press

Scott J C (1998) *Seeing Like a State: How Certain Schemes to Improve the Human Condition Have Failed*. New Haven, CT: Yale University Press

Shrestha M L, Joshi S P, Bhuju U R, Joshi D B and Gautam M (1995) *Community Forestry Manual*. Kathmandu: HMG Ministry of Forests and Soils Conservation

Sivaramakrishnan K and Agrawal A (2003) *Regional Modernities: The Cultural Politics of Development in India*. Stanford, CA: Stanford University Press

Watts M (2003) Development and governmentality. *Singapore Journal of Tropical Geography* 24:6–34

Wenger K F (ed) (1984) *Forestry Handbook*. New York: Wiley

Andrea Nightingale is a Lecturer in Environmental Geography at the University of Edinburgh. Drawing from feminist, neo-Marxist and post-structural theory, her work has focused on the management of common pool resources in Nepal and Scotland. She has particular interests in thinking through the nature–society nexus both theoretically and empirically. Her most recent research is focused around subjectivity and environment in relation to fisheries management in western Scotland.

Chapter 10

Working the Spaces of Neoliberalism

Marcus Power

Although we often hear a great deal about the current unprecedented hegemony of the International Financial Institutions and the ideology of neoliberalism in the global South, the messiness, unevenness and hybridity of neoliberal developmentalism seem to have somehow slipped off the agenda. This collection explores the production of the globalised spaces of neoliberal governance but it does so with a view to drawing out some of the complexities and contradictions associated with neoliberal professionalisation in a variety of localities. The editors are to be commended then for their attempt to open up and enact dialogue across the contested North–South divide and for establishing some interesting and fruitful connections between different areas of the discipline. Rather than marking out a distinct space for the "Third World"/"developing world", this collection illustrates global similarities and convergences in response to neoliberalism and reminds us that the North–South flow of ideas and resources is not unidirectional.

My sense is that, collectively, the contributions assembled here offer an alternative framework for analysis, one which stresses the ambiguities and ambivalences within neoliberalism, around experiences of governance and in the construction of neoliberal subjectivities. In exploring how activism can become tied up with processes of professionalisation, each contribution raises crucial questions about power and representation, about negotiation and embodiment and about the "scaling up" of policy making. In particular, I welcome the focus on how the spaces of neoliberalism are "worked" in a variety of senses, through incorporation, internalisation, co-optation, resistance and subversion.

Laurie, Andolina and Radcliffe focus on the ambivalent position of social movements in "mainstream development". Rather than exploring this through work on the colonisation of development imaginaries, the debate is shifted in new and creative directions through an exploration of issues of knowledge production and governmentality and by an examination of how indigenous engagement with the cultural politics of neoliberalism in Ecuador "has generated new ways of presenting indigenous cultures, knowledges and forms of organisation". What is particularly insightful here is the rather more fluid way in which indigenous knowledge is conceptualised, as more than just concepts but also as "issues of resources, institutions and social relations". Additionally, the concept of neoliberal multiculturalism is also touched upon, throwing light on how rigid criteria and categories are applied in the Latin American context in order to illustrate how indigenous/non-indigenous distinctions are maintained and policed. Drawing upon Michael Watts' notion of governable spaces of identity, these authors look at the institutionalisation of indigenous professionalisation and how this has produced challenges to state forms of governmentality in the specific arena of education (although they accord more agency to the state in their conception of how governable spaces are constituted and see this process as more multiscalar and complex transnationally). The professionalisation of development has been a key issue in the literature for some time but what is important about this contribution is that it explores this theme in a particular region and around a particular ethnicity and the concern to "make development sensitive to Indian needs". Rather than seeking to rehearse the now all too familiar story of an all-conquering and universal neoliberal development orthodoxy and its increasing reach within the Andean region, the complex spatiality of power relations is highlighted here as is the possibility that in some contexts neoliberalism is opening up the space of the indigenous to challenge and resistance as well as to participation.

Whilst the authors suggest that terms like ethnodevelopment and "development-with-identity" pre-date the rise of neoliberal development policies, the complex colonial and post-colonial genealogies of these terms and concepts is not really explored here (but this is a theme touched upon by Uma Kothari). The authors do however focus on the (transnational) tensions and struggles between the generalist, almost Orientalist, work of contemporary development "experts" and the need for specific, indigenous specialist knowledges. A particularly interesting theme here concerns the vision that global development agencies have of the wider potential of indigenous knowledges and the need to transfer "best practice" between places and localities. They rightly suggest that this is partly motivated (as ever with agencies like the World Bank) by the concern to realise and exploit the "untapped" commercial potential of indigenous knowledges and communities. The subtle (and not always emancipatory) ways in which indigenous knowledge production is drawn into and articulates with transnational development discourses and networks is a relatively neglected theme in the literature and the authors offer something quite innovative in this regard.

Linking the increase in professionalisation within international development directly to the expansion of the neoliberal agenda, Uma Kothari highlights the co-optation of so called "alternative approaches" through processes of "technicalisation" and shows how critical and dissenting voices are silenced and conscripted into neoliberal discourses and practices. What is particularly instructive here is the focus on how competing discourses of development are "managed", ordered and hierarchised under neoliberalism such that competing ways of knowing and dissenting voices are "edited out". Additionally, the professionalisation of development expertise is seen to reinforce classifications of difference, such as "developed" and "developing" and to reinforce the embodiment of inequality and the supposed "enlightenment" of British foreign aid and development. The construction of the development expert as an authority, it is argued, reflects a form of cultural imperialism characterised by a highly gendered and racialised eurocentrism. More specifically, Kothari rightly asserts that the construction and reiteration of this expertise continues to rely on *technicalisation* and the unequal power relations within donor–recipient relations as well as on the assumption that the expertise of foreign or Western "experts" must automatically be more advanced than anything else that might be available. Additionally, Kothari's account very effectively draws out how the construction of the development expert has a long and complex genealogy, and consequently is able to get at something of the nuanced and subtle ways in which the transition between colonialism and development involved a certain deferral of power as well as the displacement of certain assumptions. This transition is not seen here as a unilateral trajectory but more, following Edward Said, as a case of intertwinement and imbrication. I particularly welcomed the useful suggestion that more work was needed on how, following decolonisation, the West is able to maintain its authority and how many post-colonial knowledges are constructed as "neutral" and universal through the mobilisation of discourses of humanitarianism, philanthropy and poverty alleviation.

The insight here into how colonial officers were trained to understand colonial administration is fascinating as is the discussion of how many felt deeply suspicious about the new cadre of post-colonial experts. This contribution is particularly good at exploring the role of neoliberal technocrats in disseminating development and in incorporating, co-opting and technicalising participatory approaches (especially the Bretton Woods institutions). The ways in which expertise has assumed an importance which dwarfs and overshadows the stated objective of poverty reduction is also carefully drawn out here, as are the ways in which complexity and messiness in participatory approaches are submerged in favour of (more manageable) linearity and sterility. The intrinsically one-sided nature of much that passes as "participatory" development is also well highlighted, although it is not clear exactly how international development agencies might make more use of "existing expertise within aid-receiving countries". I wholeheartedly agree, however, that the fundamental issue here is how to ensure that more critical voices are heard and that the spaces available to locate development outside the dominant technocratic frame (so enthusiastically articulated by the IFIs) are opened up.

Rebecca Dolhinow, in many ways, does begin to hint at how we might go about doing this by exploring the ways in which neoliberal preferences for self-help projects and a focus on individual needs can overshadow more collective forms of social change. In particular, she shows how NGOs often "obscure and limit the discussion of alternative discourses of development and social change" by focusing on neoliberal governance solutions, through the use of techniques of professionalisation and by avoiding activities which deal with the causes of marginalisation or the need for political mobilisation. The pressures placed on NGOs by donors are seen here to push NGOs further away from a concern with community and towards a managerialism and professionalisation that prioritises paperwork, accounting and "endless meetings". The important roles of women in the *colonias* of the US–Mexico border regions are highlighted, exploring the dynamics of their position(s) as activists and in leading struggles but also in experiencing the absence of basic services most directly and intimately. Dolhinow rightly suggests that NGOs can play a crucial role in repositioning responsibility such that women are led to "take a greater responsibility in the processes of social reproduction" (a theme echoed in a number of contributions). The enthusiasm of NGOs in supporting *colonia* projects that centre upon "practical" needs whilst obscuring more "strategic" interests is also highlighted, although Dolhinow's suggestion of an alternative approach (one centred on basic human rights) seems a little unclear.

The work of Gramsci and Foucault on theories of the state and governmentality is drawn upon to tease out the various tensions and contradictions in the role of NGOs in the *colonias* and to theorise civil society as an ambiguous space which has the potential to be both liberating and oppressive. Dolhinow suggests that the demands of "mainstream civil society appear too strong to resist" for many NGOs, many of which encourage leaders to organise their communities around neoliberalised self-help projects and even contribute to the production of neoliberal leadership, ensuring political subjects which continue to choose neoliberal solutions. This research is a particularly good example of how to develop a focus on specific and local manifestations of neoliberalism as well as how these local specificities might be situated within global processes and structures. In particular, the way in which NGOs fill the needs left open by the state's withdrawal from service provision, producing a "shadow state apparatus", is far from being a situation unique to the *colonias*. In their misunderstandings and misrepresentations NGOs can actually silence the already marginalised voices of *colonia* residents and "decentre the more political questions of rights and resources". Do NGOs really just "lie at the mercy of the capitalist system" or are they central to the very development of capitalism? Can there ever be such a thing as "politically progressive NGOs" and given their overwhelming focus on neoliberal governance and the needs of professionalisation, can NGOs "nurture and develop" the activism of women in truly progressive political ways?

Speculating on the contours of a "post-neoliberal" social governance in Aotearoa (where it is claimed that neoliberalism has been replaced by a new form of "joined up", "inclusive" governance) Wendy Larner and David Craig interrogate a new emphasis on partnership in New Zealand. In particular, they draw out the ways in which the meaning of the term "partnership" is constructed by discourse and contested in a number of ways, partly in an attempt to show neoliberalism as something more than just a monolithic political project with a preference for minimalist states. The contradictions and historically contingent features of neoliberal partnerships are highlighted here and the assertion that an understanding of the specificities of partnership can enable a more effective conceptualisation of neoliberalism is well founded. Additionally, the sense of new and contradictory governmental spaces and subjects beginning to emerge with the evolution of neoliberalism is carefully explicated here. Their focus on the social characteristics, backgrounds and skills of the exponents ("strategic brokers") and practitioners of partnership also seems original and insightful.

As with several other contributions, this work notes how professionalisation has increasingly drawn community activists into new roles in ways which can facilitate the more effective management of marginality and social exclusion. Larner and Craig see the concern with partnerships in historical perspective and carefully highlight the changing emphases on the role of different partners over time. In particular, the implications of a context of "competitive contractualism" are discussed here with a concern to show how social movements and activists adapted to and managed to survive the changing climate of engagement. The idea of partnership as a "mandatory tool" that is codified, formalised and made governmental also has a number of parallels in the forms neoliberalism has taken in a number of countries of the "global South" as is the shift in policy towards more of a concern with the discourse of "social capital". The ways in which

official discourses of partnership "nurture the expansion of partnership working" also have much wider relevance and the work by Uma
Kothari brings out how this can contradict and "technicalise" the
desire to find more citizen-focused and collaborative forms of
participation. The performance of partnership is crucial here as the
authenticity of a policy or strategy is measured by evidence of
collaboration/consultation.

Kate Simpson also explores how a seemingly rebellious and anti-
establishment act (taking a "gap year") can be neutralised and become
part of the UK's neoliberal market place through the emergence of an
institutionally accepted commercial gap year industry. Here, Simpson
discerns a notable shift produced by increasing professionalisation from
collective idealism to the "infinitely more saleable values of individual
career development". Research on the theme of volunteer development
projects (many of which are very much commercial enterprises) is in its
infancy and so this contribution is particularly useful. The formalisation
and professionalisation of youth travel and the invocation of neoliberal
understandings of education and citizenship are seen to have led to
an increasingly corporate focus and the goal of producing (and
commodifying) a professional, self-governing careerist persona for volunteers. In the UK, Simpson shows that the gap year industry creates a
particular geography for participants to visit and markets itself as operating in spaces which are simultaneously "safe" and "dangerous", allowing
participants to claim authentic knowledges of distant others and to
"collect" experiences of those engagements with the "Third World" other.

Naively, a simple short period of contact with the other is seen to be
enough to break down stereotypes, although Simpson shows how
other stereotypes can be constructed to replace them and to obscure
issues of social responsibility. The gap year industry is seen to
promote the transfer of cultural capital and to package and market
difference to volunteers, leaving behind in the process any presumed
connection to charity or the work of NGOs. What would have helped
to situate these arguments, however, is more of a sense of this
industry (and the imagined geographies it creates) in historical perspective, with more focus on the roots of voluntary work in the UK
and on its connections to colonialism and the work of missionaries.
Colonial and Orientalist constructions of self/other binaries are discussed here, however, and Simpson notes how the historical "mystery"
of colonial travel experiences can be invoked in order to legitimate
and even inspire contemporary forms of voluntary work. What is
particularly interesting about this contribution is the way in which
the gap year industry is seen to offer the traveller a prescribed,
simplistic and consumable experience of "Third World" difference
alongside a set of indicators to guarantee and authenticate their
consumption. The material on parental perceptions of difficulty,

safety and danger is also fascinating and sheds light on some of the other geographical imaginations at work here. I would also welcome Simpson's suggestion that the (myopic) professional gaze of the industry needs to be turned more directly on the practices of such programmes and towards an engagement of the "colonised and colonising geographies that it reproduces". There is also much further work that could be conducted on the construction of volunteer travellers as "experts" and on the presumed role of this expertise in the process of "doing development work".

Andrea Nightingale examines the promotion of expert knowledge through an examination of the professionalisation of community forestry in Nepal. By exploring the increasing prevalence of neoliberal ideologies in environment-development programmes, this author also brings out the importance of contestation and struggle between the supposedly "backward" knowledges of locals and the more professional "scientific" knowledge of "experts". The conflation of knowledge with development (a theme covered in several other contributions in this collection) is also discussed here. The implications of this struggle for the (re)inscription of key social relations like caste and gender are well highlighted as is the way in which the professionalisation of forestry in Nepal "authorises particular kinds of knowledges, discourses and practices". Once again, the process of professionalisation is seen to be wrought with tensions and contradictions, where "community" projects contain within them goals, values and objectives that undermine each other and pull people in contrasting directions. As with the contribution by Laurie, Andolina and Radcliffe, the (messy) expansion of neoliberal practices is seen, to an extent, to create a space for resistance and requires certain identities and ideologies to be internalised. Additionally, both contributions usefully highlight the ways in which the artificial distinction between "professional" and "local" knowledges is exploited by a variety of interest groups in order to claim authority or to exert power and resistance. A focus on social hierarchies and subjectivities enables Nightingale to view resource management as embedded in power relations and everyday practices and to raise some important questions about the mobilisation of particular discourses (eg of poverty or of scientific understanding and literacy). The concern with caste and issues of racial hierarchy also adds a different dimension to the account and represents a theme that has often been neglected in the literature. This particular managerialist science of development (like so many others) is seen as incapable of producing what people "really want", as of limited use in securing futures and to be authored elsewhere or to be grounded in the histories, ecologies and models of other countries. Perhaps these are also some of the ways in which neoliberal spaces of development are increasingly "worked" out.

Chapter 11

No Way Out? Incorporating and Restructuring the Voluntary Sector within Spaces of Neoliberalism

Katy Jenkins

This commentary focuses principally on the contributions by Liz Bondi and Nicholas Fyfe, complemented by some additional discussion on the work of Diane Richardson and Uma Kothari, with the aim of drawing out the contrasts, common preoccupations, key themes, and novel perspectives of their various approaches. Bondi's and Fyfe's research contributes to a growing sense of the encroachment of neoliberal processes and practices, once associated with purely economic development, into almost every aspect of our lives. A central concern of both these authors, echoed by many others in this collection, is the question of how to contest neoliberalism from within—with the implicit assumption that the neoliberal paradigm has incorporated voices of dissent to the extent that there are no alternative spaces from which to challenge it.

Bondi and Fyfe both present case studies demonstrating the incorporation of the Scottish voluntary sector, and its previously alternative perspectives, into a hegemonic neoliberal model. They show how the sector is being transformed by the increasing influence of new managerial tools—Bondi characterises these as "the technologies of calculation" whilst Fyfe refers to the "bureaucratic restructuring" of the sector, both highlighting the controlling mechanisms of the increasing professionalisation which has accompanied the unprecedented progress of neoliberal practices. Both authors, in common with many in this collection, conceptualise this process of professionalisation as a key instrument of the neoliberal project, contributing to the co-optation, incorporation, and neutralisation of alternative ideologies and ways of being. Kothari extends these discussions into the global arena, with her focus on the rise of the international development expert (see also Nightingale), whilst Richardson's work brings to the fore the added dimension of sexual identity within neoliberalism. This makes for an incredibly stimulating and wide-ranging collection of contributions which presents an increasingly common scenario from a variety of vantage points.

Bondi and Fyfe use their case studies to critically engage with the concept of professionalisation in its diverse guises, and to explore the potential these cases present for forging new subversive spaces *within* neoliberalism. Both writers argue very coherently on their respective topics, though Fyfe is perhaps a little drier in terms of his subject matter and approach, compared with the rich voices that emerge from Bondi's account.

In her discussion of counselling as a space in which neoliberal identities are produced, Bondi wears her two hats of voluntary counsellor and academic very adeptly, combining the insights and reflexivity of each approach to produce an engaging and intriguing piece. I say intriguing, as few people would immediately connect the sphere of counselling with the extension of the neoliberal paradigm. Yet Bondi argues this convincingly, highlighting the way in which the counselling process simultaneously strengthens and, to a lesser extent, challenges the neoliberal model. Drawing on the work of Rose (1990), Bondi's point of departure is that psychotherapeutic discourses such as counselling "constitute influential vehicles through which neoliberal governance is dispersed". She asserts that the strong focus of counsellors on their clients' empowerment primarily creates autonomous, decision-making, self-governing and self-monitoring individuals (the ideal neoliberal subject, as discussed in Richardson's piece in this issue), albeit tempered with an underlying sense of collective identity—perhaps facilitating the elusive "moments of resistance" to which Bondi aspires. However, I am left with some uncertainty about whether these "moments of resistance" are manifested clearly enough in Bondi's work or are drawn more from a general sense of optimism, perhaps based on her own experiences as a counsellor. Bondi's work therefore, suggests a need for greater engagement with methodological issues in the future, particularly in relation to the politics and positionality of academics who are engaged in diverse neoliberal processes of professionalisation, often as both researchers and activists.

To this individualising and subjectivising account of the counselling process, Bondi adds a "deeply ambivalent engagement with the process of professionalisation"—a sentiment in evidence throughout much of the work collected here (including Kothari and Fyfe). Bondi builds on her previous work on the professionalisation of counselling in order to situate this process of professionalisation at the heart of the neoliberal project. She highlights three main ways in which this process manifests itself—in "the development of systems of voluntary self-regulation"; in the "academicisation" of counselling expertise in the form of training courses; and in increased opportunities within the labour market as "counsellor" becomes recognised as a legitimate occupation. These neoliberalising aspects of professionalisation are reflected, in very different scenarios, in the work of Fyfe, and his discussion of regulatory compacts developed between government and the voluntary sector, and in Richardson's discussion of the rise of lesbian and gay expertise in academia and business. Bondi's piece has other interesting parallels with Richardson's work, which are largely unexpected given their disparate starting points. Bondi, like Richardson, highlights normalisation through neoliberal practices—in this case in the creation of the ideal "normal" neoliberal citizen-consumer through exposure to the subjectivising counselling process. Bondi holds on to the hope of the political engagement of voluntary counsellors as potentially providing some sort of panacea to the predominance of neoliberalising tendencies within the counselling sector. However, Richardson restricts herself to critiquing this politics of normalisation and does not attempt to address the form that any resistance might take—merely flagging up the need for further critical engagement with the topic.

Fyfe fleshes out the wider context of the Scottish voluntary sector—the setting for both his and Bondi's case studies—and complements Bondi's work with his own thoughtful analysis, critically evaluating claims that third sector organisations can contribute to the "reinvigoration of civic life". He highlights the misgivings of many of us in relation to the transfer of the burden of welfare provision to professionalised voluntary and civil society organisations. Like Bondi, Fyfe underlines the contradictions and tensions inherent in a neoliberal world which incorporates all dissent within its boundaries, leaving little or no room for truly alternative ways of being (a scenario emphasised by Richardson in her discussion of the incorporation of "normal" lesbians and gay men within neoliberal discourses).

Taking a broader sweep of the voluntary sector than Bondi, Fyfe engages with the implementation of New Labour's "Third Way", exemplified in the incorporation of third sector organisations—those organisations lying within "the cornerstones of ... the state, the market and the informal sector"—within a discourse of neo-communitarianism. That is, a reliance on and the transfer of welfare responsibilities to the voluntary sector, through discourses of partnership, good governance and citizenship—the mantras of New Labour—in order to tap into the perceived social cohesion and economic vitality of civil society. In particular, Fyfe examines the implementation of national and local level compacts between voluntary agencies and the government, drawing the third sector into partnership with the state. Exploring this process provides a more obvious "way in" to conceptualising the links between neoliberalism and professionalisation, as it is echoed in the rolling out of neoliberalism in diverse contexts across both the developing and developed world, leading to the professionalisation of voluntary sector organisations and NGOs as they are reconfigured to meet the demands of new managerial neoliberalism (see also the contribution by Kothari; Townsend, Porter and Mawdsley 2002). This professionalisation of the third sector in the UK exemplifies a global move towards a one size fits all approach, whereby local geographical and cultural knowledge is eschewed in favour of a technical managerial approach implemented by "experts":

> What counts as professional expertise in development is not primarily founded on in-depth geographical knowledge about other places and people but is located in technical know-how. This new kind of development skill is increasingly recognised globally and reflects the universalising principles of the neoliberal agenda. (Kothari this issue)

Issues of experts, expertise and knowledge production are central in framing the professionalisation debate in both the developed and developing world. These themes are further explored by Laurie, Andolina and Radcliffe, in relation to Andean ethnodevelopment policies, and Nightingale, in her discussions of hierarchies of knowledge in community forestry in Nepal.

In emphasising the impact of this universalising agenda in the UK, Fyfe highlights the prominence of discourses of social capital—a dubious, fuzzy and pervasive concept, ubiquitously deployed by multi-lateral institutions such as the World Bank (see Laurie, Andolina and Radcliffe this issue). However, Fyfe focuses on the use of a very specific social capital, not the rich overlapping social fabric of a society founded on reciprocity, common well-being and dense networks, but a narrow social capital based on social cohesion and flows of information in the pursuit of efficient service delivery—bridging or scaled up social capital. He demonstrates the way that these attributes of social capital are becoming another instrument of new managerial techniques, rather than being desirable in and of themselves.

Fyfe presents evidence (from Maloney, Smith and Stoker 1999) of differential levels of trust and flows of information (here equated to social capital) between local voluntary organisations and Glasgow city council. He asserts that those organisations, which are more involved in consultative forums and liaising with council officials, and for whom a city council grant is an important source of income, demonstrate, perhaps unsurprisingly, greater trust of the council and of other voluntary organisations, and report good flows of information between themselves and the council. Fyfe suggests a process of polarisation between those organisations that are professionalising and becoming an integral part of the government's strategy—with all the bureaucratic restructuring that this implies—and the organisations that remain independent, working at grassroots level without the high levels of government financial support enjoyed by their professionalised counterparts. This polarisation is something I have seen in

my own work with voluntary and professionalised development
organisations in Lima, Peru, although in this context the role of the
state is minimal, with the impetus to professionalise stemming mainly
from multilateral and bilateral donors (Jenkins 2005). As Fyfe
suggests, this professionalisation of voluntary organisations under
the rubric of neoliberalism often means the demise of the "unprofessional" voluntary worker and the employment of a professionally
qualified staff. Thus, these practices effectively destroy the social
capital that they aimed to exploit, built as it is upon the antithesis of
the neoliberal approach: "'self-governing associations of people who
have joined together to take action for public benefit', that are
independent, do not distribute profits and are governed by non-paid
volunteers (Taylor 1992:171)" (Fyfe). By incorporating third sector
organisations into the neoliberal project as service providers, their
dynamism is effectively neutralised, as Fyfe himself concludes:

> ... it is clear that organisations who do professionalise and restruc-
> ture their services run the risk of disempowering citizens both within
> organisations as a result of developing a hierarchical structure with
> clear divisions between volunteers and paid staff, and outside
> organisations by reproducing the bureaucrat–client relationship
> characteristic of government organisations. Such a scenario means
> that third sector organisations often fail to contribute to the govern-
> ment's wider neo-communitarian agenda of fostering active citizen-
> ship and "the reinvigoration of civic life" (Boateng 1992:3). (Fyfe
> this issue)

Fyfe highlights the predominance of mechanisms promoting only the
passive citizenship of citizen-consumers amongst these professionalised,
"corporatist" third sector organisations. In contrast, being one step
removed from the rigours and constraints of such formalised partnership with government, Bondi's example suggests that the counselling
sector *may* be able to maintain more of an autonomous space for itself,
albeit firmly within the neoliberal sphere. Perhaps, as Bondi hopes, this
space can provide more potential for active citizenship and "moments of
resistance", working alongside those third sector organisations,
highlighted by Fyfe, which are marginalised from engaging in
government service delivery, and therefore remain independent and
engaged at grassroots level, although lacking resources.

    In examining these various actors and agents involved in the
professionalisation of the Scottish voluntary sector, Bondi and Fyfe
both skilfully distil a wide variety of topics into their discussions,
contributing to a debate which calls for more in-depth research into
the ambiguities created by the combined processes of neoliberalism
and professionalisation. In looking at how professionalisation
intersects with the neoliberal project in diverse contexts, both at

local and global levels, we begin to see the attempted exertion of increased control over our sexual, social, emotional and political lives (Bondi; Fyfe; Kothari; and Richardson), beneath an overarching discourse of self-governance and autonomy. The central question all these contributions leave us with is how to subvert and take control of the professionalisation processes with which we are all engaged, in order to provoke a process of deliberalisation from within by politically engaged actors.

References

Jenkins K (2005) "Developing grassroots experts? The progress and professionalisation of a group of Peruvian health promoters." Unpublished PhD dissertation, University of Newcastle, UK

Maloney W, Smith G and Stoker G (1999) "Social capital and urban governance: Civic engagement in Birmingham and Glasgow." Paper presented at the Annual Meeting of the American Political Science Association, Atlanta, GA

Rose N (1990) *Governing the Soul*. London: Routledge

Townsend J G, Porter G and Mawdsley E (2002) The role of the transnational community of non-governmental organisations: Governance or poverty reduction? *Journal of International Development* 14(6):829–839

Chapter 12

Professional Geographies

Nicholas Blomley

I will focus my remarks on four of the contributions in the collection—those written by Andrea Nightingale, Liz Bondi, Rebecca Dolhinow and Kate Simpson. All explore, in intriguing and valuable ways, the nature of work, professionalization and neoliberalism. They offer grounded, empirical accounts, drawn from diverse parts of the world. They demonstrate that the connection between the powerful logics of professionalization and neoliberalization, while often limiting progressive possibilities, may also create paradoxical spaces of opposition and creative difference.

These contributions ask, in various ways, how the tensions between activism, professionalization and neoliberal governance are expressed and navigated. They answer this question in different, but intersecting ways. Liz Bondi draws from her own experiences as a voluntary counselor in Scotland to explore other counselors' reflections on their practice, and on growing pressures to professionalize. She argues that both the practices of counseling and the logic of professionalization may reproduce a concept of the human subject consonant with neoliberal subjectivity. Yet she also uncovers alternative possibilities that depart from an individualized and self-directing model of autonomy. Rebecca Dolhinow, conversely, is less optimistic about the progressive possibilities associated with the neoliberal professional. In her account of NGOs, working in the Mexican-American communities of the US Southwest, she argues that a logic of professionalism can alienate and disempower the poor. Moreover, what she terms a "cycle of professionalism" can create state–NGO relationships that further distance organizations from progressive and democratic change. Andrea Nightingale focuses on the ways in which community members in Nepal buy in to, strategically appropriate, or are distanced by the professional logics of "community forest" projects. She highlights the ways in which such neoliberal forms of professionalization overlay, and can often help sustain, internal differences in caste, gender and education within rural villages. Like Dolhinow, she raises concerns at the efficacy and inclusiveness of such interventions, while also noting that they can serve to unsettle internal hierarchies. Finally, Kate Simpson takes us between North and South, in an examination of the "gap year", a particularly British institution that takes middle class youths overseas on programs designed to immerse participants in transformative encounters with foreign cultures. Not only has a professional industry sprung up to serve these new grand tours, but the gap experience itself, Simpson notes, has become marketed as essential to the production of the incipient professional, poised to enter the middle-class world of university and work. It is a gap in name only, it seems.

Much has been written, of late, on neoliberal governance. Rather than revisiting what seems like well-trodden terrain, I thought it useful to briefly comment on the ways in which these authors shed light on professionalization. This, it seems to me, is something that we spend less time thinking about, perhaps because it is so close to home (though of Castree 2000). Indeed, the very act of writing these few words for an academic journal (a version of which was presented at a professional meeting) attests to the ways in which professional standing and practices (mine, yours, ours) have become central to everyday life as a geographer. More on this later.

Professional standing signals at least one, and usually two things. First, it may entail a formal, recognized status. Lawyers, for example, are designated "professionals": they undergo elaborate programs of accreditation and induction, often involving arcane ceremonies, and are, to a degree, self-regulating, with internal codes and sanctions for unprofessional conduct, the most significant of which are suspension and expulsion. While academic geographers are somewhat more relaxed, we still require—like the ancient guilds—long periods of apprenticeship before a novice can be invested with the mysteries of the craft. We also seek to regulate who, or what, can be designated as geography through teaching, publishing protocols and journal review procedures. Second, to become a professional is to attain middle-class standing: it is to be inducted into the white-collar society, explored by C Wright Mills, Pierre Bourdieu and other observers of the middle class. The divide between professionals and trades, of course, still comprises a crucial social fault line. I vividly remember my English classmates and I being streamed into different academic paths at school. Kids that I had regarded as my friends were suddenly to be treated differently. They specialized in technical drawing or metalwork, and were expected to leave school at 16: I was pointed towards "O" levels in appropriate subjects, such as maths, French and English, and then dispatched (obviously) to university.

Professional standing, then, first and foremost, relies upon and presupposes distinction. A professional, most importantly, is not a non-professional. Distinction is something that must be internalized, shaping the production of the self. Yet at the same time, professional distinctiveness requires recognition by others. The emergence of the field of urban planning in the early twentieth century, for example, saw fascinating discussions amongst practitioners, as they struggled to articulate who they were (and who they were *not*), as a profession, while they negotiated with universities and municipalities to ensure an acceptance of their professional distinction and employability. This dynamic is evident, in varying degrees, in these contributions. In some cases, it would seem that the production of distinction, not surprisingly, leads to the production and reproduction of social distance. Thus, in Nepal, Nightingale found that higher-caste villagers proved adept at claiming positions of authority within local community forestry user groups based on their pre-existent caste status and their literacy skills. However, Bondi points to other possibilities. Here, some counselors resist professionalization, given a fear that it will erode distinction. As one respondent put it, professionalization "forces people into boxes". The fear is that counseling, a movement that has defined itself against prevailing professional cultures, will lose its distinctiveness and, presumably, encourage participants to define themselves and their practice in more orthodox ways.

Professionalization also implicates the state, both directly and at a remove. Frequently, the state is the arbiter or facilitator of professional standing; a profession is also often defined as such given its relative autonomy from the state, being granted sovereign powers of self-regulation and accreditation. Neoliberal forms of rule, these essays note, are well served by the professions, encouraging liberal freedom and government at a distance. For some authors, this can be destructive. Dolhinow notes the ways in which a neoliberal market logic impels NGOs to do the state's bidding in ways that do not always serve local needs. Yet there are undoubtedly other possibilities. Accredited (ie professional) child-care centers in British Columbia, where I live, have long been leaders in the battles over funding cuts, arguing for the expansion of state subsidies. Practitioners have been skilled at mobilizing expert knowledges (including the professional languages of early childhood education) against the state.

Professionalization also entails a particular relation to the body. In particular, it seems to connote a disembodied detachment from the world. Professional labour is mental (or "non-manual") labour. It is this, in part, that has provided the ideological basis for the exclusion of women from the professions. There is, perhaps, an echo here of the historical link between religion and the professional. A professional, etymologically, is one who makes a profession; that is, takes solemn religious vows. We can still catch a whiff of the cloister, with its code of detachment, discipline and a life of the mind, in contemporary understandings of the professional. Certainly, the worship of the text, and the assumed link between literacy and standing, appear as crucial to the creation of professional hierarchies in Nepal as they are to the Western professoriate. Yet again some intriguing tensions and paradoxes are highlighted. Kate Simpson's account of the ways in which discourses of danger and risk valorize the gap experience suggest that professional culture also values embodied ("real world") experience, at least prior to taking up an economics degree. Geography, as we know, has also long celebrated "field" experience (although always placing it below cerebral practice). Similarly, while the social hierarchies found within Nepali villages rest on people's relative position to manual work, Nightingale also notes the ways in which lower-caste men used illiteracy tactically against the professional claims of village elites.

Let me close by noting a couple of things I would have loved to have heard more about in relation to the profession. As noted above, as professional academics, we are not simply observers of neoliberal professionalization. We are also active, if ambivalent, participants. I am engaged in a professional enactment as I write this piece. This short article will be included in my curriculum vitae (the story of my professional life, as well as my passport). We know a lot about performance, yet we don't seem to reflect on what it means to "perform" the profession we are members of (or seek entry to).[1]

It would also be interesting to think through the geographies of professionalism: that is, the ways in which space is organized and mobilized to buttress professional hierarchies and sustain professional distinction. For example, the designs and attendant rituals of university campuses can inscribe professional self-conceptions and distinctions in the landscape. Graduation ceremonies at my university, for example, in which waves of begowned academics and professionals-in-waiting (the graduands) descend from a ziggurat-like hill into a temple-like arena, led by a bagpipe band and a bearer of a claymore and a mace, are obvious, if extreme, examples. Beyond the university, we academics are also adept at producing professional spaces. Global networks—instantiated in this collection—that tenure and promotion committees value as a marker of "international standing" are another telling example. Yet as these contributions note, professionalism need not produce hierarchy. Similarly, professional geographies can be put to work for other, more progressive ends.

Endnote
[1] Look, an endnote! How professional. Worse, I'm going to cite myself, and thus buttress my professional standing. See Blomley (2002).

Reference

Blomley N (2002) The rules. *Geoforum* 33(2):149–151
Castree N (2000) Professionalization, activism and the university: Whither "critical geography"? *Environmental Planning A* 32:955–970

Chapter 13

Partners in Crime? Neoliberalism and the Production of New Political Subjectivities

Cindi Katz

The contributions in this publication individually and collectively address the contradictions and possibilities of political activism and its professionalization under the conditions of contemporary neoliberal capitalism. Each piece deals differently with the making of appropriate professional subjects and the contradictory ways they are placed in relation to an evolving neoliberalism. The authors show the skill-enhancing and effectiveness-increasing aspects of professionalization, but also the ways that this process—over a differentiated and shifting neoliberal context—also reins in, if not outright contains, its new subjects. This focus raises several interesting and disturbing questions for understanding the social, political and economic relations of neoliberalism in various locales and across scale. Among these concerns are the role of the acquisition and use of skills and knowledge, the defanging of oppositional practices and positions, the reliance on newly professionalized activists to compensate for the losses associated with neoliberal policies, the ways the rhetoric and practices of "partnerships" can mask and even create an alibi for the degradations of neoliberalism, and the ascendence of various forms of individualism alongside a devalorization of the collective. At the core of each piece is a nuanced analysis of what is gained and lost in the course of professionalization, imagined everywhere in terms of the political possibilities for resistance and reworking that infiltrate these material social practices.

Each contribution asks, who is the subject of professionalization and how are these subjects produced and made sensible in the course of neoliberal restructuring? Wendy Larner and David Craig focus on the rise and evolution of local partnerships in the vanguard of state neoliberalism in Aotearoa New Zealand. These authors attend most centrally to the various actors engaged in partnerships through the shifting iterations of neoliberalism. They focus on "strategic brokers", who are the linchpins of a growing array of partnerships at the cusp of community activism and governance. Larner and Craig show how the drive toward partnerships fairly relentlessly incorporates activists into the maw of neoliberal agendas, but also how many of these social actors are fully aware of the contradictory bargain they are striking in order to reorient the course of neoliberal "roll back" to enhance community well-being.

The term "strategic brokerage", wherein these people move from a community-based activist agenda to a much more circumscribed one as they become professional brokers, grant-writers, and advocates, has many entailments. Drawing on their long-term research concerning neoliberal partnerships, Larner and Craig examine how "strategic brokers" are "governmentalised", not only in their professional roles but well beyond them into their personal commitments. As I was reading their careful assessment of this process, I kept scribbling "momism" in the margins. This dreadful word was the clearest shorthand I could come up with to make sense of the costs and compensatory mechanisms of "governmentalisation". Strategic brokers were valued for their skills at building and maintaining relationships, their "nurturing" of partners and the partnership as an entity, their intimate knowledge of their communities, their facilitation and lubrication of all manner of social process, and so on. As Larner and Craig note, it is not surprising that most of the brokers were women. While it is terrific that these skills are valorized in the form of compensation, the authors note that the women in these positions were generally underpaid as they were put in the position of "minimising the fallout from earlier phases of neoliberalism". As is customary in the relationship between production and social reproduction under capitalism, women absorb and pick up the slack of deteriorations in the social wage. In the case of the local partnerships examined by Larner and Craig, this situation is rehearsed albeit in a new guise. Their subject of neoliberal professionalism taps into and reworks familiar repertoires of subjectivity with results that may differ by scale but not by effect.

The authors in this collection also highlight the important and contradictory role of knowledge acquisition and use in the course of neoliberal restructuring. As professionalization proceeds, a growing number of community-based "partners", many of whom came to this role as grassroots activists, are formally trained, enter degree programs, or otherwise acquire specialized knowledge and skills in more structured and credentialized settings. As intended, this training enables them to better manage and deploy the resources of their particular partnership, but it also alters their sense of themselves as social actors. Nina Laurie, Robert Andolina, and Sarah Radcliffe examine the possibilities of this pivotal position in their work on indigenous education in the Andes, which will be discussed below.

Larner and Craig look at the contradictory stance of increasingly professionalized participants who come from the ranks of those wily enough to have survived two decades of lean, mean "competitive contractualism" in an array of community groups. Their survival skills were as crucial to their partnerships as their new-found skills. The authors question whether these canny subjects of professionalism should be seen in "'positive liberal' terms of newly capable, active liberal subjects" or perhaps in a more compromised light. This question reverberates in the piece by Laurie and her colleagues as well.

Larner and Craig show that as these social actors are being professionalized through training and credentials, they are also being asked to tap into social, political, and cultural skills that may advance their agendas but at the same time grease the wheels of ascendant neoliberalism. The recourse to what I am calling "momism" and other contradictory subject positions intimates some of the ways that oppositional agendas may be re-routed in the course of professionalization. Not only do these strategic brokers pick up the slack, but somehow in order to be made sensible to those with money and resources—to be codified as (worthy) "partners"—activists almost inevitability lose a large part of their critical edge, whether through credentialization, the demands of "competitive contractualism", or other processes that bolster their "social capital" over and against common well-being. It's not clear that this loss is recuperated in the partnership process. The oxymoron of "social democratic neoliberalism" suggests the nature of the loss, but as Larner and Craig indicate, there is a seething resistance to the process.

Professionalization has a slightly different twist in Diane Richardson's piece on sexual citizenship. Richardson focuses on the "professionalization of sexual politics", wherein particular kinds of knowledge production—in both the academy and more commercial spheres—construct lesbians and gay men as "normalized" "consumer-citizens", creating new forms of political subjectivity and practice at various scales. A "neoliberal politics of normalization" has been key to this process, and can be seen in the trajectory of sexual politics through the latter half of the twentieth century. Richardson traces shifts in the ambitions of the more professionalized gay and lesbian rights movements operating since the 1990s, exposing the ways they were vastly different from those of earlier periods. In the 1960s and 1970s, for instance, the struggle was for recognition—"we're here, we're queer, deal with it!" The differences between straight and lesbian/gay sensibilities—to the extent these can be named as such—were a point of pride. Indeed, a key aspect of "gay pride" was its critique—expressed and implied—of the cultural forms and material social practices of heteronormativity. In the 1990s, however, the struggles were for inclusion in the social fabric of mainstream society, however tattered or questionable that fabric was. These shifts were reflected in how many of the movements' demands were focused around "equal rights of citizenship", including the right to marry or share in the rights associated with state sanctioned marriage and family, to serve in the military, and to have the same property, inheritance, and custodial rights as those in non-gay and lesbian relationships. These demands are a far cry from the right to recognition, especially given that the earlier demands were used as a means to question the very bases by which gay and lesbian social subjects were excluded; the ways heteronormativity eclipsed and devalorized non-dominant social relations.

Far from questioning heteronormativity or its psychological and cultural consequences, contemporary gay and lesbian sexual politics often focuses on "normalization". Yet, as Richardson points out, unlike the politics of normalization that was characteristic of the 1950s, the neoliberal version emphasizes "the rights of individuals rather than gay rights and seeks equality with, rather than tolerance from, the mainstream". She reveals how the concerns of "sexual citizenship" blur, confuse, and call into question the distinction between public and private in everyday life and how these ambiguities can dovetail with a neoliberal agenda. For instance, in a twist on "scaling up", much of the motion around sexual citizenship has been scale collapsing under neoliberalism. Around issues of health and control of the body, the responsibility of care—often under the banner of privatization—has shifted from higher to lower scales while at the same time there is increasing surveillance and regulation of the home and body. In other words, the economic impetus of neoliberalism drives the state (and corporations) to abdicate responsibility for such things as health and dependent care, leaving it to individuals and families to scramble to provide them. This much is well known, but at the same time as the state is in fiscal retreat, the cultural politics of neoliberalism tends toward increased state intervention in the regulation of domestic and personal life. Richardson aptly uses the instance of AIDS education as a case in point, demonstrating how current policy depends upon a self-regulating subject who has internalized safer sex norms and practices to minimize HIV transmission, while HIV testing (like drug testing) works as a form of "surveillance medicine".

Contemporary sexual politics also ricochets around the contradictions of privatization and self-regulation expressed in economic versus cultural registers. For example, Richardson suggests that neoliberal states may have an interest in supporting gay marriage because it helps offload responsibility for care in the myriad ways that families are a "a form of private welfare, providing economic interdependency and support". Beyond this troubling convergence of interests, she warns that as lesbians and gay men achieve the rights of citizenship associated with marriage and civil unions, the threat they posed to the larger society and its assumptions of "normal" is "rendered governable". As she sharply observes, when sexual politics revolves so much around sexual citizenship and normalization, it is troubling that "(good) citizenship is increasingly constituted through the voluntary governance of the self". The agenda of professionalization, which is a cornerstone of these politics, here again compromises more radical agendas and blunts the power of opposition.

In a completely different arena, the contribution on ethnodevelopment in the Andes by Laurie, Andolina, and Radcliffe raises some similar concerns around the professionalization of knowledge, the subjects of professionalization, and the rerouting of political imperatives. Like the other authors in this collection, Laurie and her colleagues are concerned with neoliberal professionalization and the production of particular kinds of knowledge and sanctioned knowers. Focusing on indigeneity and contemporary development discourse and practice, their work carefully examines the relationship between neoliberalism and governmentality, focusing on the self-regulating subject in ways that resonate with Richardson and on the activist-cum-expert in ways that correspond to Larner and Craig. Laurie and colleagues make the case that through managing the contradictory interests of development actors at various scales, the subjects of indigenous professionalization warranted by transnational interests in ethnodevelopment have been able to mobilize to make claims against the local and national state and contest some of the harsher aspects of neoliberal reforms, producing what they—after Michael Watts—call "governable spaces of indigeneity".

The role of knowledge production and exchange is at the heart of their analysis, which looks at the productive tension that erupts where neoliberal development interests, national political economies, and indigenous social movements rub against each other. They view the neoliberal state as weakened from both ends—by transnational donors and financial institutions and by the various social movements galvanized by neoliberal restructuring. They demonstrate how within these contradictory social relations of power "governable spaces of indigeneity" can be—and have been—produced across "complex geographies and multiple scales". This scale skipping "partnership" (between the transnational indigenous and donor communities) seems to have been critical to the successful claims making of the indigenous groups. It stands in contrast (and perhaps inspiration) to the partnerships in Aotearoa New Zealand examined by Larner and Craig in which the neoliberal state often *was* the partner and could use bureaucratic (and other) means to accommodate particular claims and not others.

In the Andes case, donor interest in the latest preoccupation of the development industry, "ethnodevelopment", has been crucial in the support of "culturally appropriate education", which also responds to long-standing demands of indigenous social movements and their advocates for recognition around such things as knowledge, resource claims, values, political structures and leadership, and social organization. In struggles over ethnodevelopment, "transnational professionalization spaces" have been produced wherein indigenous organizations operate their own training schools to share knowledge, promote leadership skills, and create "ethnodevelopment experts" who have a chance of "shaping and sometimes contesting neoliberal development and notions of governable space and subjects".

As subjects of professionalization, indigenous social actors have been able to garner international donor support for their educational institutions and practices. If donors see their support as building indigenous "social capital", their partners in extensive and well developed indigenous educational networks see it as a means to rework "authoritative histories and knowledges". As the authors point out, there is a long tradition of Freireian popular education in the Andes that in recent years has begun to "focus more explicitly on indigenous concerns". At the same time these educational institutions have become more formal thanks to the training impetus of ethnodevelopment so that they simultaneously offer curricula shaped by the interests of indigenous social movements *and* credentials to their students. Thus professionalization works to foster new leaders—often women—but not at the expense of the interests of indigenous and poor communities who are engaged in new modes of "decentralized development planning".

The training programs assessed by Laurie, Andolina, and Radcliffe have managed to rework what constitutes knowledge, expertise, authority, and legitimate history at the same time as they maintain lively connections between activist oppositional agendas and the interests of professionalization. In so doing they are crucial to the construction, maintenance, and transnational expansion of "governable spaces of indigeneity" from which indigenous social actors can contest—if not always successfully—what counts as knowledge, who counts as knowledgeable, how resources are constituted and deployed, and what development outcomes are appropriate and for whom. As Laurie and colleagues make clear, the outcomes of these contests are indeterminate. The relationships among donors, indigenous social movements and NGOs, and the neoliberal state are ambiguous and can be "uncomfortable". As expectations are raised about the possibilities of professionalization, the ways they may be incompatible come to the fore, revealing the power dynamics and tensions at the heart of "ethnodevelopment". They argue that these outcomes depend on whether and how "ethnodevelopment" networks can shift the power relations of knowledge production and exchange. The history of how previous preoccupations of the development industry have unfolded do not warrant much optimism, but to foreclose the possibility that "subjects of professionalization" can appropriate knowledge consciously to create spaces of self determination is to evacuate their agency, give up on social transformation, and render struggles over what it means to know anything hollow.

As these contributions all make clear, the power of professionalization is a double-edged sword and each piece has dealt with its various contradictions. Becoming a subject of professionalization *might* mean—though it often does not—that in the course of becoming appropriate subjects of professionalization the "chickens get to guard the chicken coop". While this is always a possibility, these contributions make clear how delicate that prospect is. In each piece the dominant political groups—the groups with the resources—defined and supported a realm of appropriate subjectivity. But if being "hailed" or recognized as a subject comes with a particular terrain of practice, then by definition agency is curtailed—undermining the stated goals of such programs. In these ways and others professionalization tends to be homogenizing, defanging in its rush to the middle (of nowhere), and focused on defining, fixing, and through this, containing, what "good" "appropriate" political actors are. Of course, as these contributions show, there is plenty of play in this—long-term activists are not easily defanged, and anything is possible. But it is important to recognize the potential limits to this kind of "politics of recognition". As suggested above, the interests of international donors bent on multiculturalism and indigenous groups concerned with self determination have managed to be largely synergistic, but donor support may be contingent upon particular modes of being indigenous, and while—as Laurie and her colleagues suggest—indigenous people in the Andes have not been above a little strategic essentialism, their "governable spaces" may be constrained by these modes of recognition. What if indigenous social movements reached out, not to others hailed as indigenous, but to forge alliances with trade unionists? Would the transnational donor community, smitten with multiculturalism, ethnodevelopment, and developing *indigenous* social capital, look upon this favorably? I am not sure. And yet if social capital is not to be fixed dead capital, but rather—to push the metaphor—circulate, available for investment, then its subjects can appropriate it as they wish, creating altered grounds for their own (and others') agency. Here is where the limits of "neoliberal social governance" may be reached.

If my treatment of neoliberal politics and the sorts of professionalization it calls forth suggests a deep antipathy to neoliberalism's pernicious agenda, these authors have provoked me to recognize that contemporary neoliberalism is not monolithic and to see how its economic and cultural imperatives may work at cross purposes. Here I don't want to soft-pedal or in any way minimize the destructive effects of an increasingly hegemonic neoliberalism that has pushed the privatization of public goods and services, the demise of any semblance of a welfare state, the shriveling of gains in the social wage won over a century, and the market as the measure of all things. It reflects a concerted agenda of capitalists and their allies working on a global scale that exacts its myriad tolls individually. But nothing, not even neoliberalism, is airtight. If the fiscal imperatives of neoliberalism produce difficult conditions on the ground, its cultural politics can call forth something different. While discourses valorizing multiculturalism and "stakeholder participation" may be deployed to wash down, veil, and shed responsibility for coping with the harsh effects of neoliberal reform, the various subjects of neoliberal professionalization can and do make something potent of these discursive formations as was seen in both the Andes and to a lesser extent Aotearoa New Zealand cases. It works both ways of course. As Richardson points out, the cultural agenda of gay marriage, which is central to the sexual politics of normalization, dovetails quite nicely with the economic imperatives of the neoliberal state. While this convergence may well give lesbian and gay social movements pause, it also suggests the contradictory impulses of neoliberalism, which at the very least provide opportunities for opposition and alternative practice.

Finally, these contributions percolate with spatial implications, and reading across them raises some potentially productive areas of cross pollination. The question of scale, for instance, was addressed in different ways in each piece. Apart from the scale-collapsing effects of neoliberal impulses to privatize responsibility for social reproduction noted by all the authors, there is also a scalar downshift in the neoliberal discourses of governmentality. Larner and Craig note a shift in policy documents from concern with community development to social capital such that "communities" become sites where the public, private, and voluntary sectors meet. Within this frame, community organizations and individuals may be strengthened through training and other forms of "investment", but at the same time they can be unhinged from larger organizational (and geographical) frameworks and under regimes of "competitive contractualism" discouraged from cooperating across sectors or localities. In another realm, the professionalization of sexual politics has altered—and muted—the terrain of practice as reaching (monied) national and international networks is accomplished through a dilution of demands. In both cases the "scaling up" effects of the professionalized indigenous organizations in the Andes might offer some inspiration and guidance.

Turning on its head the ways indigenous knowledge has so long been constituted as acutely local, these leaders and educators have been able to tap into and rework their own transnational indigenous networks to control "how their knowledge is valued and represented in development". The "northern" activists in Aotearoa New Zealand might similarly reappropriate their knowledge "of and about" their communities not to survive—let along grease the wheels of—neoliberal reforms, but to refuse their terms. Similarly, those engaged in professionalizing sexual politics might recognize how their new-found mediated representations not only diminish their accountability to diverse historic constituencies, but also operate as means to contain and control them.

These contributions recognize the deeply contradictory politics of belonging, both of being inside and thus being recognized whether as partners or as sexual citizens "equalizing up", and the value and indeterminate possibilities of playing the game. In the face of numbingly endless "local" iterations of neoliberalism gone global, it is incumbent upon us to analyze—as these authors have all done—what the seductions of belonging are, how these seductions are enacted, how belonging can be transformative or resistant, what the long-term costs of being on the "inside" are, and where agency becomes alchemically compromised as "the enemy becomes us". Neoliberal politics relies on the assumption that there is "no alternative". In showing the multiple and porous forms of neoliberalism and the potent—if often compromised—material social practices of its "subjects", these contributions go a long way to confounding that assumption.

Index

Antipode

A Radical Journal of Geography

Edited by Noel Castree and Melissa W. Wright

For more than 30 years *Antipode* has published dissenting scholarship that explores and utilizes key geographical ideas like space, scale, place and landscape. It aims to challenge dominant and orthodox views of the world through debate, scholarship and politically-committed research, creating new spaces and envisioning new futures. *Antipode* welcomes the infusion of new ideas and the shaking up of old positions, without being committed to just one view of radical analysis or politics.

In addition to publishing academic papers, *Antipode* publishes short polemical interventions and longer, more reflective, explorations of radical geography in particular fields or locations.

* Essential reading for critical social scientists

* Publishes cutting-edge radical theory and research

* The only left-wing journal dedicated to exploring the geographical constitution of power and resistance

* Explores how space, place and landscape both shape and are shaped by unequal social relations

Visit the *Antipode* home page for up-to-date contents listings, editorial details, submission guidelines and ordering information:
www.blackwellpublishing.com/journals/anti

ISSN: 0066-4812

9600 Garsington Road, Oxford OX4 2DQ, UK I 350 Main Street, Malden, MA 02148, USA

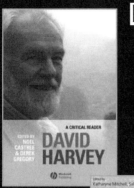